# SUBSEQUENT PERFORMANCES

Jonathan Miller

# SUBSEQUENT PERFORMANCES

Elisabeth Sifton Books/Viking

ELISABETH SIFTON BOOKS · VIKING
Viking Penguin Inc.
40 West 23rd Street,
New York, New York 10010, U.S.A.

First American Edition
Published in 1986

ISBN 0–670–81234–X
Library of Congress Catalog Card Number 86–40003 CIP Data available

Designed by Derek Birdsall
Printed in Great Britain by
Jolly & Barber Ltd Rugby Warwickshire

# Contents

## List of Illustrations and Acknowledgements

# Introduction

In this book I have assembled ideas, arguments and experiences derived from more than twenty years' work in the performing arts. Some of them were delivered during the course of the T. S. Eliot Lectures at Kent University, and others were developed in the Clark Lectures given under the auspices of Trinity College, Cambridge. In some cases they were written down and read out, and then transcribed more or less verbatim, but at Kent some of the themes were improvised at the time, largely in response to questions asked during seminars and discussions. Any inconsistency in style is the result of putting together these somewhat disparate forms of discourse.

With hindsight, I can see that several themes have recurred. In the Eliot Lectures, I tried to tackle the issues involved in producing dramatic works that had outlasted the life of their own authors, and that posed awkward problems of re-creation and interpretation. In the Clark Lectures, I returned to this subject in the context of the novel, and the legitimacy of adapting such works for the stage or screen. As a twentieth-century director I have been forced to confront the problem of subsequent performance in the theatre, in opera, and in television, and I have found it necessary to identify something that I can describe only as the 'afterlife' of the literary work. This struck me as an appropriate theme for the Eliot Lectures since it gave an unexpected emphasis to Eliot's preoccupation with the relationship between tradition and the individual talent. The invitation to deliver the Clark Lectures at Cambridge allowed me to approach the subject from a somewhat different angle, and my original concern was now complicated by an interest in the visual experience associated with reading representational prose, and with the curious discrepancy that seems to exist between the experience of reading a novel and seeing it realized in a dramatized form on the screen – an unexpected and, to my mind, questionable form of afterlife.

The text is unavoidably autobiographical; although I have tried to transcend any personal interests in the matter, I found it difficult to avoid making explicit references to my own productions. This is not because I favour these at the expense of my colleagues' but simply because my own interpretative thought processes are the only ones to which I have direct, introspective access. I have tried to balance necessarily abstract theory with anecdotal material drawn from the daily experience of rehearsing and mounting one production after another.

It has taken ten years to conceive and develop these ideas, and the fact that they have at last seen the light of day is largely the result of patient obstetric assistance provided in the first case by Linda Taylor and, in the most heroic subsequent performance of all, by Frances Coady of Faber. I would also like to thank the Master and Fellows of Eliot College, not only for their original invitation but also for their hospitality and interest on the occasion of my return to Kent University for a series of further discussions and seminars. I am also grateful to the Trustees of the Clark Lectures, and to the Master and Fellows of Trinity College, Cambridge.

I would also like to acknowledge the talent and friendship of designers who have been a constant source of inspiration. In the theatre I have enjoyed the long and affectionate co-operation of Patrick Robertson and Rosemary Vercoe with whom I have worked for nearly twenty years; Bernard Culshaw who designed all my productions for Kent Opera; and Philip Prowse who jolted me into a new way of thinking about the staging of Mozart. In television I was supported and advised by the admirable Colin Lowery who designed and supervised most of my Shakespeare productions for the BBC. I would also like to express my admiration for the work of David Myerscough-Jones and, although I only had the opportunity of working with him on one occasion I would like to pay tribute to Foxy Abbott who improvised a magnificent set for *Timon of Athens* at unexpectedly short notice.

Whatever ideas I have about lighting are the result of the patient and imaginative tuition I have received from Bob Bryan and David Hersey in the theatre, and from Messrs. Treays, Summers, Dennis Channon and Sam Barclay. I thank Alun Hughes for his costumes, and Julia Trevelyan Oman for her encyclopaedic sense of scenic detail. Germano Facetti taught me the value of detailed visual research, and his voluminous files of postcards, reproductions and paper ephemera provided many unacknowledged sources of decorative authenticity. In thinking about the formal problems of the theatre I owe an enormous debt to Nelson Goodman's *Languages of Art*, and to long and companionable discussions in which he generously gave me the benefit of his thought on the subject of scripts and scores. Finally, I would like to express my gratitude to the psychologists and linguists whose company I enjoyed whilst I was in receipt of a Leverhulme Research Fellowship at the University of Sussex.

Derek Birdsall is responsible for this book looking as nice as it does, but apart from his originality as a designer he is to be thanked for the service that he has rendered to the public in providing the only comprehensive collection of art postcards at his shop in Neal Street, London.

*Jonathan Miller 1985*

# List of Works

## Stage Productions

1962 UNDER PLAIN COVER (Royal Court Theatre)

1964 THE OLD GLORY (American Place Theater, New York)

1966 COME LIVE WITH ME (New Haven, Conn.)

1967 BENITO CERENO (Yale University)

1967 PROMETHEUS BOUND (Yale University)

1968 BENITO CERENO (Mermaid Theatre)

1968 SCHOOL FOR SCANDAL (Nottingham Playhouse)

1969 THE SEAGULL (Nottingham Playhouse)

1969 KING LEAR (Nottingham Playhouse)

1970 HAMLET (Arts Theatre, Cambridge)

1970 THE TEMPEST (Mermaid Theatre)

1970 KING LEAR (National Theatre, Old Vic)

1970 THE MERCHANT OF VENICE (National Theatre, Old Vic; ATV production, 1973)

1971 PROMETHEUS BOUND (National Theatre, Old Vic)

1971 DANTON'S DEATH (National Theatre, Old Vic)

1972 SCHOOL FOR SCANDAL (National Theatre, Old Vic)

1972 THE TAMING OF THE SHREW (Chichester)

1973 THE MALCONTENT (Nottingham Playhouse)

1973 THE SEAGULL (Chichester)

1974 MEASURE FOR MEASURE (National Theatre, Old Vic)

1974 THE MARRIAGE OF FIGARO (National Theatre, Old Vic)

1974 THE FREEWAY (National Theatre, Old Vic)

1974 FAMILY ROMANCES: GHOSTS; THE SEAGULL; HAMLET (Greenwich Theatre)

1974 ARDEN MUST DIE (Sadler's Wells Theatre)

1975 THE IMPORTANCE OF BEING EARNEST (Greenwich Theatre)

1975 ALL'S WELL THAT ENDS WELL (Greenwich Theatre)

1975 COSÌ FAN TUTTE (Kent Opera)

1975 RIGOLETTO (Kent Opera)

1975 THE CUNNING LITTLE VIXEN (Glyndebourne; revived 1977)

1976 LA FAVOLA D'ORFEO (Kent Opera; BBC TV presentation, 1979)

1976 PLEASURE AT HER MAJESTY'S (Amnesty benefit, Her Majesty's Theatre, filmed by Roger Graef)

1976 THE THREE SISTERS (Cambridge)

1977 EUGENE ONEGIN (Kent Opera)

1978 THE MARRIAGE OF FIGARO (English National Opera)

| 1979 | LA TRAVIATA (Kent Opera) |
|------|------|
| 1979 | SHE WOULD IF SHE COULD (Greenwich Theatre) |
| 1979 | THE FLYING DUTCHMAN (Frankfurt) |
| 1979 | THE TURN OF THE SCREW (English National Opera) |
| 1980 | ARABELLA (English National Opera) |
| 1980–1 | FALSTAFF (Kent Opera) |
| 1981 | OTELLO (English National Opera) |
| 1982 | RIGOLETTO (English National Opera; Thames TV production, 1983) |
| 1982 | COSÌ FAN TUTTE (St Louis, Missouri) |
| 1982 | HAMLET (Donmar Warehouse) |
| 1982–3 | FIDELIO (Kent Opera) |
| 1983 | THE MAGIC FLUTE (Scottish Opera) |
| 1985 | DON GIOVANNI (English National Opera) |

## Film and Television

| 1962–3 | WHAT'S GOING ON NOW (TV series, New York) *director* |
|------|------|
| 1964 | ONE WAY PENDULUM (Woodfall Films, dir. Peter Yates) *actor* |
| 1964–5 | MONITOR (BBC TV) *series editor/presenter* |
| 1965 | PROFILES IN COURAGE: ANNE HUTCHINSON (TV New York, dir. José Quintero) *writer* |
| 1965 | THE DRINKING PARTY (PLATO'S SYMPOSIUM) (BBC TV 'Sunday Night' film) *producer-director* |
| 1966 | ALICE IN WONDERLAND (BBC TV film) *producer-director* |
| 1967 | SCOTCH (documentary film for John Walker & Sons) *writer-director* |
| 1968 | OH WHISTLE AND I'LL COME TO YOU (BBC TV 'Omnibus' film) *producer-director* |
| 1970 | TAKE A GIRL LIKE YOU (Columbia Pictures) *director* |
| 1973 | CLAY (BBC TV 'Full House' film) *director* |
| 1975 | KING LEAR (BBC TV 'Play of the Month') *director* |
| 1977 | THE BODY IN QUESTION (BBC TV 13-part series) *writer-presenter* |
| 1980 | THE TAMING OF THE SHREW (The BBC Television Shakespeare) *producer-director* |

1980    THE MERCHANT OF VENICE (The BBC Television Shakespeare, dir. Jack Gold) *producer*

1980    ALL'S WELL THAT ENDS WELL (BBC Television Shakespeare, dir. Elija Moshinsky) *producer*

1980    A WINTER'S TALE (BBC Television Shakespeare, dir. Jane Howell) *producer*

1980    ANTONY AND CLEOPATRA (BBC Television Shakespeare) *producer-director*

1981    TIMON OF ATHENS (BBC Television Shakespeare) *producer-director*

1981    OTHELLO (BBC Television Shakespeare) *producer-director*

1981    TROILUS AND CRESSIDA (BBC Television Shakespeare) *producer-director*

1981    A MIDSUMMER NIGHT'S DREAM (BBC Television Shakespeare, dir. Elija Moshinsky) *producer*

1981    HENRY VI: PARTS I–III (BBC Television Shakespeare, dir. Jane Howell) *producer*

1982    KING LEAR (BBC Television Shakespeare) *director*

1982    STATES OF MIND (BBC TV, 15-part series) *writer-presenter*

1983    RIGOLETTO (Thames TV/Channel 4) *introduced/collaborated on TV version of English National Opera production*

1984    THE BEGGAR'S OPERA (BBC TV) *producer-director*

1984    IVAN (BBC TV 'Horizon' documentary, with Ivan Vaughan and Jonathan Miller) *presenter*

1985    COSÌ FAN TUTTE (BBC TV) *director*

# I: *THE AFTERLIFE*

# I

In 1977 when I was unexpectedly invited to deliver the T. S. Eliot Memorial Lectures at the University of Kent, the only subject that I felt qualified to discuss was the role of the director in the theatre, and the fate of plays as they underwent revival from one generation to the next. The sense of honour that I felt in being invited to give these lectures was followed by the disabling suspicion that the arguments I might develop would almost certainly have struck Mr Eliot as a questionable form of tribute. What made me uneasy was recognizing that many of his remarks about literary criticism could be even more damagingly applied to the efforts of the modern theatrical producer, and that he would have deplored the fate of classic texts in the so-called director's theatre as the inevitable result of giving undue emphasis to the 'trifling oddities' of the second-rate artist.

For Eliot had a protective regard for the 'distinguished reputations' of the past and insisted that anyone who took it upon himself to communicate the meaning of a great writer's work had a duty to 'discipline his personal prejudices and cranks . . . and compose his differences with as many of his fellows as possible, in the common pursuit of true judgement'. Although this was written in the context of literary criticism I suspect that he would have recommended the same sort of reticence when it came to theatrical production, and that he would have been dismayed to discover that the modern director, far from composing his differences with as many of his fellows as possible, takes pride in asserting the trifling differences that are his distinction.

My suspicions were confirmed by an essay by one of Eliot's most distinguished sponsors. In one of her Charles Eliot Norton lectures, Helen Gardner draws an unfavourable comparison between modern productions of Shakespeare and the ones that were staged in the 'classic' period of the English theatre. Dame Helen attributes the deterioration to the intervention of the over-imaginative producer and points out that, in the 'great' productions she enjoyed before 1960, the reticence of the producer was such that she had 'no idea' who he was:

> *I remember Gielgud's two Hamlets and the* Romeo and Juliet *in which he and Olivier exchanged the roles of Romeo and Mercutio and Peggy Ashcroft played Juliet to Edith Evans as the Nurse. I remember that the costumes were by a firm called Motley and were extremely beautiful. I do not remember, if indeed I ever knew, who produced Robeson in* Othello *with Peggy Ashcroft as an exquisite Desdemona. And, in the fifties, when Byam Shaw was producing at Stratford, nobody spoke of Byam Shaw's* Macbeth *or his* As You Like It, *but of Olivier's* Macbeth, *the greatest Macbeth I have ever seen, and of Peggy Ashcroft's heavenly Rosalind.*

According to this view, the sudden rise of the director who is often, as she says, rather direly university trained and eager to push his own ideas, introduces a screen of interpretation that intervenes between the text and the performer. Now this line of argument implies both that the great actor has an intuitive sense of how to render Shakespeare's text, and that the director is most profitably employed when he is anonymously creating an atmosphere within which the performer is free to develop these intuitions. When this argument is taken up within the theatrical profession, the actors' instincts are, in their view, constitutionally more reliable than those of directors, and the best results are obtained when the director is either excluded altogether or kept firmly on the periphery as a consultant so that the performers can decide among themselves how the play is to be performed.

In the case of Shakespeare there is a potent myth that he wrote in the light of his experience as an actor and that his wisdom and dramatic imagination can, therefore, be intuitively understood by the acting profession. Actors who uphold this claim often refer to Shakespeare as 'Will', and in recent years some of them have inaugurated special companies in which strenuous efforts have been made to eliminate the type of interpretations imposed by ambitious 'theorists'. What happens then? Well, by some sort of democratic discussion amongst themselves, and by pooling their collective wisdom as actors they will, in theory at least, put themselves in touch with Shakespeare's imagination and deliver the lines as they were intended to be performed.

This assumes that the text has some sort of quantum of intrinsic meaning that can be identified with something elusive called 'the intention of the author' which can be discovered and restored in an ideal performance. As I hope to show in the course of the book, this critical notion is fraught with contradictions when it comes to deciding how to perform a play. First of all, it conjures up a completely unrealistic and utopian idea of what an 'actors' company' would be like. A director must inevitably emerge after a few days, simply because the most imaginative and most eloquent actor, or the one with the most prestige or the loudest voice, assumes the role of chairman – or master interpreter – and the less eloquent and the less forceful simply submit.

Many actors feel that the director has a crucial and indispensable role not as the interpreter but as an employee who provides the actors with his knowledge of the world of the play and its performing traditions. Here is the idea of an actors' company which admits the presence of a director on probation. Instead of being the inaugurator of the production, who then hires the actors in the light of the ideas he has about how the play should be performed, the system is reversed: a group of actors undertakes to do the play and then hires the director to reconcile differences amongst a number of powerful and persuasive individuals. He is an editor who eliminates gestures, intonations and styles of performance that are inconsistent with a hypothetical ideal of the life of the play, or the world of the playwright. The director attends simply as a human encyclopaedia to provide necessary information about stance and expression, in the light of *his* reading of the antiquity from which the play comes. This variation has yet to be tested in practice, but it too assumes that a direct line of communication can be opened between performer and author through which the ideal performance – or that approximating the author's intention most closely – will be released.

To judge by the reaction of the critics, many of whom greeted with considerable enthusiasm the prospect of encouraging actors to stage Shakespeare without the help of a director, the result has not been altogether successful. In fact, productions have often been described as rudderless and uninteresting. But imaginative productions have almost always been associated with institutions in which generous public subsidies have allowed the management to offer the promise of long rehearsals and competitive salaries. Lacking these resources, newly founded actors' companies have been at a serious disadvantage when it comes to recruiting the best available talent. To make matters worse, many of the performers who enrol in such companies are prompted by a reactionary hostility to the influence of imaginative 'concepts', a negative attitude often associated with a determination to turn the clock back to the 'good old days'. It is not surprising that the productions come across as dated rather than authentic.

Yet there is no evidence to support the claim that these experiments under more favourable circumstances would necessarily lead to the results promised by the enthusiasts. I have a sneaking suspicion that, even if actors with the best attitude are left to their own devices, they tend to introduce mannerisms just as distracting as those said to be imposed by directors. Not everyone who is irritated by the ideas introduced by clever directors is prepared to believe that the best remedy is to rely on the intuitions of seasoned performers. On the contrary, there is a well-established belief that the acting profession has an unhelpfully simple-minded view about what makes Shakespeare valuable and that, even with the finest performers, there is little to choose between the sentimental mannerisms introduced by the actor and the reductive ideas imposed by the director. In the face of this dilemma it is sometimes suggested that Shakespeare would fare much better if removed from the professional theatre altogether. In the last twenty years or so a dogma has arisen that admits that, while there can be no actual ideal performance, its nearest approximation is realized by someone who responds to the text in an unmediated way. If the nearest we get to some kind of 'ideal' performance is that which is least interfered with by clever directors or actors, then it can be argued (and often is) that the purest and most

moving performances are the ones given by amateurs or even schoolchildren.

It is easy to see the appeal of these alternatives. Schoolchildren are
considered to be too innocent to have had any elaborate or distracting
thoughts about the text and, by piping out the words as they occur on
the page, they leave the audience free to develop its own interpretations.
The argument for adult amateurs is slightly different. Their age favours a
mature understanding but, since they have not been exposed to the
corrupting influence of professional training, their delivery is thought to
be uncontaminated by actorish mannerisms. It would be wrong to
dismiss these arguments as completely absurd but it is difficult to take
either of them seriously.

As far as the schoolchild's performance is concerned, the appeal has
little to do with innocent diction revealing the essence of Shakespeare;
the principal virtue is the unintended one of incongruity. The spectacle of
titanic emotions expressed by diminutive performers who do not
understand the implications of the text provides a refreshing surrealistic
shock and forces the audience to pay attention to a text that may be over-
familiar. The idea is that as a merely competent reader of English the
child acts as a channel without structure, bringing you the text as
Shakespeare wrote and conceived it. This in itself is unrealizable, but one
has to concede that there is something refreshing and sometimes
revealing about a performance given by children. A playwright like
Marston, for example, wrote *The Malcontent* deliberately to be performed
by children and to make use of this effect. By presenting monstrous and
wicked events and actions that could not possibly have been perpetrated
by children he drew the audience's attention to their incongruity and
outrageousness. With amateur adults, I think what happens is rather
different and that any excellence that occurs is by default, in the sense
that a good performance is usually given by someone who under different
circumstances would be a professional, and is judged by the criteria of the
professional theatre. The rest of the performance is merely endured.

But these are desperate expedients and the logical conclusion of the
arguments on which they are based is that no performance can do justice
to the amplitude and complexity of Shakespeare's texts. The very act of
putting his plays on stage automatically pre-empts the alternative
meanings that would otherwise occur in the mind of the private reader.
Implicit in this idea is the notion of the primary status of the text,
particularly when it comes to Shakespeare, as a literary work. It then
follows that in some peculiar way the play is at its very best when read
quietly by the informed reader, who somehow manages to dramatize in
his or her imagination a performance that is more congruent with the
intentions of the author than *any* particular performance could ever be,
and *all* performances then represent a lapse from this ideal state. This

presupposes that there is something committal about a reading as opposed to a performance. All sorts of things can be held in suspense in the imagination and do not have to be committed either to a specific visual appearance or to a very specific and concrete tone of voice. In this suspended state the literary text can still maintain the richness of possible associations because it is not committed to any particular one.

In a very important sense great plays can be said to exist without being theatrically performed, and I cannot deny the fact that each time a play is staged the production is inevitably a limited version of the range of possible interpretations. But if the principle that plays should be read rather than performed were to be taken seriously it would dissolve the distinction between drama and all the other forms of literature, and make it difficult to understand why a writer had chosen to cast his ideas in the form of a play at all. In fact, the suggestion that plays are best left unperformed is comparable to the belief that novels can be successfully dramatized. In both cases, there is a fundamental misunderstanding about the structure and purpose of the genre. A play that has been kept unperformed has been aborted, whereas a novel that has undergone dramatization has been irreversibly mutilated. As long as we recognize and accept the argument that performance is, necessarily, a limitation, then the destiny of a great play is to undergo a series of performances each of which is incomplete, and in some cases may prove misleading and perverse. By submitting itself to the possibility of successive re-creation, however, the play passes through the development that is its birthright, and its meaning begins to be fully appreciated only when it enters a period that I shall call its *afterlife*. In the case of Shakespeare's plays, for example, what is often disputed is the form that their continued existence takes (and who should determine that form) when the plays have outlived their original creation and performance. There is a tendency to forget that for a playwright like Shakespeare the written script was not intended for publication but as an aid to performance without any view to a distant posterity.

This term and idea applies not only to plays but to other works of art that survive the period in which they were conceived and first realized. I have borrowed the word 'afterlife' from Aby Warburg, the founder of the Warburg Institute, which he described as a place where scholars could study 'the afterlife of the antique'. He was referring to the process by which classical culture was revived following its long neglect after the fall of the Western Roman Empire. This process took a peculiar course, described by one of Warburg's colleagues as 'an undulating curve of estrangements and rapprochements', culminating in the triumphant restoration that we now recognize as the Renaissance.

I find the phrase useful because it draws attention to the peculiar transformation undergone by works of art that outlive the time in which

## The Belvedere Torso

*This is a torso by default. The sculptor who created this seated figure had no reason to anticipate that it could become damaged and mutilated by time. And yet it is in this form that it has assumed its canonical status. Even if the missing parts could be recovered it is difficult to imagine a restoration that could satisfy a modern audience. The peculiar thing is that we do not see it as the representation of a damaged body, nor do we see it as a damaged representation of a complete one. In its afterlife, it has assumed a self-sufficient identity so that the restoration of the missing parts will seem just as vandalistic as the knocking off of the bits that survive.*

Marcus Aurelius

*Michelangelo has restaged a new production of an old statue. Wrenched from its original context and classical setting, placed on a rostrum that is recognizably different from the original, the work has been redramatized. Although it preserves the physical identity of the original, its dramatic function has changed by being put on to a Renaissance stage.*

IMP. CAESARI·DIVI·ANTONINI·F·DIVI·HADRIAN
NEPOTI·DIVI·TRAIANI·PARTHICI·PRONEPOTI·DIVI
NERVAE·ABNEPOTI·M·AVRELIO·ANTONINO·PIO

*Mantegna*, Le Calvaire

*There is nothing careless or sketchy about Mantegna's treatment of this small predella from the St Zeno altar-piece. But now it is isolated from the complete work, in which its significance would have been diminished by contrast to the altar-piece, it has assumed an unprecedented value as a work of art in its own right.*

*Uccello*, The Profanation of the Host
*iv. The Execution of the Repentant Woman*
*v. The Jew and his Family are Burned*
*vi. Angels and Devils Dispute over the Woman's Corpse*

*Designed as a decorative border to an altar-piece whose main part has been lost, Uccello's predella is now subject to a concentrated gaze altogether different to the one for which it was designed. In its afterlife, it has assumed a more dramatic importance than Uccello could ever have anticipated.*

they were made. If they are rediscovered after a long period of being lost or neglected, it is as if they are perceived and valued for reasons so different from those held originally that they virtually change their character and identity. There comes a point in the life of any cultural artefact, whether a play or a painting, when the continued existence of the physical token that represents it does not necessarily mean that the original identity of the work survives. In some examples of painting or sculpture the re-evaluation is the result of physical deterioration; the object may be recovered in a form that would no longer be acknowledged by its maker. The classical Greek sculptors, for example, presumably allowed for the natural process of weathering, and some of them might have welcomed the patina that their creation acquired in later years. But we cannot assume that they would have been delighted by the mutilation that befell so many of these works as a result of years of burial and neglect. When pieces of classical sculpture were recovered and collected during the Renaissance, however, part of their appeal was undoubtedly associated with their mutilation. There is little doubt that some of the charisma of the Belvedere Torso can be attributed to its suggestive incompleteness, and that the work is now being appreciated for features that would have been regarded as faults by the artists of antiquity. A sculpture, originally made to conform to certain standards of finish and perfection, resurfaces in a culture that puts a distinctive premium upon the suggestiveness of the unfinished work.

There is another reason why we esteem works that have been bequeathed to us in a badly worn or damaged condition. In this form the works in question bear witness to their own antiquity, and this is valued for its own sake. When certain ancient monuments are restored the refurbishment induces public indignation and a belief that the object no longer looks like an antique work of art. Confronted by the effects of expensive washing and re-dressing the public often feels cheated of its heritage as the work has acquired canonical status in its weathered or injured form.

The situation is made more complicated by the fact that restoration is frequently carried out insensitively so that the finished work is necessarily offensive. And yet even when performed with all the available resources of skill and scholarship we are left with the uneasy sense that a diaphanous hood of interpretation has been slipped over the repair and that, far from being restored to its original state, the object has merely provided an armature on to which the modern craftsman has imposed his own ideas about the distant past. This is analogous with the sense of disappointment underlying criticisms of the interpretation imposed upon the classics by the contemporary theatre director. Yet it is difficult to see how plays, paintings or sculptures can be restored to their original splendour without some imposition of interpretation on the part of the artist reproducing the object.

As well as the physical effects that can be inflicted upon an object, comparable social and institutional influences change the life of a work of art. The work may be transferred to a place or setting that bears no resemblance to the one where it had a recognizable social, aesthetic or religious function. It would be nonsense to talk of the object merely continuing its life; it has a new one – an afterlife. The equestrian statue of Marcus Aurelius, for example, was originally a triumphant effigy of this Roman emperor. It was then lost, or simply lay around Rome, was recovered during the Renaissance, misidentified as a portrait of Constantine, and finally placed by Michelangelo on the pedestal in the centre of the Piazza del Campidoglio in Rome as a demonstration of the Christian Imperial theme. Even if we now know its real identity, we can no longer see the statue as the original would have been seen. Apart from the fact that it is placed in a strange, and previously unthinkable, setting there are simple anomalies like the absence of stirrups. For its original audience, the dangling feet would have seemed natural but we see them as due to a peculiar lack of stirrups, which were quite unknown to the Romans of antiquity.

Some works of art are deliberately dismembered in the course of their repossession by later periods so that they take the form of unrepresentative fragments. Once again this has an irreversible effect upon the way in which they are perceived. Plunder and commerce often led to the dispersal of certain Renaissance altarpieces, for example, with the result that works that were once appreciated for their carefully designated entirety are now distributed amongst widely separated galleries. When they are disconnected in this way the perceptual effect of the fragments is altogether different from the one they would have had when displayed as part of the original integrated art work; they begin to acquire unintended values by being the subjects of an unforeseen type of scrutiny. When a predella is removed from the altarpiece to which it belongs and is displayed as an independent object in its own right, the illustrated strip acquires a significance it would never have had when subordinated to the image for which it supplied a decorative border. Visitors to the ducal palace at Urbino have become acquainted with Uccello's *Profanation of the Host* unaware of the fact that when originally attached to the lost altarpiece for which it was painted it would have dwindled to a marginal ribbon of ornament. In its afterlife it has enlarged to become a masterpiece in its own right. An even more vivid example is Mantegna's *Crucifixion* in the Louvre. Wrenched from its rightful place in a predella belonging to the great altarpiece in S. Zeno at Verona, this phosphorescent panel has assumed monumental proportions.

The fact that these works are now exhibited in galleries rather than churches has had an important part to play in transforming their identity. Apart from any decay or restoration they may have undergone, they have

The Annunciation
1. *Fra Angelico*
2. *Piero della Francesca*
3. *Alesso Baldovinetti*
4. *Master of the Barberini Panels*
5. *Sandro Botticelli*

*According to Michael Baxandall the gestures of the virgin's hands are to be read as formal representations of the successive stages of the Angelic Colloquy. Derived from handbooks on Franciscan preaching, their significance would have been sharply differentiated, but to a modern audience the semaphore has become indistinct and incidental to the overall theme of the Annunciation itself.*

been changed by social re-allocation. Something that was once intended to guide and intensify religious experience is now being enjoyed as an example of aesthetic achievement. The spectator cannot exempt himself from the role in which he has been cast by the act of entering a gallery, and the secular gaze that now falls upon the picture changes it just as much as the dust and smoke of time. Even if the picture were confronted as an aid to religious devotion today, it has entered its afterlife and many of the signs that are there as aids to the original congregation can no longer be read by a modern audience. Michael Baxandall has pointed out the specific information that is conveyed by the various positions of the Virgin's hand in quattrocento Annunciations. There are, according to him, five successive phases of the Angelic Exchange or Colloquy and each position of the Virgin's hands characteristically registers one of these.

For an audience who knows nothing of this, the positions of the Virgin's hands are no more than trivial variations on the single theme of the Annunciation, vaguely expressive perhaps, but not especially significant. An audience familiar with the possible alternatives, however, would have automatically known which of the five phases of the angelic colloquy they were being invited to meditate on: the semaphore was recognized. If a modern congregation were now to use that object as an aid to devotion, it would face it merely in a mood of generalized piety, unaware of the specific code it was there to show. Even if the language were understood, as it might be by the art historian code-breakers, the picture would still not be read as it was when first presented. We are no longer a pious audience; if we distinguish one of the five phases we do so as informed tourists.

The predicament is made even more complicated by the different policies that determine how a picture is displayed in a gallery. When a painting is exhibited alongside other works by the same artist, its appearance is altogether different from the one that it has when hung next to works done by other painters of the same period. When a painting is displayed as an instance of a genre – in an exhibition devoted to still life, for example – it looks altogether different from the way it would appear in an exhibition devoted to the many different works of a particular period. The way in which a painting is perceived is also influenced by the *way in which it is reproduced*. The appearance of many great works has been irreversibly changed by being introduced to the public in the form of photographic copies, most of which represent the work on an incorrect scale. Visitors to a gallery or a church are often shocked to discover that a picture is either much larger or much smaller than it seemed in a book of reproductions. The viewer's confusion is increased by the custom of reproducing enormously blown-up details, some of which become more attractive than the whole painting, which may seem quite disappointing by contrast.

For all these reasons it seems right and proper to describe the renewed existence of these works of art as afterlives, and to see them not simply as faint or attenuated versions of their previous existences but as full-blooded representations of their existence now. This unforeseen hereafter that we inhabit, and in which we perceive such objects, departs so much from the time of the work's original conception that it seems advisable to think of the work as a separate entity with its own peculiar conditions.

The concept of an afterlife can be usefully applied to plays on a rather different logical level. This is because there is no particular object, perishable or otherwise, with which a play can be identified. What is being referred to when someone talks about the *existence* of such a work? The continued existence of *Hamlet*, for instance, does not depend on the *existence* of any particular copy of the text since any old version will do as long as it is a reliable transcript of the original. The contrast with a painting is self-evident. Piero's *Flagellation* can be said to '*exist*' *only* if the authenticated handiwork of the artist survives. Neither copy nor forgeries will do. This is a distinction that Nelson Goodman makes in *Languages of Art*, between what he calls autographic works of art, which are identified with handwork, and those he calls allographic, which have to be re-created in performance. An autographic work, like the *Flagellation* by Piero, is one whose identity presupposes the continued existence of the physical artefact that left its maker's hand, and only with the destruction of the work itself does it cease to exist, although it may survive by imitation or copy in a forgery. The very existence of an autographic work makes forgery possible – but there cannot be a forgery of an allographic work, like a play, which does not physically exist as an object in the same way as a painting or sculpture. You might forge a manuscript but how could you counterfeit a production?

These problems apply to any work in which performance is recognized as a constitutive part of the art. As Nelson Goodman points out, an unperformed play is not quite so forlorn as an unperformed symphony. *King Lear* could have had an intelligible existence without ever having been staged, whereas the very notion of an unperformed *Winterreise* seems unimaginable. Yet there is a sense in which a play can be said to have been completed only when work has been supplied by someone other than the playwright. This does not mean that playwrights are slipshod artists, constitutionally incapable of finishing their own work, or that their relationship to the actors who perform their plays is in any way comparable to that of a great painter who leaves his assistants to apply the finishing brush strokes as, for example, Verrocchio left Leonardo to finish his *Baptism* by painting in one of the angels' heads. The craftsmanship supplied by the theatrical profession belongs to a different category from the work that went into making the script, whereas the effort that goes into revising or finishing a painting is merely a continuation of that which brought it into existence in the first place.

Of course, in a purely practical sense the continued existence of *Hamlet* depends on the survival of at least one reliable text but since it makes no difference which one it may be tempting, as Richard Wollheim points out, to identify the play with the class of all its reliable copies. This suggestion is open to several objections, one of which is that the fortunes of *Hamlet* would then fluctuate with the number of copies in existence. If there were twenty thousand copies would the play be more substantially *in existence* than if there was only one? It also ignores the possibility of performance. The alternative expedient, of identifying a play with one of its performances, will not work either because it would follow that any faults in that particular performance would apply to the play itself. And what would one want to say about a play that had never been performed?

In the effort to discover *something* in which the existence of a play could be said to consist, the suggestion is sometimes made that each work should be identified with an ideal performance, that is to say with no actual performance but with the best imaginable one. But it is always logically possible to imagine a better performance than any particular one claiming that status. This concept cannot supply the wherewithal for a play's continued existence. Besides, the notion of an ideal performance begs the very question that this book explores. It implies that an ideal performance would be unanimously recognizable if and when it occurred. This, of course, is the point at issue. Not everyone agrees with Dame Helen Gardner that the best imaginable production of *Macbeth* was the one in which Laurence Olivier performed the title role; those who were satisfied by Trevor Nunn's production of the play would almost inevitably disagree with Dame Helen. Great plays seem to be capable of an almost infinite number of alternative performances and, unless we make the improbable assumption that successive productions have a built-in tendency either to improve or to degenerate as time goes on, it is impossible to predict when and where the ideal is likely to realize itself.

The allographic work of art introduces all the ambiguities and open-endedness that give rise to the debate about the role of the director that we began with. You have a text, the purpose of which is to provide the instructions from which it is possible to produce a performance; but that, as Nelson Goodman points out, is not the text's only function in allographic works. It is also an authenticating device, the purpose of which is to provide a system of identification that allows you to say, on any given occasion, that this performance is an instance of the work in question.

It seems to me that the scripts of plays are ineffective in regard to both of these functions. The text of a play is surprisingly short on the instructions required to bring a performance into existence. Playwrights do not include – and cannot, because of a shortage of notation – all those details of prosody, inflexion, stress, tempo and rhythm. A script tells us nothing about the gestures, the stance, the facial expressions, the dress, the weight, or the grouping or the movements. So although the text is a necessary condition for the performance it is by no means a sufficient one. It is short of all these accessories which are, in a sense, the *essence* of performance. The literal act of reading the words of a script does not constitute a performance. Words are nothing more than the bare minimum when staging a play. Similarly, the script is defective as an identity card unless we accept that a play is fully performed simply when all the words are given in the right order.

I remember standing in the wings one night at a performance of *Hamlet* when the actors came off stage complaining bitterly about having seen a man in the front row following the performance with a text. Quite apart from the fact that they felt it was rude not to have their performance *watched*, they also felt anxious that their lines and words were being checked. While they were relieved to hear from the stage manager's report that they were word perfect I wonder how they would have felt if the text had contained considerably more. After all, if the play is an identifying document, and not merely an enabling one, they would have had no reason to feel relieved merely because they had given the words in the right order, as the prosodic instructions that Shakespeare might have included would be just as constitutive of its identity as the sequence of words. An actor who gave a slightly querulous intonation to a line that Shakespeare had instructed to be spoken in an assertive and bold way, would have just as much reason for feeling guilt as he might at having omitted some of the words.

In a sense, one of the measures of a great play is that it has the capacity to generate an almost infinite series of unforeseeable inflexions. Had Shakespeare, by virtue of some sort of notational resource as yet undiscovered, been able to write down all these things he would have pre-empted the possibility of this successive enrichment which occurs from one performance to the next. One of the reasons why Shakespeare continues to be performed is not that there *is* a central realizable intention in each play that we still continue to value, but because we are still looking for the possibility of unforeseen meanings.

There are ways in which this ambiguity can be abused. If, for example, an interpretation that derived in performance turned Claudius into a shining hero, and Hamlet into a treacherous villain, it would have violated the genre within which the playwright was working. While I am arguing that these plays are apparently open-ended, and that to pre-empt such open-endedness is perverse and would guarantee the work's early death, I admit that they are not totally malleable and should not be subject to an infinite number of possible interpretations. Common sense, tact and literary sensitivity *should* prevent the director or actor from introducing interpretations or versions of the play that are profoundly inconsistent with the range of meanings understood as constitutive of the play's genre. So that although I sponsor the idea that the afterlife of a play is a process of emergent evolution, during which meanings and emphases develop that might not have been apparent at the time of writing, even to the author, this does not imply that the text is a Rorschach inkblot into whose indeterminate outlines the director can project whatever he wants. On the contrary, the developmental possibilities are constrained and although it is difficult to make these constraints explicit it is usually easy to identify a performance in which the deep structure of its inherent meanings has been dislocated. In fact, by using the phrase 'emergent evolution' I have drawn considerable inspiration from the biological model of organic change.

In the phylogenetic history of an evolving organism it is always possible to recognize the existence of a morphological prototype and while this may undergo extensive transformation, with the unexpected enlargement of one part accompanied by a proportional shrinkage of another, the structural relationships are preserved so that it is easy to recognize the underlying affinity of many different examples. As Darwin pointed out, careful analysis shows that the fin of a porpoise, the paw of a lion, the hoof of a horse and the wing of a bird or bat are all related to one another by their common descent from a prototypical vertebrate limb. The successive performances of a play or an opera can be compared to this process; and although the works may undergo changes that are sometimes tantamount to anamorphic distortions, something equivalent to topological propriety is preserved from one instance to the next.

Another model that I find useful is the procedure used by cartographers

*D'Arcy Thompson from* On Growth and Form

*As biological evolution progresses, the proportions of an organism may be stretched and shrunk but it is still possible to trace the line of descent and to identify the modern form as an altered version of the ancestral prototype.*

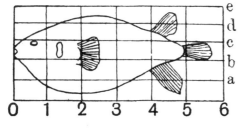

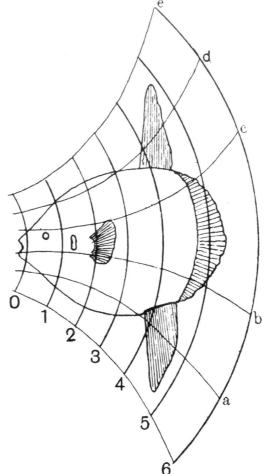

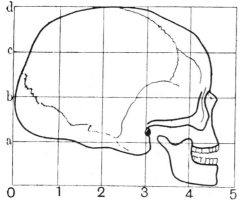

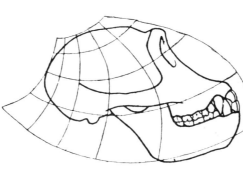

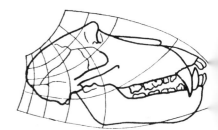

when transferring a map of the world from a spherical globe on to the flat surface of a page. The oceans and continents preserve the topological continuities of the original but can do so only at the expense of considerable changes in their relative proportions. The point is that as long as the director observes some intuitive sense of topological decorum his own production, albeit different from those of his predecessors, can be mapped on to them and through them can be mapped finally on to the structures of meaning that are inherent in the original text.

In recent years these proprieties have often been set aside to allow productions in which there would seem to be no limits to the director's imaginative energy. In the kind of production that I have in mind, many of which seem to originate in Germany, it is difficult to identify any organic continuity between the production in question and its predecessors, and the work appears to be quoted rather than produced. These productions are so fractured that it becomes impossible to map them on to anything inherent in the text. When that happens I feel as if I am confronted by something that resembles a foetal abnormality – in which the orderly process of emergent development has been arrested and distorted by morbid processes working against the long-term interests of the work in question. Unfortunately critical fashion has often favoured these bizarre aberrations, and productions that have developed along more organic lines may be dismissed as boringly obvious.

*As a play is transformed from one revival to the next it can undergo enormous alterations in shape and proportion so that characters and scenes that seemed unimportant in one production loom unexpectedly large in the next. But as in a Mercator projection, the topological relations are preserved, and the work still has the narrative consistency of the original. Even if the work is distorted, it should be possible to map its internal relationships on to those of the original.*

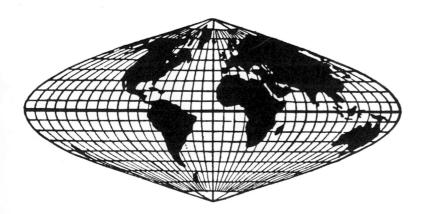

We can imagine that confronted by an all-male version of *As You Like It* Shakespeare might have some difficulty in recognizing it as the play that he wrote and had performed in 1594. In fact, if the theatrical illustrations of any one Shakespearean play were arranged around in chronological order they would look so different that it may be easier to recognize the period of the picture than the identity of the play. Yet all these performances were generated by the same script and its failure to give rise to identical products means that its status as a set of instructions is somewhat ambiguous. Scripts may contain clearly instructive passages, such as stage directions which prescribe certain physical actions – '*Konstantin moves rapidly upstage, opens the French windows and vanishes on to the veranda. He returns accompanied by Nina*' – but the bulk of the text is made up of speeches, and the sense in which these should be regarded as instructions is much less clear. This becomes more apparent when you contrast such notation with, for example, the following passage assigned to the clarinet in Mozart's Quintet in A, K581, where it is difficult to regard the symbols as anything *other* than a set of instructions.

*Score showing the clarinet passage from Mozart's quintet, K581*

*For each of the notes written down on the stave of a Mozart score there is an acoustic event that complies or fails to comply with it. In this respect, the score is notational; the characters are unambiguously distinct from one another as are the corresponding sound events. But since there is no notational system for representing the style of the piece, the performance is left to the discretion of the players, and the question of whether any given performance is a satisfactory instance of the work becomes the subject of debate that cannot be settled by reference to what the composer has written. With scripts, as opposed to scores, the relationship between notation and performance is much more ambiguous since the range of acoustic events that count as an instance of what the author has written down is much more debatable.*

While a script is an example of a notation, and in that sense at least resembles the inscriptions in a knitting pattern or a musical score, it is very important not to be seduced by this analogy between words and music. Angered by a floridly conceptual production of a play, critics sometimes point out that no one would ever dare to take such liberties with the performance of a Mozart symphony and that the modern director should pay as much respect to a script as a conductor does to a great classical score. According to those who exploit this analogy, re-staging *Hamlet* in modern dress is comparable to re-scoring the 'Haffner' for brass band and Moog synthesizer, and, since no one in his right mind would dream of doing that, why should anyone take the liberty of vandalizing the work of a great playwright? The frequency with which this argument recurs suggests that there is an illuminating similarity between symphonies and plays and that, because the performance of both depends on the obedient following of scripted instructions, the decorum that is observed in one is indistinguishable from the etiquette that applies to the other. This view is misleading and unhelpful. It assumes that successive performances of any one musical work are much more standard-ized than in fact they are. But the important point is that the so-called *language of music* cannot be usefully compared to the language of human discourse. People speak glibly of the language of music, and although this is only a figure of speech, I think it has encouraged a critical assumption that words and music lie on the same level of interpretability. The extent to which music can be regarded as a language at all is highly questionable. We might accept that a score, like a script, relies on notation, the forming of 'phrases', a syntax, and that music can conjure up images – the third movement of Beethoven's 'Pastoral' Symphony skilfully re-creates the impression of a storm. It can evoke moods and, in its own idiosyncratic way, it can also represent colourful scenes and natural events but, since it can neither assert nor deny, there is no way in which music can *describe* the scenes that it represents.

Nor is there anything in music, for example, that corresponds to a word: there are no recognizable units or segments for which one can substitute alternative bits with equivalent meanings. Perhaps the best way of highlighting the differences is that you cannot even imagine a paraphrase in music. We talk about phrases in music and we talk about phrases in language, but it is central to language that phrases can be paraphrased. The meaning that is expressed by a sentence can remain more or less constant under paraphrase. We can think of the first line of *Anna Karenina*, for example, and know that it will survive not merely paraphrase in Russian but translation into English. It is impossible, however, to imagine what would count as a paraphrase of the opening bars of Beethoven's 'Hammerklavier' because there is no central, under-lying proposition that would remain constant and survive an alternative expression in another series of notes. Music is syntactical but not semantic. Despite the fact that we talk about 'the composition of music' there are no *rules* of composition; what one composes in music are its elements. Those elements can, in fact, have significance by being composed but they do not refer to another domain of propositions that survive transformation into a different composition.

This is not the only reason why the comparison between scripts and scores turns out to be unworkable. In contrast to musical phrases, the sentences in a script represent the utterances of a particular character and there is an important distinction to be made between the meaning of the sentence and the meaning that it has for the person who utters it. Recognizing what someone means by a particular phrase calls for something over and above the linguistic knowledge that enables us to produce a synonymous expression. It is necessary to take into account who spoke it, to whom and under what circumstances. The artist who plays the solo instrument in Haydn's Cello Concerto in D can successfully perform the part without having to imagine being anything other than a cellist; she does not have to pretend to be Haydn or some person imagined by Haydn. The actor who plays the part of Claudius, on the other hand, can expect to succeed only if he imagines a person who consistently means something by the lines that appear opposite his name in the script. Claudius's speeches could be said to have a meaning that is independent of any particular person who might utter them but their full significance becomes apparent only when put into the mouth of a recognizable character who cannot be identified on the evidence of the scripted speeches alone. For example, on one level it is quite easy to recognize the meaning of Claudius's famous soliloquy which begins with the words, '*O! my offence is rank*', and it would be perverse to deny that these were the thoughts of a remorseful murderer. It is only by disregarding this and other written evidence that Cavafy was able to represent Claudius as an innocent victim slain by his deluded nephew. But the fact that the script leaves us in no doubt as to Claudius's resourceful villainy, by showing us, his readiness to commit further crimes in order to cover up the original one, does not mean that his character is unquestionably determined. On the contrary, there are several alternative ways of personifying him and with each of these portrayals the speeches begin to assume a different significance.

Similarly in *King Lear* it may be possible to identify what I can only describe as a sea level of meaning from the sentence, '*O! reason not the need*', and that irreducible level may remain unaffected by uttering this line in a hoarse whisper, in a guttural French growl or the electronic tones of the computer Hal in the film *2001*. Yet the purpose that this sentence serves in the play demands a more subtle identification of its meaning, and the inscription that Shakespeare provides to represent this line does not give enough phonetic instruction to identify its further reference in the domain of meaning. The point here is that although the meaning of the sentence may not be altered very much by the changed tone of voice, what Lear meant by speaking the sentence undoubtedly is. He could speak the line as if to say, 'Oh, for God's *sake*, let's not go into hair-splitting assessments of necessity', or as if to say, 'Jesus Christ, don't let's get into a discussion about *need*'. And yet Shakespeare's written script contains no explicit marks referring to the prosodic features that would make this difference clear. There is nothing referring to stress, pitch or intonation and, since the line is spaced according to the printer's conventions, there is nothing to indicate a pause or a crucial syncopation. There is no reference to facial expression or manual gesture, and yet all of these variables have a bearing on the sense or tone of the line.

The differences that I am referring to are not just colourful variations. They can alter the meaning of what is said and the character of the person who speaks. A relatively small change in pitch, stress and timbre of the way in which 'melt' is spoken in Hamlet's '*O! that this too too solid flesh would melt*', can make all the difference between exasperated disgust at being 'too too solid', and palely interesting melancholy. An actor who commits himself to the first reading has automatically biased his choice when it comes to the alternative readings of other lines, since a character who is angrily disgusted by the situation in which he finds himself will act and speak differently from someone who beautifies his despair.

The point is lucidly demonstrated by John Searle, when he invites the reader to imagine a situation in the Second World War in which an American soldier is ambushed by Italian troops and wishes to give them the impression that he is one of their German allies. What he would like to do is to express the meaning that is conveyed in the German phrase '*Ich bin ein deutsche Soldat*' but, unfortunately, the only German phrase that he knows – one he remembers from a freshman course in modern languages – is '*Kennst du das Land wo die Zitronen blühn?*' His intention in using this sentence is to make his non-German-speaking Italian captors believe that what he has actually said is: 'I am a German soldier' but this is not what the sentence itself means. As a well-formed German phrase, it means what Goethe meant it to mean, namely: 'Knowest thou the land where the lemon trees bloom?' Nevertheless, although the meaning of the phrase is *constrained* by the rules that determine the reference of its constituent words, its force varies according to the circumstances in which it is used and cannot be retrieved by parsing it. Let me give another example. The phrase 'This room needs painting' has an intelligible meaning regardless of the circumstances in which it is uttered. This means that, even taken out of context, it can be understood by anyone who speaks English. It cannot, for example, be used to express the idea 'This room needs demolishing' or, 'I could do with a drink'. But the force that it has is

41

quite a different question. If it is spoken by an estate agent who is trying to convince a reluctant client that an apartment is worth leasing in spite of its dingy appearance, the phrase might well be taken as an apologetic recommendation, tantamount to saying, 'This room could be quite attractive if it were painted. Disregard its dingy appearance and try to imagine what it would be like if it were redecorated.' But if it is spoken by a commanding officer in the course of a routine inspection, his underling would be wise to take it as an order. The same phrase is used to achieve two altogether different types of speech act: an apologetic recommendation on the one hand, and a menacingly veiled command on the other. And, although the circumstances are enough to distinguish the two types of speech act, the speaker of each one would reinforce the distinction by using the appropriate intonation. If all that was required to extract the speaker's meaning from a phrase were the rules of English composition there would be no room for irony or metaphor.

When someone says: 'Can you pass the salt?' – and you apply the rules of grammar as a merely competent speaker of English rather than a competent member of the English-speaking community – you would extract nothing other than a phrase that could be paraphrased: 'Are you able to pass the salt? Are you competent at salt-passing?' The rules of English would enable you to extract from that phrase only something about competence. Whereas you know that a speaker who asks this question is not inquiring about your ability to pass the salt, but is actually asking you to pass the salt. In other words, he's not making an enquiry, but a request. The humorous schoolboy answer is to say yes to such a request, and this itself is a joke about the difference between utterance meaning and speaker's meaning. This is an extremely simple example, and there are all sorts of very complicated elaborations of which metaphor is one. If you hear the advice: 'Put a Tiger in Your Tank' . . . and you were to extract the meaning on the basis of English composition alone, you would in fact have to undertake an elaborate programme of cramming a striped carnivore into a motor-car petrol tank. It is only a knowledge of the English community, car-owners, and assumptions about tigers having a fierceness that might apply to the power of petrol that enables us to see that this is not, in fact, an order to go out and track tigers for the boot of the car. That is an example of a collective level of speaker meaning.

The theory of speech acts is directly relevant to the problem of theatrical performance. Despite the fact that the speeches included in a script can be spoken more or less intelligibly, without having to take into account who uttered them, to whom and under what circumstances, knowing how to perform them so that the audience can recognize what the character means calls for something over and above a sensitive understanding of Tudor English. The lines that Claudius addresses to

Hamlet in Act I, scene 2, for example, have a meaning that can be identified without having to consider the context in which they occur.

> *Though yet of Hamlet our dear brother's death*
> *The memory be green; and that it us befitted*
> *To bear our hearts in grief and our whole kingdom*
> *To be contracted in one brow of woe;*
> *Yet so far hath discretion fought with nature,*
> *That we with wisest sorrow think on him,*
> *Together with remembrance of ourselves.*

Recited as an isolated poem, the lines may be taken to express the proposition that death comes to everyone and it is inappropriate to over-indulge a grief. In order to express these sentiments unambiguously, the speaker would have to distribute the stresses in the right way with the help of the poetic metre. But when it comes to speaking the lines *in the play*, and especially in a particular production of the play, the diction is much less determined than some critics seem to suppose. How the actor delivers the speech depends not only on the sentiments that it expresses but also on the effect that Claudius wishes to have on Hamlet at that particular moment in the play. And that, in turn, depends on what sort of person the actor and director suppose Claudius to be. Yet the argument that an accurate recognition of the character's personality will specify how the lines should be delivered is at best impractical. Claudius is a fictional person and his character is not decidable as it might be if it were based upon someone who had actually lived. As the play unfolds we learn all there is to know about him. Since all that exists of the character is in the play Shakespeare wrote it is pointless to ask for further biographical details. However, the actor who is cast in the role cannot afford to luxuriate in this interesting indeterminacy. Fictional though Claudius may be, the actor who plays him must convince the audience that his actions and speeches are determined by actual motives and must improvise his characterization on the understanding that the portrait that he then offers is, at best, an interesting and plausible conjecture.

The actor's performance as a particular character requires hypothesis. Critics often object to the introduction of hypothesis without realizing that, far from it being some kind of *contaminating* influence, it is in the nature of *all* perception. There are no perceptions without hypothesis but some may strike us as more outlandish and unacceptable than others. What happens when an actor approaches a part is something rather like the process used by scientists when they improvise and test a theory. In other words, although the text fails to portray the character that it is said to represent it will usually suggest some sort of hypothesis on the basis of which the actor can make a start. More often than not, the hypothesis goes a long way beyond the information that is given by the text and cannot, therefore, be justified by straightforwardly referring to the lines that the author has written. This applies also to the conjectures that must, at one time, have formed the basis of the traditional and widely accepted theatrical representations of the character in question. The difference is that the conjectural model that the modern actor uses as the basis of characterization is recognized as such and, instead of sticking to it through thick and thin, he or she consistently modifies and redesigns it in the name of some *emergent principle*. To borrow Karl Popper's phrase, the process is one of conjecture and refutation alternating with one another as the rehearsal develops. This is presumably what underlies hostile critics' impatient dismissal of modern productions for being unduly influenced by 'ideas'.

What do people mean when they say that one actor's performance is not an acceptable characterization? One answer, of course, is that they dislike the breaking of precedent. In the history of a frequently performed classic, certain characters speak and behave as if the profession had signed some sort of agreement with respect to his or her personality. Naturally the impersonations vary quite widely from one production to the next but none the less leave the impression that they cluster round one broad hypothetical prototype. And although no single performance of the part displays each and every feature of the prototype, it is so easy to recognize a family resemblance amongst them all that it is tempting to conclude that the profession as a whole shares a collective image of the ideal representation. It is with the help of this model or scheme that the actor approaches the task of deciding how to deliver each of the lines that has been written for the character he is to play. And each time a performance is given in accordance with this scheme it becomes more and more difficult to dislodge it from the imagination of the regular theatregoer. After a time, the actor in the role of Claudius, together with most audiences, becomes reluctant to accept any version that departs too widely from the inherited prototype. It is as if the fictional status of the character has been replaced by an actual one, and novelties are criticized for being breaches of biographical truth.

Claudius is not the only Shakespearean character who has fallen victim to this process of dynastic consolidation. Hamlet himself has shared the same fate; so has Ophelia. In fact, the more often a play appears in the repertoire the more likely it is for each of its characters to become stereotyped, and when a contradictory performance is given it is often treated as an impudent pretence, like one of those people who pop up from time to time claiming to be the Grand Duchess Anastasia.

It is sometimes argued that many of the answers to these problems, as to how to deliver a line or play 'in character', are implicitly represented, and that an intelligent reading of what is written supplies all the necessary information. Shakespearean scholars, for example, often insist that the metrical structure of the verse automatically distributes the stresses to convey the meanings that Shakespeare had in mind, and to eliminate the unacceptable alternatives. Now, while there is a great deal to be said in favour of this argument, in so far as a disregard for metre usually leads to a misconstruction of meaning, the structure of the verse does not specify as much as the scholars believe, and playgoers are often startled to discover that metrically indistinguishable readings are, none the less, enjoyably different. The question all these points raise is: *why do playwrights submit their work in such a remarkably indeterminate condition?* Musical scores, after all, leave much less to the imagination of the sight-reader. Over and above the accurate specifications of pitch, key and rhythm, composers often make detailed references about loudness, energy and overall phrasing. Changes of pace are indicated and the tone of a passage is often identified by reference to a rich, descriptive vocabulary. Nothing comparable is to be found in the text of one of Shakespeare's plays.

There are at least two possible reasons for these glaring deficiencies: one technical and the other cultural. The technical reason is connected with the difficulty of devising a notational system rich enough to represent all the variables I have just mentioned. In the area of prosody, for example, the phonetic distinctions that can make a difference to the meaning of a sentence are so small that it would take an almost infinite set of written characters to represent them all. Such a notation would be so dense that it would be difficult for the eye to distinguish the different characters from one another. It would be like trying to tell the time on a clock dial that depicted nanoseconds. And since prosody involves several independent variables, each one of which would probably require its own dense notation, the script would become wellnigh illegible. It is difficult to imagine any actor sight-reading such a 'score'.

The problem becomes even more complicated when one takes the gestural aspects of language into consideration. Choreographers have tried, with varying degrees of success, to evolve notations for representing the essential aspects of a dance routine. Apart from the fact that most of these schemes pose a serious problem of legibility, it is questionable whether they successfully represent anything more than the crude outlines of a dance. Choreographers who make use of these schemes, in order to revive dances that have dropped out of the repertoire, succeed only when they are able to consult their memory of the original version. When it comes to devising a notational scheme for facial expression, the problem seems almost insoluble. Experts in 'body language' have tried to analyse facial movements into a set of discrete particles – so-called kimemes – in an effort to identify some gestural counterpart to the phonemes of spoken language. But these systems are comparatively crude

**94**

.....finalmente dopo molti sforsi esclama:

Ah!.. ah!.. ah!.. la ma le di
Ah! Ah! Ah! Now the curse is

zio
work ne!!
ing!

(sviene)

*Fine dell'Atto primo*

B M C appear from DSR to watch Rig in his agony; M picks up the mask and laughs at it.

The Policeman (Williams) appears from MSR and comes toward the trio B goes to him and pays him off with a wad of 'bills'; Cop exits

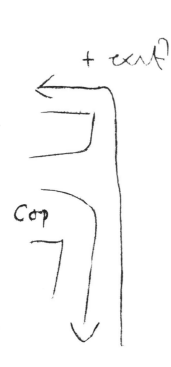

+ exit?

Cop

Note – Rig. pos'n for LX.

B·M·C shake hands and generally clap each other on the back.

– exit?

and any performance based on such 'instructions' would almost inevitably seem stilted and unconvincing. In any case, the problem of the notation's legibility would remain.

The only imaginable alternative to a notational scheme would be a discursive one. Instead of representing the intonations and gestures, item by item, it might be possible to write down, in the margin of the script, a more or less lengthy description of the emotional attitude that was to be conveyed by the speech in question. I inadvertently resorted to this technique when trying to communicate two different ways of saying, '*O! reason not the need*'. What I could have written was: ' "*O!*" to be followed by a long gap during which the eyelids are to be closed; open eyelids on beginning to say, "*reason not the*"; two-second pause while slowly shaking the head backwards and forwards, then say, "*need*" with the eyes closed again'. Whereas, what I did was to use the locution, 'as if to say'. The instruction took the form of: 'Say the line, "*O! reason not the need*", using all the phonetic and facial expressions that would naturally occur to you if you were trying to say, "Oh, for Heaven's sake . . . why do we have to get into this wearisome business of reasoning something so obvious as the need?" ' Now, although this second technique of discursive paraphrase is much more legible and intelligible than the explicitly notational one, Shakespeare makes no effort to use it and a script that included such discursive instructions would be almost unmanageably bulky. To do justice to all the attitudes of any one play by Shakespeare, each text would have to be published in a ten-volume edition.

These are some of the technical reasons why play scripts are so indeterminate. But even if these technical difficulties could be overcome, there are cultural reasons why playwrights still leave their plays in an indefinite state. Confronted by classical works, some of which have survived for several hundred years, it is easy to forget that the author did not write them for posterity. Plays, like any other art form, are created for the artist's contemporaries, which means, to some extent at least, that certain things are understood without having to be explained. When he writes for a community that shares many of his own values the author can reasonably assume that the performers will intuitively recognize many of the attitudes, which he intends to be expressed in and by speeches he wrote. In fact, playwrights sometimes write parts with specific actors in mind, almost anticipating the inflexions and gestures that such favoured performers will provide. Under these circumstances, it would be unnecessary to undertake the laborious task of either annotating or describing how the lines should be delivered. Besides, most authors participate in the production of their own plays and, by attending rehearsals, they can amplify their meaning, describe what they meant, what the attitudes of the characters are, and criticize inflexions and gestures that are inconsistent with the original purpose.

Problems begin to arise after the last performance of the play's inaugural run and, unless the playwright is available to supervise the revival, the advice that he gave to the original cast will have been lost. While a conscientious stage manager often keeps a detailed prompt copy, the stage directions that it includes fall a long way short of what is necessary to reinstate everything that was in the première unless, of course, it is consulted by people who participated in the original production. When the playwright is associated with a company, the details that are conspicuous by their absence from the written text are often conveyed from one revival to the next in the collective memory of his faithful colleagues. This tends to happen when the author has been celebrated as a daring innovator. The colleagues who were closely associated with his pioneering efforts often appoint themselves as custodians of the orthodoxy and ensure that all the remembered details of the inaugural production are preserved from one performance to the next. In many cases, this board of guardians is headed by a close relative who tries to police the performances long after the playwright's death. Such pedantic custody is not necessarily an advantage. Personal intimacy may or may not imply a privileged understanding of the author's intentions. And the inflexible determination to preserve the play in the image of its first production can sometimes do the author a terrible disservice. The play can become mummified by dogma; there is evidence to show that Chekhov suffered in this way. After his death in 1904, Chekhov's colleagues at the Moscow Arts Theatre succeeded in establishing a canonical production of each of his plays. The proprieties were supervised by his widow who extended her vigilance to the smallest detail. But the style of the company was superseded by developments in every other area of the European theatre, with the result that the orthodox production began to look quaint and even irrelevant. Something comparable happened to Wagner and to Brecht.

Inevitably with time there comes a point when the human link between the first production and any subsequent one snaps, and the bridge of reminiscence and anecdote is irreparably broken. When that happens the detailed additional instructions that had been written down in the prompt copy become curiously unintelligible, since there is no one available to explain the generative principles on which they were based. It is at this point that the play begins to enter its afterlife and the indeterminacy of the text begins to assert itself. By the time the language has become recognizably archaic, the process has become more or less irreversible.

There is an alternative scheme for recording and preserving the details of a dramatic performance; one that involves neither notation, nor description, nor personal memory – *electronic recording*. Instead of annotating or paraphrasing what happens on the stage, this technique provides a visible and audible example of it. It is, to all intents and purposes, an imperishable replica and seems automatically to overcome the deficiencies of a written script. But following an example or copying is fraught with as many difficulties as obeying a linguistic instruction, although the problems are of a different order. These can be understood only by analysing the somewhat bewildering concept of exemplification itself, or what it is for something to be an example. The most useful account is the one provided by Nelson Goodman and the argument that follows is based closely on his. As an example of an example, Goodman refers to a tailor's booklet of textiles. Each little swatch exemplifies some of its own properties but not all of them. The customer knows, when he is offered the booklet, that although each swatch illustrates colour, weave, texture and pattern, it does not provide an example of shape or size. Each piece of cloth undoubtedly has both a shape and a size but that is not what it is illustrating for the purposes of the deal. How does this apply to a video tape? How literally should one take the instruction: 'Regard every aspect of this tape as exemplary and follow it slavishly?' We know from experience that each performance contains not only regrettable flaws, but incidental features that are neither here nor there. How can we discriminate? When the tape is reviewed shortly after recording the issue can usually be settled by straightforward common sense. Or, to be more accurate, by relying on the fact that the sensibility of the viewer coincides, to a large extent, with that of the performers; so that the features that the viewer regards as exemplary are likely to be the same as the ones regarded as such by the production team. There is usually someone available to correct the mistakes – a stage manager, for example, who might point out: 'Look, that turn of the head, which you seem to like so much, was something we kept asking him not to do.' As time goes by, however, the process of discrimination becomes more and more difficult and, without the help of a personal consultant, it becomes harder to tell which aspects of the recorded performance are to be taken as exemplary and which are not.

Eventually, the sensibility of the viewer will be so different from that of the original production team that the discriminations that he or she makes are quite likely to contradict the ones made by a distant predecessor. A performance reinstated on the basis of this judgement would be recognizably different from the one that it claimed to be copying faithfully. The process of reproducing a performance by copying an electronic replica is fraught with the same problems as forging a painting. When the forger is a contemporary of the painter, he shares so many of his victim's aesthetic standards that he automatically recognizes which features of the work are to be regarded as exemplary. As long as his technical skill is sufficient, he can create a fake that is almost indistinguishable from the original. But when the forgery is done at a much later date, the aesthetic principles and features that the copyist regards as exemplary, and emphasizes, would be different from the ones identified by a predecessor.

When forgeries of the same work are arranged in chronological order, they almost invariably betray the period in which they were painted.

This principle applies to legitimate processes of art as well as to nefarious ones. When the King of Naples commissioned official pictorial records of the Roman wall paintings that had recently been uncovered at Pompeii, the artists undertook the task without any intention of defrauding posterity. The only purpose was to provide a permanent record of a perishable artefact. But, once again, the problem of exemplification asserted itself, indistinctly at first since the pictures presumably satisfied the royal patron as a faithful record of his perishable treasure. If we look at these pictures today they convey two impressions rather than one. Anyone who is familiar with the Pompeian originals can immediately tell what these are meant to be pictures *of*, but it is just as easy to tell *when* they were produced. They are second-century subjects executed in an eighteenth-century style. Restoration is contaminated in the same way. Viollet-le-Duc's efforts to restore Romanesque stonework resulted in sculpture that probably seemed convincingly medieval at the time but that is immediately recognizable, to a twentieth-century observer, as a nineteenth-century fake. This difficulty is not peculiar to the autographic arts alone. The attempt to reproduce a dramatic performance by taking an example and getting actors and designers to copy it as accurately as they can is bound to be contaminated by principles dictating which features of the model the copyist will regard as exemplary.

*E.E. Viollet-Le-Duc, initial designs for the restoration of Le Massier de Pierrefonds*

*Restoration and forgery both try to reproduce the appearance of a lost or damaged original. But the artist cannot avoid seeing the past with the eyes of the present, and it is only through hindsight that the style of the restoration is seen to be different to that of the original.*

This is vividly illustrated by the difficulties of maintaining the repertoire in a large international opera house. Productions are expected to defray their original expenses by a long series of profitable revivals. But since it is impossible to run any one production continuously over many years, it is usually necessary to reinstate the performance after a considerable lapse of time. By then, the original cast has almost certainly dispersed and, more often than not, the producer who was responsible for the première is no longer available to supervise the revival. Before the development of video tape, the prompt copy and the model book were the only available sources of information and, as I have already pointed out, such instructions are notoriously unreliable. The development of mechanical reproduction held out the hope of a more accurate record. But practical experience has shown that there are unforeseen disadvantages. When the tape is consulted less than a year after the first performance, there seems to be little difficulty in reproducing a passable replica of the original. When several years have passed, a curious problem of visibility begins to arise: what the tape shows is not necessarily what the new assistant producer sees. The vision of the aspiring copyist is now so recognizably different from that of the original production staff that, even when the most conscientious efforts are made to duplicate what is to be seen on the screen, the resulting performance departs more and more from the original. In other words, the extent to which an electronic record can be regarded as a model is limited by the perceptual capabilities of the person who tries to use it for this purpose.

If we had a video copy of the first performance of Shakespeare's *Twelfth Night*, it is no good saying it exemplifies everything that it shows because people would disagree immediately as to what it is showing.

I think the best example of this is a film shown to some Africans about twenty-five years ago. The film was set in an African village and was about hygiene so it portrayed the daily life of a village with people preparing food and repeatedly washing their hands. When members of the audience were asked what they had seen they talked only about a chicken crossing the road. The mystified makers of the film went back and ran it through very carefully to discover that after about twenty-five minutes a chicken crossed the bottom left-hand corner of the screen. This fleeting appearance had, until then, been invisible to the film-makers but to the African audience the film exemplified a chicken crossing the road in an otherwise boring picture of an African village. In the same way, if we were to have a copy of the initial performance of *Twelfth Night*, what we thought it exemplified would depend on what we found to be its salient features. If called upon to copy it we would copy what we thought was important, and in that very act would adapt the production even if we had agreed to the idea that copying meant producing something indistinguishable. The reproduction of the play would indeed look identical to us but a subsequent generation, twenty-five years later, would wonder why we had picked out various features and not others from the tape. This is why, when Van Meegeren forged Vermeer, it passed off very successfully at the time when he shared the same sensibility as his audience who saw Vermeer as exemplifying the particular qualities he copied. Now, we notice that it left out what we believe to be essential in Vermeer, and our forgeries would look different. In short, even if we regard the process of going back to the original as a possibility and an authenticating device we have to understand that forgeries are not faithful copies.

*Perception* always approaches its domain with interests, preoccupations and prejudices about what is important in a work whether of art or literature. If we agreed that the function of the director is to restore as much of the information of the original performance as he could, what he would infer as being important about the original production would not provide a faithful copy of its original but merely tell us what *he* thought was important in it. He would automatically and unavoidably be introducing an interpretation, and even at his *most* obedient would introduce preconceptions. I believe that it is better to be conscious of your preconceptions rather than simply to be the victim of them.

To reinforce this, let us just imagine for a moment that by some bizarre magical time warp we were able to duplicate the inaugural production of one of Shakespeare's plays so that a time traveller would be unable to detect the difference. Would it be right to regard these two productions as identical? According to Arthur Danto the fact that the productions are visibly and audibly indiscernible is no justification for thinking of them as such. To illustrate his point, Danto refers to a well-known experiment in aesthetic duplication. Jorge Luis Borges wrote a provocative story about the discovery of a literary fragment that duplicated a passage in Cervantes' *Don Quixote*. Borges points out that the fragment was neither plagiarism nor a transcript of the sixteenth-century prototype but an altogether original work deliberately created by a twentieth-century French poet called Pierre Menard. Borges reports Menard as saying that he was quite capable of imagining the universe without Cervantes' *Quixote* and that, for him, Cervantes' novel was a contingent work and not a necessary one: 'I can premeditate writing it. I can write it without falling into a tautology.' In Borges' story, Menard imaginatively annihilates the work of his Spanish predecessor and successfully creates a passage of prose indistinguishable from the one that Cervantes wrote four hundred years earlier.

Danto takes Borges to be saying that the indiscernibility of the two passages – one by Cervantes and the other by Menard – does not mean that they are identical, as although visibly indistinguishable, the two passages display a vivid contrast in style. Borges himself points out that,

'The archaic style of Menard – quite foreign after all – suffers from a certain affectation. Not so that of his forerunner who handles with ease the current Spanish of his time.' The point is that the two passages were written at different times by different authors, and although this fact may not be detectable in the printed words it serves to distinguish them as altogether different. As far as Danto is concerned, 'The works are, in part, constituted by their location in the history of literature as well as by their relationships to their authors . . . and so, graphic congruities notwithstanding, they are deeply different works.' Even if you could theoretically avoid those artefacts of interpretation that are built into the process of copying and forging, the hypothetical and unachievable perfect copy would probably strike a contemporary reader as quaint rather than authentic, and even if struck by the work's authenticity this itself would distance him from the experience of a contemporary reader of the original as the very idea of authenticity would have been irrelevant. The claim that something is authentic has already pre-empted the possibility of having an authentic experience.

If the notion of theatrical authenticity means anything at all, we might think that the more closely a production duplicates the details of the one supervised and approved by the author the more accurately it conveys his intended meaning. But of course there is no guarantee that any of the contemporary productions expressed everything that Shakespeare had in mind when he conceived and wrote his plays. On the contrary, in the speech that Hamlet delivers to the players, there is evidence to show that the performances were not always what the author hoped they might have been. '*Speak the speech, I pray you, as I pronounced it to you, trippingly on the tongue . . . Suit the action to the word, the word to the action . . .*' Yet the mere fact that Shakespeare was in a position to administer such criticisms is often understood to mean that the subsequent performance should have come closer to fulfilling his ambitions than any production supervised by a modern director. Even if it could be proved that his advice had not been followed in every detail, the fact that he wrote for a particular type of theatre and for a characteristic form of acting means, according to this view, that a duplicate of the original production would be a more favourable version than any alternative. But would we accept it?

If we were sitting now watching the supposed duplicate of the Elizabethan première of *Twelfth Night* we would find much of it impenetrable. Like a work of religious art placed in a modern gallery, we would see many signs and a rhetorical style of acting that would be very hard for us to read. If this preservation was realizable, it may well be that Shakespeare's work would no longer be performed and could well have spent an afterlife in the forlorn library condition to which unperformed plays are consigned. The notion of performance would be altered if we were bound by the one canonical production, and plays would, like pictures, become autographic works of art. As a consequence the theatre would become rather like a museum or a church in which the audiences would be subtly changed into congregations, witnesses of a rite rather than spectators of a play. However interesting this might be from an archival point of view, in that the original would preserve all the idioms of the Elizabethan theatre, the play itself would be imprisoned in its own orthodoxy and prevented from developing that emergent character which is constitutive of great drama. In a paradoxical way, the preservation of the canonical performance, which many people think would express and embody Shakespeare's intentions, is more likely to cut us off from his vital dramatic imagination as we would be distracted by the foreign gestures and style of acting.

It seems to me that it is precisely because subsequent performances of Shakespeare's plays are interpretations, rather than copies, that they have survived. The amplitude of Shakespeare's imagination admits so many possible interpretations that his work has enjoyed an extraordinary after-life unforeseeable by the author at the time of writing. We overvalue the notion of the identity of the work and search fruitlessly for some hypo-thetical feature that will act as a guarantee or a token of its identity. There is nothing that satisfies that demand, and we can only recognize the minimum conditions for the performance of a play – that the words that are written must be delivered. However much we may disagree about what constitutes the identity of a play by Shakespeare, we can agree that it resides at least in his words so that a paraphrase will not do. And yet we are prepared to paraphrase so many other elements, like the stage-setting and costume, which for Shakespeare would have been a structural, not an optional, component of the work.

It was an attempt to restore a far-reaching and, I would argue, unrealizable authenticity that prompted English scholar William Poel to flout recent theatrical convention by re-instating the Elizabethan staging of Shakespeare's plays at the end of the nineteenth century. Poel recognized that the theatre had undergone a peculiar transformation shortly after the dramatist's death and that when his plays were revived after the re-opening of the theatres under the Restoration the staging was recognizably at odds with the original style of the presentation. In many respects, the subsequent performances of Shakespeare's plays over the next two hundred years were similar to that of the paintings and sculptures whose afterlives I described earlier. The unfurnished platform was replaced by a proscenium stage and the texts were often mutilated to accommodate the elaborate scene changes that were destined to become the most significant part of the eighteenth- and nineteenth-century playgoer's experience. It was to counteract these and other tendencies that Poel undertook his controversial experiments in restoring Shakespearean production to the form in which it was first given to the Elizabethan public. For obvious reasons Poel's

*William Poel's production of* Hamlet *at the Carpenters' Hall in 1900*

*Like Viollet-le-Duc, Poel set out to restore the appearance of Shakespeare's original stagings. To a modern eye, however, the late nineteenth-century style is highly visible and the whole tableau looks like a historical scene in Madame Tussaud's waxwork museum.*

experiment differed from the magical duplication that I have already tried to imagine. Two hundred years of theatrical evolution had all but destroyed the memory of the Elizabethan prototype and, until the rediscovery of the famous Swan sketch of the Globe Theatre, little was known about the physical format of the Elizabethan stage. In the absence of a visible and audible model, Poel had to undertake an imaginative reconstruction. Although this was helped by the discovery of sixteenth-century prompt copies, Poel's achievement depended on a close study of the written text from which he was able to identify the dramatic genre to which Shakespeare's plays belonged. A close study of the Quartos convinced Poel that the only theatrical format consistent with the text was the one in which the plays had been originally staged. He recognized that Shakespeare's plays were literary creations demanding rapid imaginative transition from one scene to the next and that the uninterrupted thrust was incompatible with the cumbersome changing of illusionistic scenery.

In a series of experimental productions mounted at the turn of the century, Poel abstained from expensive spectacle and substituted a bare format that gave pride of place to the events expressed in, and constituted by, the spoken utterances of a play. The experiment was not altogether welcome and audiences, whose taste had been corrupted by the picturesque tradition, felt that they had been robbed of the Shakespeare they knew and loved. To a modern eye, however, the photographic records of Poel's productions seem quaintly picturesque in their own way. If such productions were to be accurately duplicated today they would give the same sort of impression as Viollet-le-Duc's nineteenth-century restorations of Romanesque sculpture. As we have seen, the notion of authenticity is an unstable and elusive one, and yet Poel's productions were considerably less *inauthentic* than the ones that had been staged throughout the preceding century. Today it is easy to identify their late nineteenth-century aesthetic characteristics, but these seem trivial by comparison to Poel's success in reproducing the format of the sixteenth-century original.

As long as productions of Shakespeare were occasions for staging colourful historical tableaux comparable to, and in many ways indistinguishable from, the novels of Walter Scott or the romantic canvases of de la Roche, there was no temptation to consider the political or psychological implications of the text. This meant that there was no incentive to stage the plays in terms of some controlling and perhaps reductive metaphor. Ironically, by stripping away the picturesque and releasing the plays into a dramatic rather than a pictorial space, Poel revealed their essentially literary character, making them increasingly susceptible to the sort of 'conceptual' interpretations that critics so often deplore. As soon as the dramatic action was prised away from its literal historical setting, the text acquired an independence that gave subsequent directors a licence to re-set them in any period that struck their fancy.

Poel's experiments were conducted in the name of authenticity but their effect upon a twentieth-century audience was more complicated and more disturbing than he understood at the time. Quite apart from the fact that reproductions of antiquity inevitably strike the modern imagination as affectedly archaic (just as Menard's 'Cervantes' seemed to his twentieth-century contemporaries), Poel's departure from recent tradition had the unexpected effect of emphasizing the transferability of the dramatic action. For an audience that had grown accustomed to seeing Shakespeare's plays picturesquely staged in the period that was apparently suited to the action, the ease with which they could be transferred to a non-historic sixteenth-century limbo suggested that there might be no limit to the way in which these plays could be re-staged in the future.

It is true that there has not been a relapse into the pictorial traditions of the Victorian theatre, and it is still possible to identify Poel's influence in the unfurnished starkness of many modern productions, yet the twentieth century has generated more visual variety than ever before. Floridly aberrant though they may have been, the pictorial productions of the nineteenth century were more or less consistent with one another. Most of them, at least, were painstakingly 'historical'. While the visual representation of the past differed from one production to the next, the amount by which they varied was negligible in comparison to their historicism. Twentieth-century productions, however, have been characterized by a consistent inconsistency and, although 'literal' representation is conspicuous by its absence, they now tend to differ from one another almost as much as a Georgian production differed from a Victorian one. In the last twenty-five years, a regular playgoer could have seen *Julius Caesar* staged in togas, frock coats, jackboots or doublet and hose. Most of these productions were staged in a format that owes much to Poel's 'Elizabethan' experiments, but it would be foolish to pretend that such performances represent a continuation of his original initiative.

The development of the avant-garde in expressionist theatre and the constructivist décor of Meyerhold and Mayakovsky, together with the artistic revolutions of the 1900s, had an important effect on the theatre and the role of the director. Cubism, surrealism and Dada, in the 1920s, brought with them startling new attitudes to the art of the past. One of modernism's rather paradoxical characteristics was a much more self-conscious relationship to the past, which it treated as a plunderable treasure to be re-assembled in new forms. The looting of the past allowed an artist like Picasso to find elements that could be used in new combinations in collage. Many artists took fragments of Oceanic art, for example, and represented them in the art of cubism. In a similar way the director in the theatre began to emerge as someone doing 'assemblage' rather than restoration.

Apart from the transformations that a play inevitably undergoes as its

*Barry Jackson's* Hamlet, *Kingsway
Theatre, London, 1925*

*In the effort to refresh the perception of a
work which has become over-familiar in its
traditional form, twentieth-century directors
often set the plays in modern times. When
this works it is because the audience preserves
a memory of the previous style, and by
superimposing the modern image experiences
the pleasurable shock of historical stereoscopy.*

59

actions, speeches and characters are developed, certain aspects of the afterlife of a dramatic work run parallel to the changes that overtake material artefacts, such as paintings or sculptures. I am referring to the way that a play can alter its appearance, and to some extent its identity, according to how it is staged. Just as a painting changes when it is removed from the Eastern end of a church and placed in an art gallery, so a play by Shakespeare, or an opera by Mozart, changes its character according to the physical format in which it is presented. A play that started its theatrical life on the unfurnished platform of the Globe and then went on to be pictorially represented in the Victorian theatre, with further alterations in physical format when thrust on to the apron stages that developed after the 1950s, has undergone changes that are just as far reaching as the ones that result from reinterpretations of the spoken lines.

These changes are often regarded as incidental transformations in an object that otherwise retains its original identity. I admit that at one level it is true to say that each of these stagings represents an instance of the work in question – *King Lear* perhaps, the *Ring* or *Mother Courage* – but the differences in visual presentation powerfully influence the way we visualize its identity. Just as Michelangelo altered the aesthetic identity of the statue of Marcus Aurelius by placing it in the grand seigneurial setting of Campidoglio so Peter Brook by putting *A Midsummer Night's Dream* into a white gymnasium box altered its status as a dramatic event, and made it altogether different from the sort of object it was when Beerbohm Tree staged it in a realistic midnight forest. The same principle applies to the vicissitudes of Wagner's *Ring*. Pictorially produced at the time of its composition, the *Ring* was stripped of all scenery by Wieland Wagner and transplanted into a ruined industrial setting by Patrice Chereau. While there is an unarguable sense in which each of these subsequent performances was an instance of the opera originally written by Richard Wagner, the work itself developed under the influence of these alterations in theatrical format.

What is it that we are supposed to 'see' when we witness a theatrical spectacle? The whole issue is epitomized in an interesting and provocative remark made by Bernard Williams. It is, he says, reasonable to ask a member of the audience seated in Row E how far he or she was from Laurence Olivier playing Othello. But there is no answer to the question how far he or she was from the Moor, or from Desdemona. The same distinction applies to questions about the distance that separates the audience from the scenery. The spectator may be less than twenty feet from whatever represents the bedroom in Cyprus but no tape measure can tell us how far he or she was from the bedroom itself. By visiting the theatre we are participating in a representational system, and we are reading the play systematically as something that stands for what we suppose it to be. In order to do this we have to recognize the existence of a *frame* within which what is to be seen is taken as representational and beyond which everything to be seen is regarded as part of the real world.

If an outburst of unexpected strangling were to take place beyond the margins of this frame we would summon the manager and ask him to call the police – even if the scuffle was somewhat half-hearted. But when Othello begins to stifle Desdemona – not half-heartedly at all but with every sign of doing the job properly – we would summon the manager only if a member of the audience tried to stop him. The frame surrounding the theatrical event enables us to make this useful distinction. In proscenium theatres, inherited from the eighteenth and nineteenth centuries, the frame coincides with the decorative archway separating the stage from the auditorium. And with strong artificial lighting this difference is reinforced by the fact that the audience sits in the dark while the artificial events are brightly illuminated. The raising of a velvet curtain gives additional reassurance of this distinction. Both a thrust stage and a theatre in the round provide the spectator with implicit frames separating the two domains.

It is important to recognize the difference between frames and fences. What prevents the dramatic action from overflowing into real incident is not a mechanical obstacle separating the audience from the cast, as, for example, the spectators watching a lion-taming act at the circus are separated from the action by something that mechanically protects them from undergoing the risks of the courageous *dompteur*. In fact it is because it is a fence and not a frame that the spectators know that the lion-taming spectacle is real – so real indeed that it is only because there is a fence that they are happy to sit so close to it. The same distinction applies to the plate-glass window that separates the inquisitive spectator from the poisonous reptiles at the zoo. When we speak of the missing fourth wall of the theatre, however, we are referring to something that has a different logical status altogether, and the events we see through its notional transparency require, as Richard Wollheim has pointed out, a type of vision that is altogether peculiar to representational seeing. To understand this form of vision, and what it requires on the part of the spectator, it is essential to realize how representation works as a system, and it pre-supposes two worlds – the world to be represented, and the world that does the representing. The subtleties of this relationship are all too easily confused by taking illusionistic realism as the paradigm so that anything less than a convincing illusion is regarded as an impoverished version.

What there is to be seen in a representation largely depends on what we expect it to show us. An Ordnance Survey map of the Barbizon forest is just as much a representation of it as a painting by Corot, and the fact that it tells us nothing about the shimmer of the foliage or the fall of light does not jeopardize its value as a representation. On the contrary, for the purposes that we consult it, a map of the Barbizon forest represents what we want to know and although Corot's picture represents what is delightful about the forest's appearance it would not help us to find our way out of it. The length of the lines that represent the paths, and the angles at which they meet, *do* represent the length of the actual paths and the angles of their actual intersections. The fact that the lines are drawn in black or that their width conveys no information about the width of the paths is irrelevant. For someone lost in the forest the map provides the useful information he requires, and fulfils its function as a representational system.

There are many intermediate examples that may be helpful when thinking about stage scenery in the theatre. An urban developer who had designs on the Barbizon forest might make a scale model of its layout. The model could display many physical properties that resemble those of the actual forest. The metrical width of the paths might now be included, and the trees might be represented by filigreed clumps of plastic whose colour and texture bore some representational relationship to the colour and texture of the trees in the forest. If the budget ran to it the model-maker could even introduce a treatment that gave the paths a physical appearance similar to that of the original, but in terms of cost/benefit this would give more information than was necessary and in all probability the walkways would be colour coded in brown while the peripheral roads were unambiguously marked in black, because it is useful to make an unambiguous distinction between pedestrian and vehicular traffic. As Nelson Goodman has pointed out, most representational systems are composed in a somewhat hybrid way with analogue components that represent by virtue of resemblance, and digital components that represent by virtue of making unambiguous distinctions.

This analysis makes it possible to understand the different ways in which settings are represented on the theatrical stage. In anything other than the most illusionistic scenery the representation is achieved by an extremely subtle interaction between analogue and digital modes of representation. So-called abstract scenery is not simply scenery that has lost something—or falls bewilderingly short of looking like what it stands for—like a model or a map it assigns representational significance to some but not all of its physical properties. For the audience to know what is happening on a stage it is necessary for them to read the whole thing as an integrated system and to understand which properties of the representational setting are related to which properties of the represented scene.

Here is an example from my own work in designing a setting for *The Merchant of Venice*. I asked Julia Trevelyan Oman to make the Venetian streets look as real as possible, and not only were the size of the scenery walls metrically related to the size of the walls they represented but also the surface was treated so that it looked like the original. The audience was intended to read both the metrical properties and the textual properties in the analogue mode of representation. When thinking about a production of *The Taming of the Shrew* I decided to take a very different approach. Taking my inspiration from Serlio's drawing of an Italian street scene, I asked the scenic artist to represent the architectural proportions so that the shape and size of the scenic colonnades could be taken as an accurate indication of the shape and size of the actual ones although we then assembled the entire set out of untreated timber. I presume, or hope, that the audience did not read into this the assumption that Shakespeare's Padua was actually made from untreated timber.

In the afterlife of every play the manipulation of these representational variables determines the theatrical experience of the audience. It is only when the producer, director and designer understand, even if only implicitly, how these variables are interrelated that the audience can be expected to recognize the visual status of what it sees. The problems of televising plays and operas can be more clearly understood in the light of these considerations. It was only by recognizing the peculiar character of the televisual *frame* that I began to understand some of the difficulties I encountered in deciding on the most appropriate representational idiom for this medium. For plays and operas written for the stage, the frame defining the domain of their distinctive artifice is altogether different from the one that surrounds the television image. Even with stages as different as the Globe and Irving's Lyceum, or the apron stage of Chichester and the sandy arena of Brook's Bouffe du Nord, the representational frame is identical as it marks off two domains within the same physical space. While the dramatic events are prevented by aesthetic etiquette from invading the domain of the natural events (the seated audience), the spectators sit within a space that includes both domains, and actively experience the fact that the cast abstains from invading their hemisphere. The frame separating the audience from the dramatic action is shared by the spectator and the actor.

In the case of television the space the spectator sits in does not articulate with the one in which the dramatic events occur. The 'transparency' of the screen is quite unlike the notional transparency of the missing fourth wall of a proscenium stage. When the spectator's gaze penetrates the screen its line is not continued into an actual beyond any more than it is when he looks at a picture on the wall of an art gallery. While the spectator seated in the theatre is looking at actual objects that represent notional things a television viewer is looking at a *picture* of actual objects representing notional things. This creates awkward problems for the producer or director when choosing the appropriate representational idioms for a stage production on television.

In the theatre the scenery, illusionistic or otherwise, abuts directly on to the non-representational architecture of the auditorium. Even in the absence of visible walls and doors the audience can easily tell when a performer is on or off the scene. In some modern productions where actors about to make their 'entrances' are still visible, the implicit frame makes it quite clear that they are dramatically invisible. The imaginative theatre director who takes pleasure in emphasizing the distinctive artificiality of the drama can provocatively exploit this vision of the actor-as-person and the actor-as-character. In television, however, the scenery does not abut with anything and, although it may be cut off by the edges of the domestic screen, the spectator is left with the uneasy sense that the edges of the screen do not coincide with the framework of the dramatic action. There is always the suspicion that if the screen were larger, or the camera angle wider, there would be more of the same to be seen. This suspicion is confirmed when the camera pans right or left to reveal action that was previously out of view. Televising Shakespeare or Mozart forces the director to adopt an illusionistic idiom that he might otherwise resist when staging the same works in the theatre. Abstract scenery only works convincingly when the audience can see the point at which its deliberate artificiality gives way to the non-representational reality of the theatre's auditorium. A television producer who wishes, like William Poel, to revert to the non-pictorial abstraction of the Tudor stage in the effort to honour the artificiality of Shakespeare's dramatic genre has two alternatives, and neither of them is altogether successful. Recognizing that diagrammatic abstraction works only when it is visibly contrasted with the architectural reality of its surroundings he can deliberately shoot off, so that the viewer sees the studio where the production has been built, the lights, cameras and even the exit signs. But since this world beyond is not continuous with the room where the viewer sits it creates a puzzling distraction. The alternative is to build the artificial scenery in the round so that the camera can rotate through 360 degrees without ever shooting off. When this happens the viewer peers into an artificial world that is completely enclosed but as he does not have the opportunity to contrast the artificiality of this world with the actuality of the real one the theatricality of the experience is mysteriously diminished.

The only successful televisual counterpart to the Empty Space sponsored by Peter Brook that I remember was Trevor Nunn's version of *Macbeth*, originally staged at the Other Place, Stratford. The characters loomed in and out of a non-committal blackness and as there were no visual representations of place the television audience was left with the reassuring conviction that the drama was located between the faces that came and went on the screen. The success of this enterprise was largely due to the fact that *Macbeth*'s dramatic action is contained in the encounters between its characters, and where they come from or where they happen to be is unimportant. In that production, the television screen was like a devotional icon in which the representation was unambiguously confined to the surface of the screen and there was no requirement to read any depth into it. In any play where doors, walls or even natural horizons are essential to the action all this breaks down. The domestic comedies of Shakespeare are inconceivable in this kind of iconic limbo. In *The Taming of the Shrew* Petruchio must penetrate a visible household, and even in *Othello* the jealous suspicions of the play can be incubated only within the chambered privacy of rooms where doors can be closed. In spite of its mythical placelessness, *King Lear* cannot be televised without visibly representing the contrast between the boundless heath and the walled enclosures of the various palaces. A featureless blackness would make nonsense out of the scene in which Edgar as Poor Tom persuades his blind father to jump over the edge of a non-existent cliff since its non-existence has to be visible to everyone except the blind victim.

Representationalism enforces itself upon the television producer however reluctant he may be to make use of it. In the television productions of Shakespeare for which I was responsible I am embarrassed to admit that the most successful were those in which the scenery was more real and more pictorial than the nineteenth-century stage versions I have reacted violently against when directing in the theatre. For reasons that I cannot explain this realism did not strike me as offensive when confined to interiors, and in my production of *Othello* where the set was carefully based on the rooms in the palace at Urbino, the drama seemed all the more convincing because of its scenic realism. But such realism seems quite absurd when the action calls for an outdoor setting. In the BBC production of *As You Like It* filmed in the gardens of Glamis castle the realistic foliage clashed distractingly with the artificiality of the pastoral verse. In both film and television I suspect that the afterlife of plays and operas is undergoing an uneasy passage, and that eventually we will see this interlude as a somewhat anomalous episode in the subsequent life of theatrical works written for audiences who were expected to breathe the same air as the performers.

When appearing on the screen, plays and operas undergo yet another change that transforms them into something recognizably different from their previous incarnation on the stage. In the theatre, the audience witnesses a physical event, and although the view is determined by the seating, the spectator sees the action in its entirety. With the invention of cutting, a television or film director can segment the action into separate parts. While the audience can synthesize these sequences, and imagine the total space in which everything occurs, each shot momentarily precludes the possibility of seeing anything else that is happening at the same time, and this transforms the work into something quite different from the one imagined by its original author or composer. If the editor is successful the spectator sees the drama without ever being aware of the abrupt succession of shots from which it is made. Yet if you stand in a darkened road and look at a television through the window of a house on the opposite side of the street all that you can see is the staccato alternation of brightness as one shot gives way to the next. Without the momentum of an intelligible story the only visible property of the programme is the abrupt succession of its component shots.

After years of trial and error, film editors have evolved practical rules of assembly so that when the eye is directed unaccountably towards one group of characters, excluding all the others, the viewer's sense of narrative continuity is left undisturbed. It is the very success of this surreptitious technique that irreversibly changes the dramatic identity of the stage work. Some critics have suggested that this action is no different from that of the spectator in the theatre when he shifts his gaze from one part of the spectacle to another but this parallel does not work. Physiologists can demonstrate that shifts of gaze are accomplished with a rapidity comparable to the cuts in a film from one shot to the next, but in the theatre the unattended part of the vista is still visible to the spectator so that peripheral events on the stage subliminally modify the experience of the salient ones. When a work is written for the stage – a format in which everything that happens is intended to be seen simultaneously – and is then submitted to this type of segmentation in film it is misleading to suppose that the audience is seeing the same dramatic spectacle in a somewhat different way. In order to see the drama in this segmented way and to experience it as a continuous narrative demands cognitive efforts that are altogether different from those needed to interpret events happening on a stage. In fact, although the television viewer is unaware of it, when watching the screen he undergoes an experience similar to reading narrative prose. Like sentences, which automatically exclude whatever they do not refer to, movie shots eliminate what they do not show. The reader of a written narrative is just as unaware of the succession of separate sentences as the television viewer is of the alternation of discontinuous shots. In both cases what gives the artwork its coherent textuality is the way that the reader of one and the spectator of the other can identify referential implications that cross the boundaries between consecutive but discontinuous sentences and shots.

It would be tempting to assume from this argument that while film or television are inappropriate media for the production of plays they are ideally suited for the dramatization of novels. As I hope to show in a later section this does not follow at all. On the contrary, most novels are irreversibly damaged by being dramatized as they were written without any sort of performance in mind at all, whereas for plays visible perform-ance is a constitutive part of their identity and translation from stage to screen changes their identity without actually destroying it.

In discussing the influence of film and television upon the afterlife of plays I have deliberately concentrated on the way that these new media affect the look of the works and alter their narrative structure. But there is another aspect – the repeatability of a play that has been filmed or televised. In an otherwise interesting essay on 'The Future of Art in an Age of Mechanical Reproduction', Walter Benjamin unaccountably fails to consider what happens to the identity of a play when one of its productions can be replayed as long as it survives physical storage. Until the end of the nineteenth century each production of a play disappeared with its final performance so that its afterlife depended on revival and re-production. But as soon as any performance is committed to film or tape there is at least one production of the play with an afterlife of its own that parallels to that of the play itself if it undergoes revival from one generation to the next.

It is interesting to speculate what Helen Gardner would have thought of the productions of Shakespeare she fondly remembered if they had been recorded and she had watched them again after a lapse of forty years. As Sir Frederick Bartlett demonstrated in 1932 memory is not, as was once supposed, a mechanical record of a previous experience differing from the original merely by virtue of fading or decay. To remember something is to reconstruct it in accordance with current interests; recalling is not simply a question of replaying a neurological record. We have all had the bewildering experience of disliking a film that once overwhelmed us and we remembered as brilliant. There is the even more bewildering experience of discovering ten years further on that the very same film is paradoxically brilliant once again albeit in a different way from the remembered brilliance of the original showing. This is why when the BBC set out to televise the whole of Shakespeare and hoped by excluding fashionably imaginative productions that they would guarantee the programmes an undatable permanence they began a self-defeating enterprise. As the story of Van Meegeren's Vermeers proves there is no such thing as a permanently self-effacing style. And it is one of the cruel paradoxes of theatrical art in an age of mechanical reproduction that the permanence of the record is the very thing that brings the pretentiousness of these claims to immortality to light. With the passage of time such productions run the risk of looking permanently quaint without ever having enjoyed the privilege of being briefly brilliant.

Film and television have exerted far-reaching influences on the character of dramatic works originally written for the stage but these are, in many respects, incidental to an afterlife that will, in all probability, continue to depend on active revival as opposed to mechanical repetition. Precisely because of their permanence, mechanically reproduced productions will never replace staged revivals, since (as with living organisms) it is only by undergoing the consecutive processes of death and reproduction that plays can enjoy the self-renewal without which an afterlife is inconceivable.

The relationship between scripts and performances is strikingly similar to that between genetic instructions and the biological individuals to which they give rise. At the end of the nineteenth century August Weissmann argued that there was a distinction to be made between the characteristics that a living individual owed to its genetic inheritance, and the features that it acquired under the influence of environmental factors during its early growth and development. A similar distinction can be recognized in the continuing life of a play or an opera. Each performance is constrained by the script but in the process of being brought to life as a living production it acquires characteristics that are due to the interpretive efforts of the performers and producers, not to mention those brought about by staging it in different formats. Once the production has died with its final performance it sheds its acquired characteristics and theoretically reverts to the condition of the script or score from which a new production can be revived. But this is where the comparison between plays and living organisms breaks down. Weissmann insisted that characteristics acquired during the lifetime of an organism could not be inherited since the genetic text remained unaltered by the environmental influences – the children of blacksmiths are not born with brawny muscles developed by the exertion of their fathers. With plays, however, acquired characteristics are often to be found in subsequent productions. This is not because the text has been altered but because human culture is influenced by imitation. The revival or re-production of a play could never take place in complete ignorance of its previous incarnations, so that although the text has remained unchanged by the vicissitudes of various productions, the memory of previous performances exerts a powerful influence on the shape of subsequent ones.

The influence of precedent, for which there is no counterpart in biology, extends from slavish imitation to radical renovation. But even when the effect of imitation is at its strongest, the mere fact that revival is a reproductive process guarantees the appearance of novelty. During conservative or so called classical periods in the theatre there is still a natural tendency for the production of plays and operas to depart from the inaugural prototype. For complicated reasons the tempo of this natural evolution can change unexpectedly, and Helen Gardner has vividly chronicled the sometimes abrupt alteration in the evolution of Shakespeare upon the stage. But even if we take these rapid changes into consideration, there is a striking difference between the ones that overtook the theatre during its classical period and those introduced in the last fifty years, and Helen Gardner rightly identified the intervention of something altogether new.

In the productions leading up to the ones she enjoyed in the 1940s and 1950s, the appearance of Shakespeare's plays changed as unsolicited novelties imperceptibly infiltrated themselves into each revival. Each production was realized according to the fashion of the day and, although performers and managers presumably took pride in adding something of their own, originality was painlessly constrained by the influence of precedent. With the emergence of the director, however, plays and operas began to be reproduced with an explicit interest in originality and for the first time in theatrical history it is both legitimate and useful to apply the argument of Paley's watch.

During the high tide of natural theology at the beginning of the nineteenth century, Bishop Paley developed a famous analogy to explain the functional design of living organisms. According to him, if someone who knew nothing about timekeeping were to find a watch lying on the seashore he would find it impossible to account for its efficient mechanism without stipulating the existence of someone who had deliberately designed it. And for this reason he thought it necessary to postulate a supernatural craftsman whose skill guaranteed the efficiency of living things. With Darwin's discovery of the cooperation between unsolicited variation and natural selection this analogy became defunct. It is, however, applicable to the structure and function of modern theatrical productions.

In contrast to a pre-war revival of a Shakespearian play, different though it may have been from its Georgian or Victorian predecessor, productions after 1960 are recognizably produced and in some cases the evidence of explicit design is so prominent that the work in question seems to have been quoted rather than revived. To some extent this is the commendable result of recognizing that the revival of a dramatic work from the distant past is a conceptual problem and not simply a theatrical task. It is as if these theatrical bequests were now visualized as alien artefacts, and it is understood that they cannot be reproduced without making a conscious effort to reconcile what is foreign and incomprehensible with what is permanent and readily intelligible.

We are witnessing, in our own time, something comparable to what happened during the fifteenth century when the artefacts of classical antiquity were repossessed by the culture of early modern Europe. As Erwin Panofsky has pointed out, the success of the Renaissance presupposed the recognition of a fundamental discontinuity between the culture of the present and that of the distant past. One of the reasons why the proto-renaissances of the ninth, tenth and twelfth centuries were so tentative and short-lived was that this historical discontinuity was still somewhat blurred. It was only when the artefacts of the classical past were seen to be recognizably different that they could be confidently approached and re-incorporated. Panofsky's idea can be usefully applied to the enthusiastic renovations that classical plays and operas have undergone in the last half of the twentieth century.

Until dramatic works from the past were judged to have come from a world that was recognizably different from the one in which they were to be revived, variations in performance appeared by default rather than by design. Of course, a Hanoverian production of *King Lear* looked and sounded different from a Tudor one, but the distinction cannot be explained by someone having consciously faced the problem of what the play meant or what was meant by trying to put it on in the first place.

But in the last part of the twentieth century even the comparatively recent past is visualized as a foreign country where people do things differently. Taking care of the sounds in the performance of a play no longer guarantees that the sense will take care of itself. In fact the very notion that the sense of a play is unambiguously readable in its text is both problematic and controversial.

It is difficult to explain why all this should have happened now and not before. After all, the interval between a Victorian production of *King Lear* and the first time it was staged is much longer than the period separating the Victorian production from one staged last year. The recognizable discontinuity is not simply a question of the amount of time that has elapsed; the staging of a play written by Chekhov as recently as 1904 is also recognized as a problem.

To explain this in terms of the unwelcome arrival of the director is to put the cart before the horse. Why did the director emerge when he did? Why has his influence now become so strong? The obvious answer is that historical change has accelerated so much in the last fifty years that the differences between 'now' and even a quite recent 'then' are much more noticeable, and the bequests of the past arouse our interpretive energies as never before. Besides, as Clifford Geertz argues, the life of the mind has now taken a distinctively 'interpretive turn', and with the development of self-consciously hermeneutic interests the problem of meaning assumes a paramount importance. Nowadays almost any institution, action, image, utterance or ritual is seen as requiring interpretation.

In its ordinary use, the word 'interpretation' is usually taken to imply the existence of a determinable meaning and one might suppose that the development of the 'interpretive turn' would have led by now to a large yield of commonly agreed readings. But the very opposite has happened. In the study of law, scripture and literature, the emergence of interpretation as a distinct enterprise has coincided with the growth of conflict rather than a consensus. In fact, the very notion of interpretation has itself become a subject of controversy, and although some critics continue to uphold the idea of determinable meanings, there are just as many who claim that this is an unrealistic aim, and that the text – literary, dramatic or whatever – sustains an almost unlimited range of possible readings.

As E. D. Hirsch points out, 'it became fashionable to talk about a critic's "reading" of a text . . . [and] the word seems to imply that if the author had been banished, the critic still remained and his new, original, urbane, ingenious or relevant "reading" carried its own interest.' According to Hirsch, the disadvantage of this particular twist of the 'interpretive turn' is that there are no reliable criteria for distinguishing frivolous readings from ones which 'really' make sense. The only way of quieting the Babel of interpretation is to restore the author as the determiner of the text's meaning since this is 'the only compelling normative principle which could lend validity to an interpretation'. Hirsch then goes on to counter the arguments which have been developed against the author as the final authority.

With texts that come from the more or less distant past, it is often claimed that their meaning inevitably changes with the passage of time, and that it is only profitable to read them for contemporary meanings or for meanings which are interestingly relevant to the modern imagination. Hirsch points out that if this attitude is taken to its logical conclusion the reader encounters no one but himself each time he engages with a text, or an utterance, from the distant past. In any case, it is not the meaning of the text that changes with the passage of time but its significance. The mere fact that a modern reader can recognize implications which would have been unrecognizable to the original author does not imply that its meaning has altered. It is sometimes argued that the author himself can re-identify the meaning of his own work, and that on a subsequent reading he can recognize meanings that were not apparent to him at the time of writing. But the fact that an author can revise his opinion, cannot be counted as evidence for or against the identity of his original meaning. He has simply had second thoughts about the meanings which he originally conceived.

The authority of the writer has also been threatened by the development and popularization of psychoanalytic theory according to which the poet or playwright, like anyone else, is under the influence of urges and impulses that he is in no position to recognize or even control. Any conscious meanings that might be expressed in his text are small by comparison to the unconscious ones which lurk beneath its easily readable surface. The problem is that, as with psychoanalytic theory itself, there is no reliable criterion for judging whether a given meaning belongs to the mind to which it has been attributed. In the absence of such a criterion, there is virtually no limit to the intentions that are perceivable in any particular work. And although the author is nominally credited with them, thereby apparently restoring him to his rightful role of the determiner of the text meaning, the authorship is now uneasily distributed between two imaginations and it is impossible to make a reliable judgement with regard to intellectual royalties.

As this hermeneutic curiosity intensifies, cultures that might once have been thought of as almost indistinguishable from our own are increasingly seen to be different and therefore in need of interpretation. The paradox is that at the very moment when one group of critics is laying claim to Shakespeare as our contemporary, there are just as many who recognize his enigmatic difference.

Another factor complicates the issue. Apart from the fact that each play from the past is now seen to be the legitimate subject of interpretation, the director's importance is also emphasized by the unprecedented development of a theoretical attitude to the significance of theatre itself. Many of the transformations that we have witnessed in the last fifty years have been the direct result of conflicting theories about the nature of drama itself; the role of make-believe; the meaning of artificiality and the legitimacy of various forms of representation.

Workers in the theatre now confront the question of what sort of event a play or an opera is, and what sort of staging best realizes the identity assigned to it. While texts have been penetrated by theories that bear upon their meaning, the aesthetic identity of the theatrical experience is now in a state of permanent reappraisal. When Peter Brook restaged *King Lear* or *A Midsummer Night's Dream*, the result was determined not only by his substantive theories about the meaning of the text and about the motives of the characters but also by his resolution to change the identity of plays in general. The Empty Space was not simply a new way of staging old plays but, much more radically, a coercive device designed to give the audience a self-conscious awareness of the peculiarity of their predicament as witnesses of a dramatic spectacle.

II: *SUBSEQUENT PERFORMANCES*

# II: i

As an inexperienced young director entering the theatre in the 1960s I was very excited by this idea that the productions of the classics need no longer be slavish reconstructions but are re-creations. The past, which is in many ways unvisitable, no longer reduces the director to the role of a failing archaeologist but offers actor and director alike the possibility of re-making a work of art that is essentially emergent. As I hope to show, recognition that a play is an emergent object need not mean that in its re-creation it becomes either 'contemporary' or an excuse for a director's egomania.

My first professional theatrical involvement was not as a director but as a performer. It all began at Cambridge where I appeared in the Footlights and was then asked, together with Peter Cook, Dudley Moore, and Alan Bennett, to appear in *Beyond the Fringe*. I was still working at a medical job at University College and saw the offer as a vacation from work in medicine rather than the beginning of a dramatic career. The man behind the show was John Bassett, Robert Ponsonby's assistant. They had both grown tired of the success enjoyed by the Fringe productions and wanted to launch an official show at the Edinburgh Festival in 1960 that would be better or 'Beyond' the Fringe. In 1961 we played for a year in London and then went on to Broadway. This was my first experience of the theatre outside Cambridge, where I had acted very little, and it was atypical in that the material was not true drama but tiny comic vignettes. It was a collaborative exercise and there was no director in the conventional sense. Despite the fact that the show was labelled a satire we were not self-consciously satirical in our approach, and although we wanted to attack certain institutions and attitudes our main aim was simply to be as grimly amusing as we could without needing too much musical accompaniment or dancing girls in fishnet tights.

We would sit around a table and work on the material collectively, record it and type it up for submission to the Lord Chamberlain. Each of us had our particular pieces but the big set numbers, like the Shakespeare sketch and those on the Second World War and civil defence, were devised by us all. The scripts were then the basis of the show and, with the exception of Peter Cook, who used to improvise his miner sketch every night (a preliminary to E. L. Wisty), we kept fairly closely to what we had written. I do not know now to what extent we calculated that our material might survive and remain amusing, but with hindsight we seem to have chosen topics that are relevant today: certain aspects of the class structure, the H-bomb, civil defence, the monarchy, idiocies in the performance of Shakespeare, the church, and nostalgia for the Second World War.

It was rather surprising that the Americans were so amused by our particular kind of English absurdity. We did not change *Beyond the Fringe* at all for New York, and it may have survived both changes in time and place because it went down to the roots of humour rather than being tied to specific personalities of that particular moment. But it was very unlike the fast, wry American comedy that was popular at about the same time in Chicago's Second City and with comedians like Lenny Bruce who were the precursors to *Saturday Night Live*. *Beyond the Fringe* had no effect on that line of American humour, and although it may have had some influence on British comedy, the *Monty Python* team went far beyond us in developing the surrealist and absurd. Watching *Monty Python* or *Spitting Image*, what now seems most striking about *Beyond the Fringe* is that only twenty years ago we were still having to deliver our scripts for the Lord Chamberlain's approval.

It was not until 1962 that I directed my first professional production, at the Royal Court Theatre, around the time that the director is generally assumed to have seized theatrical power. The shifting attitudes towards the classics and the past were not the result of a sudden wind of change in 1959/60 that swept the fate of the theatrical profession at large into the sinister hands of a few aggressive new directors. There had been a general weakening of the influence of tradition in performance and production for some years, and I think this goes back to the widespread cultural changes already detectable in the decade following the Second World War. It is difficult to summarize these changes, and even harder to demonstrate the impact that they had on the social structure of the theatrical profession. But it seems reasonable to assume that the processes that culminated in the Labour landslide of 1945 had an irreversible influence upon the way in which actors and directors regarded the task of reviving theatrical classics. The authority of precedent had already been undermined in the area of politics, and when a triumphant socialist politician rallied his colleagues with the cry, 'We are the masters now', echoes of this claim were heard far beyond Westminster, not least in the theatre, which had already successfully recruited writers and performers who were recognizably different from the ones who ruled the roost in the pre-war years.

This tendency was most marked in the output of new plays, of which the most emblematic example was John Osborne's *Look Back in Anger*, but the success of working-class actors as they began to replace their more genteel seniors cannot be overlooked. Theatregoers were having to tune their ears to much rougher accents than the ones to which they had grown accustomed. It was not just a question of flat vowels and unmelodious voices – the moral attitude also had changed. The actors emerging from post-war drama schools were refreshingly disrespectful about the roles they undertook, approaching them as if they had sprung into existence without any previous occupants. Many of these young performers came to the stage armed with the same impatient indignation that had overturned the Conservative majority in 1945, and when they stepped into the roles of Shakespeare's captains and kings they were rarely willing to perpetuate the stereotypes that had proved so acceptable to the audiences of Baldwin's England.

It was no longer assumed that the correct speaking of verse would automatically deliver the author's meaning, or that if the sounds were taken care of the sense would simply follow. Influenced by the sort of textual scrutiny that had been so conspicuously encouraged by critics like F. R. Leavis, directors and performers collaborated in the task of systematic reconstruction, dis-establishing traditional characterizations and replacing them by ones that insisted on new ways of phrasing old speeches. In some cases this led to a regrettable disregard for metrical orthodoxy and the language of the classical texts was sometimes unforgivably defaced. But such Cromwellian atrocities were the exception rather than the rule and, since many of the new directors had been influenced and encouraged by George Rylands just as much as they had been excited by the textual scrutiny of F. R. Leavis, post-war productions of Shakespeare were, more often than not, refreshing blends of expert diction and intelligent character analysis.

By questioning the authority of the prototype, the acting profession as a whole set itself a much more difficult task than the one that previously existed. Instead of inheriting a model of this or that character, it now became necessary to build one more or less from scratch, which led to an interesting dilemma – where to begin? As I have pointed out, knowing how to speak the lines depends on already knowing what the character means by them. And since the character in question has no existence apart from the lines with which he or she is supplied, the actor is forced to construct someone on the basis of evidence whose significance has still to be interpreted. Admittedly, something is to be learnt from the fact that the character says this rather than that. By retrieving the literal meaning of the words one might suppose that it was possible to go some way towards deciding the identity of the character and how he or she might phrase the speeches. But, on the other hand, the lines do not tell us all that much about the character until we can imagine *how* they are uttered and what was meant by uttering them in the first place. It is quite easy to become paralysed by such a double bind, and this is one of the reasons why modern rehearsals are so much more exhausting than the ones in which the actors and actresses used to turn up dressed in the sort of clothes that would secure them a table at the Ritz.

Another influence that helped this change was the development of a popularized version of psychology. It was no longer enough to speak the verse properly and be metrically orthodox. In order to identify the character by his or her speech acts, and deliver the lines appropriately, actors felt they had to plunge into the consciousness and even the unconscious of the character. The combination of textual scrutiny, as introduced by Leavis, with psychiatric and psychological scrutiny, sponsored by Freud (although done without his advice by Stanislavsky), provided a very powerful pincer attack on the theatre which opened up the whole organism of the play. It became a terrain to be explored, a truly emergent object, rather than a stable entity.

A final ingredient, and perhaps the umbrella under which these alterations were taking shape, was a sense of scepticism focused on the recent rather than remote past. In an atmosphere of social change all over Europe, but of particular intensity in England, the old gentilities of the 1930s performer held little charm for the modern actor or director who felt this style to be as irrelevant as the social institutions that had been overturned with the Labour landslide itself.

In England, the most distinguished pioneer of this theatrical revolution was the Cambridge graduate, Peter Hall. Ably assisted by his colleague, John Barton, Hall ushered in a new era in the afterlife of Shakespeare's plays. At the theatre in Stratford, he inaugurated a memorial to Shakespeare that was all the more successful for not being a cenotaph. I can still remember the delighted shock of witnessing the phoenix of Henry V brought to life by Ian Holm under Hall's supervision. The famous lines were spoken with meticulous regard for Shakespeare's metre and yet the person who uttered them seemed as unfamiliar as the lines themselves. The noble patriot had been successfully usurped by an energetic runt, and although his speeches linguistically meant what they always had, what he meant by them was something that I had never heard before.

The *King Lear* jointly created by Peter Brook and Paul Scofield in 1962 was another landmark in the reconstruction of Shakespeare's characters. Audiences who had grown accustomed to the Druidical stereotype, which had perpetuated itself in a clone for the best part of a hundred years, were startled to hear the lines spoken by a cantankerous bullet-headed warrior. From that moment it was difficult to imagine how the figure who is so aptly caricatured in Ronald Harwood's play *The Dresser* could have taken possession of these lines in the first place. As someone who witnessed Donald Wolfit's supposedly definitive performance of the part, as well as John Gielgud and several other admired and traditional portrayals, I find it difficult to sympathize with discontented claims to the effect that the Scofield–Brook collaboration yielded a performance diminished by pretentious theory. On the contrary I felt, like many other theatregoers of my generation, that the speeches had been possessed by a rightful claimant and that the lines seemed to make rich sense for the first time.

This does not mean, however, that I regard the Brook–Scofield *Lear* as definitive or that I dismiss Donald Wolfit's for not being. Although some critics still use the phrase 'definitive performance', the concept now seems irrelevant and unhelpful. Each time a classical play is revived, actors and directors approach the characters on the understanding that who they are and how they speak is something to be discovered in the course of rehearsal. We now take it for granted, or so it seems to me, that the speeches that succeed one another are not, in any sense, the record of how some particular person expressed him or herself but are unowned phrases waiting to be claimed by someone who could consistently mean this or that by speaking them.

Actors and directors working on classic plays remind me of creative breeders. In just the same way that a new iris can be seen to be a florid development of the original wild flower, successive productions cross-pollinate and introduce new varieties that are still visibly related to the original play. Despite certain notable exceptions where it is really very hard to identify the relationship of the performance to the original text, I think that most of the rich variations that have grown up in the last twenty or thirty years are breeders' very elaborate varieties of the original form. One of the exciting things about the theatre in the last thirty years is that this process of selective cross-breeding has become the prevailing form.

Why George Devine invited me to direct one half of a double bill at the Royal Court in 1962, I shall never know. I had no reputation or experience as a professional director when I began work on John Osborne's *Under Plain Cover*. I have always assumed that I was chosen because no one else agreed. There was a tremendous discrepancy between my lack of experience as a young unknown director and the reputation of John Osborne, who was not only a very well-established playwright but also a cult figure in post-war theatre. I was extremely cautious and hesitant to introduce what I thought might appear to be eccentric interpretations bearing no relation to Osborne's imagination. But I was never tempted to take the work and re-fashion it in my own image. As the rehearsals went on, I brought to light aspects of the play with which he identified but that were unfamiliar until he saw them on the stage. As far as I can remember, the number of occasions when he looked at something in rehearsal and said, 'How could you possibly have felt that that was what I meant?' were rare. On the whole, he was delighted to see what it was that he had meant. But Osborne was far more explicit than Robert Lowell.

It was while working with Robert Lowell in 1964 on *The Old Glory* that I came face to face with something that I have since realized is also true for playwrights who are dead, namely, the difficulty of extracting from an author what he means by the play he writes. Critics are often obsessed with this idea of the 'author's intention' and I would have thought that living as closely as I did with Lowell during rehearsals it offered an admirable opportunity to discover from him precisely what he meant by what he wrote. It is difficult to imagine a more articulate and more

*Robert Lowell's* The Old Glory *at the American Place Theatre in 1964*

In The Old Glory *a twentieth-century poet took the novella of a mid-nineteenth century author who was himself writing about an early nineteenth-century event. It is difficult to know what would have counted as an authentic staging. As the inaugural production of the play my own version is in some senses the prototype, but it would be foolish to assume, simply because Lowell approved and applauded this version, that any subsequent staging represents a deplorable lapse from its canonical form.*

interesting mind than Lowell's and yet, in long and often very intrusive inquiries on my part, I never succeeded in hearing answers that elucidated exactly what he intended. In fact, in this particular case, it was the other way round. He was constantly surprised to find that in the process of rehearsal meanings with which he was previously unacquainted were disclosed by his own play. Now it may well be that he was considerably more tolerant, accommodating and flexible than a playwright such as Pinter who is extremely explicit about what he means, and will allow very little other interpretation. It may also have been due in part to Lowell's innocence, his inexperience in the theatre, and relief that the play was put on at all. But another reason for his openness to interpretation might be more positive and interesting.

As a poet, who worked with complex allusions and extremely elaborate references and traditions, he acknowledged the idea that in writing you are never fully aware of the meanings that are present in a work you make. Although there is a sense in which the maker of a work is in a privileged position to say what he might or might not mean by what he wrote, an intelligent and imaginative person like Lowell, who was committed to the notion of the unconscious sources of his own ideas, was prepared to accept the possibility of alternative interpretations and to identify very closely with them once they became apparent in the course of rehearsal. The English, as a whole, tend to be less friendly to the idea of undivulged and unfamiliar sources of their own inspiration, perhaps because we are still suspicious of the notion of the unconscious. Anglo-Saxons assume with a sort of Johnsonian common sense that what you know is what you write, and there is thought to be a complete symmetry between the two. In contrast, a poet like Lowell who had himself been exposed to analytic ideas, and had undergone analysis, was much more prepared not only to accept but to welcome the idea that the play's contents might be larger than its volume implied – rather like the Tardis telephone box in *Doctor Who*. He was impressed by his own creativity, and the production of his work, rather than being irritated by mine.

Angry critics and actors usually cite revivals of the classics as examples of directors who abuse their power by feeling free to impose fanciful ideas when interpreting a play. One explanation for this is that the director is allowed to run wild with no playwright in attendance to curb his interpretive energies. It may also be that works from the past seem to need more interpretation as the significance of the work – its range of possible meanings – requires greater exegesis the more remote in time the play's origins become. But these arguments deny what my own experience of classical and contemporary drama reveals – that a play, whether new or old, is an emergent object that can be realized only in its many subsequent performances. The fact that since the 1960s I have tended to stay with plays from the past happened by default rather than choice, but my experiences as a director with the playwrights at rehearsal did not change my approach to the staging of the plays.

I enjoy having the playwright at rehearsals but it is important to have days when he or she is absent so that the rehearsal can develop freely and the results are then submitted for editing and reconsideration. John Osborne would come into rehearsal every three or four days but Robert Lowell was so delighted to be there that he came every day. *The Old Glory* was a re-working of two (originally three) stories: *My Kinsman Major Molineux* by Hawthorne, and the longer one, which has survived as a play in its own right, came from Herman Melville's novella *Benito Cereno*. Lowell saw these plays as allegories of modern America. He was interested in the route to the American mind and excavated these archaeological shards trying to make something modern out of them. When I revived *Benito Cereno* a few years later in England, it was very unpopular and mistakenly seen as a straightforward allegory of the Vietnam War, whereas in America the two plays were highly praised.

I worked again with Lowell in 1967 on his translations of Aeschylus' *Prometheus Bound* at the Yale Drama School with Kenneth Haig and Irene Worth. Once again this piece, like the two in *The Old Glory*, was not literally a translation or an adaptation; they were all what Lowell himself called imitations, transformations based on the original. During the course of rehearsals he never rewrote but, particularly in the case of *Prometheus Bound*, which was too long, he allowed cuts. This was in contrast to John Osborne who resisted cuts as a Christian Scientist resists surgery.

When Lowell presented me with his script of *Prometheus Bound*, which nominally takes place on a Caucasian mountaintop in some sort of primeval antiquity, I was immediately struck by the enormous difficulty of staging the play. The idea of an actor tethered to a rock in the middle of the Caucasus is not a very promising start to a theatrical evening, and although this might sound a sweeping generalization it is invariably true that nature looks atrocious on stage. This problem made me think about changing the play's setting, despite the fact that Lowell's stage directions described the mountaintop as Aeschylus had intended. Here is an example of interpretation that might have been seen as typical of the modern director's cavalier attitude towards the author's intention and a trick he would never dare perpetrate with the author in attendance. But the opposite happened when I discussed this with Lowell. He saw that it would be awkward in practice and, with his enthusiastic collaboration, we came up with an alternative setting.

I looked for a metaphorical counterpart that would suggest some sort of constraint and imprisonment but would allow this complicated historical dialogue to take place without the embarrassment of a nasty piece of nineteenth-century naturalism. The Greeks themselves would not have staged the play literally so I did not feel that we were violating a

*Robert Lowell,* Prometheus Bound *at Yale University in 1967*

*Lowell's version of Aeschylus'* Prometheus Bound *is twice as long as the original, and it is difficult to tell whether it counts as a translation or not. When Lowell wrote his version, he visualized it in the classical setting referred to in the original text. But when I came to stage it, I superimposed yet another level of translation by setting it in a seventeenth-century limbo. Lowell was pleased to discover that his own work, not to mention that of Aeschylus, contained more than either he or his Greek antecedent had knowingly put into it. So what can one make of the claim that the author's intention is the only reliable criterion by which the validity of interpretation is to be judged?*

theatrically 'authentic' staging. I searched for a way of boxing the work that would allow the production to make references to antiquity, but in some sort of dramatic parenthesis. Having read Frances Yates's *Art of Memory*, I had some ideas about memory theatres and realized that it might be possible to set the play, not in the place where it is said to occur, but in some sort of theatrical limbo that could refer to the rock without representing it. Working with the designer Michael Annals, we set the play in a late Renaissance limbo in the world of the seventeenth century, and on the edges of the Thirty Years War. This meant we could start by suggesting that an atrocious and terrible execution or torture had just taken place from which a prisoner is brought in accompanied by Force and Power, so named in the text but not necessarily represented as such on stage. By putting the play inside a vast ruined Renaissance courtyard, with walls reaching up into the flies and down into the basement, we used a mnemonic device whose architecture referred to antiquity without requiring a slavish representation of it. In the niches of this great theatre, as Frances Yates suggests, we placed shattered statues, images reminiscent of the characters in the play. The audience could then see Prometheus and Io, with her horns, so that they were put in mind of the myth itself while what they saw enacted on the stage was not the myth but a mnemonic of it. In the same way that Lowell's interpretation of Aeschylus was an imitation, a mnemonic of the original work, so the staging served to place the play inside an ironic framework which released us from a literal production.

The actor playing Prometheus was on a tiny pedestal poised in the middle of the pit and surrounded by the shattered architecture of the courtyard. As we had excavated and removed the stage to extend the towering walls below ground level there was only a narrow catwalk leading to the platform from the back of the theatre. The staging evoked a feeling that some great unknown social disaster might occur; it was as if a war had been waged out of sight but nearby. From the beginning to the end of the play Prometheus could not move off the rock but was free to move around on the tiny rostrum. This suggested his imprisonment without him having to lie back for two and a half hours in a position that would have made it impossible for him to express the wit and variety of rhetoric that Lowell had provided.

While it would be unwise to conclude from the enthusiasm with which Lowell accepted this radical interpretation of his work that Shakespeare would have agreed to comparable ideas from a director, it does demonstrate the unfinished nature of the script in relation to a performance which takes shape under the eye and protection of the author. I suspect that playwrights fall into two distinct categories with regard to the interpretability of their work. There are writers, like Lowell, who are more explicitly poetic and for whom the possibility of undisclosed meanings is part and parcel of their philosophy of art; and a second group with a much more intolerant attitude to interpretation who believe, perhaps with good reason, that they are in the best possible position to know everything about the meaning and intention of their work. This attitude is expressed most clearly in the work of the American critic E. D. Hirsch, for whom the notion of an author's intention is a guiding principle regulating all future interpretations. Hirsch writes about the interpretation of poems, not plays, but the consequence of his argument is applicable. In his view, it is only by reference to an author's intention that you can actually prevent the possibility of a chaos of interpretations – a veritable slum of alternative ideas about what the work in general means. While there is something to be said for what Hirsch implies, I think he is over-optimistic about the extent to which any artist knows what he means, certainly the extent to which a complex and interesting artist knows what he means. I do not then assume that the work is open to any and every interpretation that may appeal to the director. There *must* be a notion of a constraint – and this is introduced by the language, and by the notion of genre. If the genre within which the playwright is working is not recognized as a constraint it is possible to misidentify the play and to start to stage it in ways that denature the work.

In 1974 I directed *The Freeway* by Peter Nichols, another contemporary dramatist, who belongs to the second category of authors – those who are intolerant of interpretations other than the ones that originate from them explicitly. I detected this early on, and worked with him carefully on the script, listening scrupulously to everything he said, and trying wherever possible to reproduce his intentions on stage. Again, he was present at almost every rehearsal so that whatever I introduced was subject to his criticism and I was *very* careful in this particular case *not* to let my imagination run riot. The possibility of this happening was limited by the much more detailed readability of the social details written into the play: it took place in contemporary England or in some future world that could be closely reconstructed from the present. There was no reason to think that the play could take place in an alternative location as Nichols's setting was a constitutive part of the play's action, which had to happen on a slip road, or a giant freeway, in the middle of a traffic jam. *The Freeway* was a social satire, and it would have been a gratuitous violence to the text to have introduced any other alternative, but it was not a happy experience. The play was badly received and closed rapidly. I am sure that in such an instance the playwright feels let down by the director and I find it hard now to pinpoint why it was such a failure.

\*

I often find modern English writing disappointing, and in the last five years America seems to have produced far more exciting playwrights than England. I am thinking of David Rabe, Sam Shepard and David Mamet in particular, writers who take pride in hitting the detailed diction of rough, fast, creative and witty American street talk. Listening to their words you hear language evolving in a way that is rare in English work. Modern American plays may seem more invigorating because of shock of unfamiliarity and the ethnic richness which arises from what, even today, appears to the English as an exotic culture. Playwrights like David Hare and Howard Brenton are too didactic in their views of society and so much English work seems unnecessarily explicit, programmatic and glum. The plays that have struck me as being genuine works of imagination tend to be less naggingly political. Edward Bond's *Saved*, for example, is about a social scene but plunges into another world of darkness which is much more than a simple slice of life, and does not hector the audience with an obvious political line.

While injecting a healthy vitality into writing, the American emphasis on naturalism and contemporary living speech has a problematic aspect for any director working with actors committed to the method acting of Lee Strasberg and his followers. There is a tremendous emphasis in American acting on very close identification of the emotions of the protagonists. Actors recoil from the idea of what they would call 'affectation' and we would refer to, rather less pejoratively, as artificiality and a high degree of convention. It is as if their integrity is being questioned when they are asked to represent a character with whom they cannot identify socially. This is one of the reasons why Americans are not altogether happy with European drama, and find it hard to speak artificial lines in verse. They tend to lack what I can best describe as the wonderfully affected nimbleness that English actors have no difficulty reproducing – I use the word affectation here in its best sense. The American preference for a rather more naturalistically slipshod style is very effective for contemporary drama but hopeless when representing a culture quite different from their own. The actors have little ability to identify with values that differ from those prevailing in America today, and this encourages a tendency to put Shakespeare through a sort of blender so that his plays appear in a form that is readily consumable by a very suburban American audience. Having said this, however, I would not want to obliterate or disparage American idioms of performance or encourage them to make terrible impersonations of admired English actors. But as a director I have never been able to reconcile the natural pride of the American actors in their own skills with the requirements of a play that demands, particularly in the case of European drama, certain forms of artificiality and highly technical skills. With Restoration plays, for example, there is a certain delicacy, irony and lightness of touch that can be recognized only if some pleasure is taken in the artificiality of the diction. These plays are not cast in modern language, and an enthusiastic adoption of the idioms in which they are written must prevail, otherwise the plays are denatured and will fail.

The problem for any serious director working in America is the commercial system epitomized by Broadway, where I had one particularly disastrous experience with a comedy called *Come Live with Me* which closed after a couple of days. The big commercial theatre in America is in a dire condition, like its English counterpart, the West End, and consists of very expensive, extravagant revivals of American musicals with only the occasional new play. Most of the interesting new work appears in places like Chicago, or way Off Broadway. Beyond the paralysing box-office pressures on Broadway there is a whole world of regional theatre where a wide repertoire of English and European plays is performed. This two-tier arrangement and a disease called the star system affects theatre in England in less blatant and slightly different ways. The energy of the 1950s and 1960s in English theatre has been dissipated. While admiring the young actors and work performed by the Joint Stock Company, and at the King's Head and Bush Theatres, I think that post-war respectability, and the growth in recognition given to the theatre, has led to a sad dullness accompanied by an unevenness in the distribution of wealth.

It is very hard to say exactly why the theatre has lost its disreputable and raffish image but the fact that, after the war, subsidy was thought worthwhile indicates how it has come to be regarded as part of the nation's health rather than as a colourful and casual entertainment. The theatre responded with a new sense of self-importance and took itself very seriously indeed. This is partly reflected in the way that it has become a perfectly creditable career for a young man or woman. Large numbers of people with university educations have gone on the stage without having been born in a band box, a laundry skip or theatrical digs. They have been exposed to expert theories of criticism, and taught about the plays as something other than performances. Before the war, there were not enough graduates in the theatre to form the rather substantial minority that they do today.

It is easy to be seen to be biting the hand that feeds me by saying that subsidized theatre over-dignifies a profession that perhaps works best when that very raffishness which we have deplored is given its full rein. It is often in that form that theatre exercises its most liberating function; and when it becomes a serious business subsidized by the state and supported by local councils, it stiffens and becomes too self-important. But on the other hand (the unbitten one) theatre *is* very expensive, and it is difficult to see how it can survive without subsidy except by succumbing entirely to the deplorable models of Broadway and our own West End.

The theatre has undergone enormous growth *because* it is taken seriously and although beneficial in some respects this attitude has encouraged feather-bedding, wastefulness and mediocrity.

In the 1960s when the National Theatre was in its comparatively modest setting at the Old Vic, and the Royal Shakespeare Company (RSC) was at the Aldwych, these two places had an exemplary importance but they were not as greedy as they are today. There was plenty of vitality to be found on stages beyond these two, and I did some of my best work as a director in the provinces when I worked at Nottingham in the 1960s and early 1970s. At that time, there was a much more even distribution of work, talent and money between the provinces and London. Over the last twenty years, this balance has been lost. The National Theatre is now a great big three-auditorium complex on the South Bank, while the RSC has moved to the Barbican and expanded in size. The gradient between the centre and the periphery has steepened, but this has not been to the advantage of either London or the provinces. While people quite clearly enjoy the very congenial atmosphere of the new National Theatre with its river views, it may well be that we are purchasing congeniality at too great a cost.

The development of such huge centralized cathedrals of English drama has encouraged an episcopal *largeness* of style which is believed to be commensurate with the importance of the plays. The National and the RSC see themselves as flagships and centres of excellence. The result is a style of performance and production that reflects the view of the management (and those performers invited by the management) that what they are doing is too important to be performed in a slipshod, casual way. Consequently a lot of the spontaneity and fluid speed of the acting is lost. When I first worked for the National Theatre, in 1970, it was at the Old Vic under Laurence Olivier. I was not there in any official capacity but had a series of one-off engagements from *The Merchant of Venice* through to *The Freeway* and Beaumarchais's *The Marriage of Figaro*. The Old Vic then had a sort of sloppy, raffish charm and was still run by someone who had both a practical, knockabout working relationship with the stage and was familiar with everyone. We seemed to spend a great amount of time in very squalid huts in Aquinas Street, which never struck us as uncomfortable. But when the theatre became dignified with an enormous building and its own logo, it seemed to grow like any other big company, whether IBM or British Leyland, and soon became heavily official – an institution. The liberating raffishness disappeared and as the theatre became a cultural attaché representing the nation's health, it began to die.

We may now be about to enter a sort of nuclear winter of the arts, and from this bleakness and lack of shelter new and enforced developments may emerge to correct some of the current faults in the theatre. I say this because I can never forget that one of the best productions I have ever worked on was a casual, scratched together touring show of *Measure for Measure* which Laurence Olivier asked me to direct for the National's Theatre-Go-Round in 1974. He had only £500 to spare and a few actors who were not particularly prestigious. It was a wonderful experience, the atmosphere was intense and companionable without any sense of self-importance as we all knew that we had nothing to lose and everything to gain. After that life became very difficult for me at the National. This was partly due to the problems of moving into the new premises on the South Bank, but also because I came up against a form of executive ambition on the part of Peter Hall which I found totally impossible. I resigned eventually because the endless discussions about what we ought to be doing in the theatre were too boring. I do not think the theatre is important enough to bear such bureaucratic scrutiny. For me, what is attractive about the stage is contained in the name of what it is we do: it is a play and is playful. But suddenly it became an institution that was too grandly self-important. The committee approach became too engrossed in its own deliberations. In a sense, theatre becomes important only when it has imaginative spontaneity. Playful ideas are aired and should not become the subject of dreary long discussions as if they offer up major issues in structuralism for tedious debate. The validity of any idea can emerge only when it is tried out, and the one way a director can justify himself is by seeing if a production works. Imagine what it would have been like if Peter Brook had been made to print out a detailed manifesto, and to sit down to explain why he wanted a trapeze. His productions may well never have been seen, and the explanations might have sounded bizarre, heavy and didactic in discussion, whereas in performance *A Midsummer Night's Dream* was a startlingly exciting and imaginative production that worked.

Turning the theatre into an institution has had a deadening effect. Meanwhile the provinces are working on very short rations, and seem to have become repertoire mills with interesting productions every now and then. The effervescent sense of novelty that was there in the 1960s, when these theatres were receiving their subsidies for the first time, has gone. This is not solely due to the fight for finance, because there may be times when such a struggle is liberating, but when it is combined with routine requirements and a kind of boardroom bureaucracy the effect is rigor mortis.

I think the theatre should be a much more careless business of *doing* plays with a disrespectful and flamboyant energy. Peter Brook, who now works in the rather shabby Bouffe du Nord, has found his own invigorating environment and, without in any way wanting to glorify squalor, I do feel that the theatre is at its best when it maintains spontaneity and recognizes that it is a charades business. I look back with enormous excitement to Peter Brook's *A Midsummer Night's Dream*, *Marat-Sade*, *Lear* and more

*Peter Brook*, A Midsummer Night's
Dream, *1970*

*By setting* A Midsummer Night's
Dream *in a white box furnished with
trapezes, Brook did not mean to convey the
impression that Shakespeare's events took place
in a gymnasium as opposed to a midsummer
forest. He liberated the audience's
imagination by creating an empty space where
the arrangements made a metaphorical
reference that transcended the literal world
both of mossy dells and aerobic gyms.*

recently his very simplified version of *Carmen*. He was an inspiration to many directors in the sense that his determination to abolish the fripperies of 'courtesan theatre' and to reduce it to its intense dramatic essentials was very important. His great strength, however, lies in the fact that he is an extremely imaginative showbiz director who produces his best work precisely because he has an energetic and joyful sense of theatre. He combines sparkling spectacle with intense and lean representations of encounters between characters. I disagree with many of his dogmas, but his work has an essential vitality and sense of spectacle that I admire enormously. A large part of his work was done at the Royal Shakespeare Company before it, like the National, moved shop to become a flagship of excellence but in recent years he has rarely made appearances in either place.

While there is plenty of self-important pomposity within the institutionalized theatre, it does not seem to extend to the audiences. The growth of the big theatres coincided not only with economic recession, but also with a gradual waning of the public's belief in the theatre's true importance. This may be just my own weariness, but theatre now does not seem to have the energetic appeal or even glamour that it held twenty years ago. One reason for this may be that we no longer have any exotic critics who can give the theatre back that healthy sense of pride which came about partly as a result of very individual and very idio-syncratic writers like Kenneth Tynan. When the history of the theatre in the twentieth century comes to be written, Tynan's role in giving back to the theatre an image of its own importance, without in fact being self-important, will be recognized as both distinct and crucial.

Tynan, whom I first met when I was an undergraduate at Cambridge, was not just a working hack journalist. It seemed quite natural that he should be involved with the National Theatre and, although he was recruited by Olivier only in an attempt to neutralize what was otherwise a dangerous enemy, his presence was a great pinch of yeast. His influence was enormously benevolent although Olivier has gone to great lengths to deny this, partly because there were aspects of Tynan's character that led him, and the National Theatre, into some disastrous follies for which Olivier never forgave him. Tynan's advice to stage *Soldiers*, the Hochhuth play about Churchill, seemed outrageous to Olivier who was a simple-minded patriot at heart.

But despite Tynan's extravagances, he was an extremely creative figure and even his absurdities were on a grand scale comparable to that of his writing. Theatre became exotic and desirable because he thought it was. I no longer turn to the theatre pages with the excitement that I once did and although contemporaries like Alan Brien lacked Tynan's flamboyant, showstruck, star-fucking excitement, he too was an invigorating critic to read. Tynan managed both to belong and be a

marvellous host to the theatre when he threw great parties. The parties and his newspaper columns were inseparable; the column was simply the party carried on the morning after. Theatrical in his own life, he wrote well about the theatre. Tynan's outrageous puns about the theatre were fresh and I will always remember his review of John Van Druten's *I am a Camera*, for which the heading was simply 'No Leica!'. These sort of puns tend to be repeated but have faded and grown stale.

Why Tynan was influential within the theatre is hard to explain. He did not influence me as a director but his advice was often very useful. Sitting in the stalls during a dress rehearsal he would see where something needed to be cut, or where pace was inadequate and, more often than not, his technical advice was helpful because he had an intrinsic understanding of the hurly-burly of the theatre. Whatever was virtuous about him was welded inseparably to what was a vice in him. There was a certain gullible, vulgar extravagance about his writing that is also part of the attraction of the theatre itself. Having Tynan present at rehearsals was like having Diaghilev sit in. There was an astrakhan-collared vulgarity about his presence and, with all that was unlikeable about that, it gave the proceedings a lift.

When you look back to the eighteenth century in England it is very hard to identify any playwright of great importance with the exception of Sheridan, and Goldsmith, who was not celebrated in his lifetime. Again, nineteenth-century England witnessed little excitement in the theatre and produced some playwrights at its end but not at its beginning. By conscientious efforts at resuscitation, we can go back to a work like *Wild Oats* and make something quite joyful out of it. I do not believe, however, that the theatre itself has failed in any way. It has simply gone through one of the natural seasons of growth and relative senescence, but I find it quite hard to work in today. There are some very talented people with good ideas but one of the reasons I have been away from the profession recently is because I felt that it was no longer as interesting. Perhaps there are just too many of us doing it now. It expanded too quickly and has become an occupation rather than a vocation.

In a curious way, we may expect too much of the theatre now precisely because it has become an institution dominated by enormous companies. We think of it in the same way as any successful industrial enterprise that turns out a product with a high degree of technical expertise and finish. The production line never ceases, and every now and again there will be an exciting new model. In the light of this attitude the theatre becomes as boring as car manufacture. I think we ought to recognize that theatre is as intermittent as any other art and goes through a period of great excitement and joy in its own new-found abilities, and then falls into routine perhaps for as long as twenty or thirty years, dwindling in social importance as its image becomes less prominent in the public eye.

*Kenneth Tynan, Beverly Hills, 1979*

# II: ii

When I began directing I had experience as a performer, a fairly intuitive sense of what was plausible and amusing, and a strong natural sense of observation, which is essential. A director must have the capacity to *remind* performers – not to constrain them by enforcing particular inflexions or intonations. When asked to summarize the work of a director in a few words I have always said that as far as acting is concerned the function of a director is to remind people of things they know but have forgotten, and to encourage them to forget things they should never have known in the first place. At any given moment in a rehearsal the director, like a good analyst, might say, 'Have you ever noticed that under these circumstances people do this or that?' or remind the actor or actress of how people respond and behave. I find it very difficult to talk about the process of rehearsal because it somehow implies that the director has a secret strategy that he or she uses in order to bring the play into existence. As I have grown older the reverse is true, and I have less and less in the way of specific procedures.

It is often assumed that an imaginative director is someone who arrives with a rigid model of the production in mind, and has imagined every detail. I find that although I will imagine ways of staging the play, the model that has led me to cast this actor, rather than any other, is *provisional*. Casting is a conjectural process, based on an intuition I might have about the way in which a particular speech could be spoken. When I read a play, I begin to have some intimation of how the speech acts might sound, and that will put them into the mouths of certain actors or actresses. But this is not the same as having a complete picture of the final production in my mind, and trying to fill out the characters accordingly.

What happens is that the casting effects an introduction, a blind date between a text and a living person, in the hope that the chosen actor will, in coming to inhabit the lines, invest them with meaning which neither of you can foresee at the outset of rehearsal. The process is rather like choosing a rose bush from a nursery where the plants on display have been trimmed right back, and carry little notes telling you their names and what they will be. The director begins to know what kind of flowerbed he has selected only once the actor has been planted in the text, watered, and sustained throughout rehearsal. For example, when I cast John Cleese as Petruchio in *The Taming of the Shrew* it was not because I had seen him fully-flowered and blossomed in the character of Basil Fawlty. I chose him because I had seen him in various guises in *Monty Python* and spotted a vigorous stock there, without any leaves or flowers but highly suggestive of what might develop when planted and nourished by a classic text.

Before rehearsals begin, I will have worked on a metaphorical level looking for similarities and affinities between the structures in the play and other works of art of the period. But these are very preliminary intimations of what might happen in the rehearsal period – sketches and suggestions about how things might proceed. They introduce guidance and limitations but not tyrannies. The director who approaches the work having apparently imagined everything has literally conceived everything but imagined nothing, thus missing the crucial point of directing: you must imagine very richly but you must also be capable of conceding, admitting and allowing to the same degree. It may be that actors regret, and resent, that they have not taken this initiative, and see themselves as *objets trouvés* assembled by the director in a collage of his making. But I do not think that this is a fair assessment because, although they are *objets trouvés* to the extent that the director identifies particular properties they have before the play starts, the actors show all sorts of completely unexpected features, which develop in the course of rehearsal. It is nearly always the case that the director is surprised by what the actors bring to rehearsal. What follows is *adaptation* and *discussion*, and these two words describe the process of directing itself.

I like to let people start reading the play, and to wait for alternative inflexions to appear during the course of rehearsal, which I then edit, revise and emphasize. In this way salient features can emerge, or be introduced, as the production grows. I used to begin rehearsals with some long erudite lecture, but now I say less and less. I show the set, hand round the costume drawings and give thumbnail sketches of what I think the characters might be, and why I have chosen particular actors for the parts. People tend to believe in the pre-existence of the fictional characters, and mistakenly think of rehearsals as nothing more than the process of bringing these characters back to life. But I start out the rehearsals treating the speeches in the text as if they are premises to let that are to be occupied by persons as yet unknown. When casting, I may have advertised for a particular type of tenant but I cannot tell exactly how they will inhabit the role.

During rehearsals, the director and actors make visible something that is there but in some way obscured. The only point that I ever emphasize now is that the characters – Hamlet, Claudius, Troilus, Cleopatra, or whoever – are extremely indeterminate people. They are signposts pointing in a certain direction; indications of where there might be a character if the rehearsals go well and they come into existence. Another analogy, which I think of in order to describe rehearsals to myself, is that they are like seances. In the process of getting the actors to speak their lines, characters begin to take possession and to inhabit the speeches. By the time the rehearsals come to an end, the lines seem to be spoken by someone with whom the actor was unfamiliar at the outset but has come to know in the process of speaking the lines. As a director who is outside the play, for whom the lines have an objective existence, I have vague intimations as to what is in them but defer to, and rely on, the actors to bring characters out of those lines. It is only by inhabiting the lines, by being inside them, by speaking them and beginning to act through them, that a direct knowledge of what they mean emerges in rehearsal.

The language we speak spontaneously, like the language that has been written down for someone else to speak artificially, has a double existence. The words have an objective existence for an outside hearer, who may infer something about what is meant by them, but they also have a subjective existence for anyone who speaks them. Obviously, their subjective existence is spontaneously created by the speaker because he or she knows what it is he or she wants to convey by speaking them. In the case of lines that pre-exist, because an author has left them behind him, their subjective identity has to be discovered by the conjectural process of speaking them. Merely reading a speech does not always tell you what is possible in the lines. Their full possibilities cannot become apparent until they are spoken.

An actor is someone whose imagination is galvanized and stimulated by taking the plunge and inhabiting the lines from within, not by reading them from the outside. Often the actor begins to make discoveries only by taking the risk of speaking the lines without having the faintest idea of what they mean. It is then the director's responsibility to notice and encourage consistent or interesting trends developing in the diction. In this way, confusing, conflicting or less interesting alternatives are gradually whittled away so that a cleft is made in the language. As the rehearsals continue, and the director encourages one implication rather than another, meaning opens out rather as if you have made fissures in the language itself.

From moment to moment in rehearsals all sorts of things happen that are not apparent when I read the text over to myself. When someone is up on their feet saying the words I hear new intonations because of an intuitive inflexion introduced by the actor, and I point it out. This is where the analytic function of the director begins, and there is a kind of vigilant inactivity on the part of a good director by which he or she lets the rehearsals go on and simply records intonations as they occur from day to day. By gradually picking out and reintroducing often unconscious deliveries given by a particular actor, the rehearsal develops. This reminds me of an ambiguous pictorial figure where, by developing and shading in the interpretation that favours one particular configuration rather than another, a new image begins to emerge from the old format. As the other alternatives are minimized, the perspective alters giving prominence to the one interpretation that gradually becomes visible. It is like the Necker cube; a skeletal outline of a cube in which no face is obviously nearer or farther than another so that the front and back faces appear to alternate and perception tends to oscillate unstably between the two alternatives. It is up to the director to point out the alternatives in the text, and to observe which one is emerging in rehearsal. By providing the actors with extra information one interpretation can be solidified and the visibility of the alternatives diminished.

I used to start off rehearsals with a formal reading simply because I submitted to the tradition that you sat around on day one and read the play through from beginning to end. I have abandoned this approach because it exposes the cast to unnecessary risks of embarrassment and humiliation, which arise inevitably when one actor appears, at the outset, to have a more definitive reading than the others. This confidence may not be a good thing if it means that those who are still stumbling and finding their way are put off or paralysed on the first day. Now I tend to split the reading into small sections and, with two or three actors, read scenes that are not necessarily at the start of the play. Often the most productive implications about a character emerge when you begin with scenes half-way through the play – as though you have dropped rather casually into the middle of an event. The ideas that develop as a result of that reading may extend backwards into the, as yet, unread beginning of the play. In other words, I am increasingly tempted to allow the play to develop gradually, so that from little buds or islands the ideas grow out as if from quite separate centres and eventually meet to form a continent of meanings which comprise the contours of the whole work.

At the start of rehearsal the play has an existence rather like an objective continent that is waiting to be discovered, and it is terribly hard to decide where to start to put the boats ashore. I am less and less tempted to start with a frontal attack on a play because it is so daunting, and can defeat the imagination of everyone concerned. In a way, the problem is very similar to the one that philosophers such as Wittgenstein have raised. It was he who said, and here I paraphrase, that you get mental cramps if you attempt a frontal assault on a large philosophical question like the meaning of meaning. But if you can first tackle a smaller, manageable question, and ask: what sort of meanings are there? and: what are the uses we put a particular word to? then we become familiar with the fact that meaning is a cluster of concepts rather than one concept that can be penetrated. In the same way, the play seems to be a cluster of characters whose nature will be discovered by attempting an assault on some element that may, at first, seem to be peripheral to its larger meaning. Gradually, by allowing one or two actors the experience of inhabiting the lines from inside, the daunting objective entirety of the work is broken down.

In an intelligent, well-conducted and convivial rehearsal the cast is improvising by simply acting a scene in a way that allows you to see that

*The Necker cube*

*The speeches written down by an author have a literal meaning which is constrained by the rules of grammar and the entries in an English dictionary, but the meanings expressible within the limits of these constraints are comparable to the different figures that are visible in the geometrically unchanging form of the Necker cube. New characters can leap into three-dimensional perspective as a result of speaking the lines in different ways. And although it is impossible to represent Claudius as a kindly uncle, just as it is impossible to see Necker's lines as the representation of a hollow sphere, the lines assigned to Claudius can give his character many alternative appearances.*

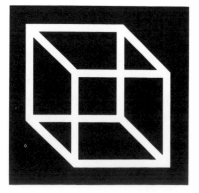

its outcome is not yet determined. Improvisation in itself does not benefit rehearsal. I cannot see how improvising in a vacuum can possibly increase our knowledge of the play, as we are still confronted with the problem of how to tackle and approach the script. In rehearsal, the unforeseen and unforeseeable implications of a scene will sometimes emerge as a result of solving an incidental, technical problem that seemed quite trivial at the time. For example, in the fourth act of Chekhov's *Three Sisters* there is a beguiling moment of bathos when Masha's cuckolded husband, Koolyghin, tries to console her grief at the forthcoming departure of her lover, Vershinin, by suddenly appearing in a woolly beard confiscated from one of his pupils. The actor playing Koolyghin wanted to know when he should take the beard off, and I found it difficult to say when exactly. 'Keep it on for a moment,' I told him, having nothing better in mind at that time. 'Brazen it out and we'll see what happens.' So for a moment, he continued to wear the beard, not in his role as Koolyghin but as an actor who could think of nowhere else to put it. As we went on rehearsing the prop reinstated itself as a feature in the play and the actress playing Masha, in her role as Masha, suddenly took note of this woolly concealment, and at the moment when she said, 'It's time to go' she walked across to her husband and unhooked the beard from his ears only to discover, beneath its absurdity, the serious concerned face of her hitherto neglected spouse. It was as if by concealing himself under a deliberately assumed absurdity, he could reappear transfigured. In some mysterious way, the actor had gone into the beard as an insensitive clown and, because Masha had taken it off him, he emerged from its disguise appearing before her eyes as a man of dignity, kindness and patience. But all this happened as a result of solving an apparently trivial problem of when to take off a false beard.

Another moment in rehearsal: Olga and Vershinin are standing together in the garden studiously avoiding any reference to the dreadful moment when Masha will enter to bid Vershinin farewell. Janet Suzman had dreaded this moment almost as much as the character she was playing, and told me before we began rehearsing the scene that she would like to avoid the cliché of racing in distractedly. How to come in then? I suggested that the entrance might solve itself if she considered not so much her grief at his departure, or the distraction which that might provoke, but the embarrassment of farewells in general. She arrived, therefore, at the downstage corner of the scene suddenly reluctant to draw attention to her own presence, wishing to be found, wishing to imply: 'I know you care less about our parting than I do so I won't throw myself at you, and burden you with my insufferable misery. All the same, you should be able to tell by the abject self-effacement of my stance that I am grieving and that the rest is up to you.' Alternatively, it is as if Masha anticipates that there is no written script for farewells under these circumstances. No more than there is for Vershinin who dreads the farewell for reasons that are complementary to Masha's. As far as he is concerned another brief affair is over and presumably he would like to bring it to a conclusion as rapidly as possible. How tiresome if this were to involve a scene. Paradoxically the effect of working all this through exerted a retrospective influence on the acting of the earlier relationship between the two of them. It was only by discovering the disparity of their emotions at the end of the relationship that we were able to go back to the beginning and discover aspects that had remained hidden when they were rehearsed in the chronological order of their occurrence in the play. In this respect, rehearsing a play is like constructing a novel, and in taking the events out of sequence the cast can enjoy the luxuries of analeptic conjecture.

I began by saying that as a director I do not have a secret method for rehearsals but there is one strategy I find very useful, although it might be more aptly described as an abstention from strategy. Often, when an action or speech seems difficult or puzzling to an actor, the only way to resolve how it should be performed is to encourage him to find a way while pretending that you are not doing that at all. Let me give an example. At the end of a hard afternoon's work, when nothing seems to have happened, I will call the rehearsal to an end and then suggest that we simply run over the lines to help memory. A couple of us will then go and sit down in the stalls, with or without the books, and feed each other cues. By this inadvertent method you make discoveries, and glean meanings and intonations, rather than deliberately harvest them in performance. This process is analogous to the one I saw in a patient with Parkinson's Disease, who very often found it difficult to make a deliberate assault on a task that he knew was hard for him to accomplish, but he could manage it if he pretended to do something else and literally caught himself unawares. Sometimes you have to creep up on your intention by pretending to be unintentional. Polonius' words describe this circuitous approach: '*And thus do we of wisdom and of reach,/ With windlasses, and with assays of bias,/ By indirections find directions out.*'

In the process of rehearsal, it is often by the artful creation of apparent distractions that we discover direction. But it needs the vigilant attention of a director who, at the same time, pretends not to be looking out for such signs. At the end of rehearsal he must somehow resist the temptation to say: 'I wonder if you realize that you came up with some very interesting stuff then?', because the cast will then recognize this indirection for what it is. Perhaps three days later I might say, 'Incidentally, why don't you try it like that?' knowing perfectly well that the actor has already done so, whether he remembers it explicitly or not, as the little read through will have made him familiar with a new intonation or delivery.

As I have grown older, and I hope more mature, I leave more and more of the discoveries to be made by the actors themselves. In a sense, I am doing what so many actors criticize directors for not doing, as I leave it to the imaginative talent of the performers to make the discoveries, in the only way that really interesting discoveries are to be made in texts, by inhabiting the lines subjectively and not by looking at them from the outside.

Now, this may sound as if, with time, I have abdicated all interpretative responsibility but the very reverse is the case. Despite the fact that I am confined to an objective relationship with the text I do have very useful ideas, but these take effect only if I keep on handing out little fragmentary insights, like tiny pieces of mosaic, which I leave to the actors to realize in the performance. If the director's initiative were removed altogether my role would be diminished to a consultative one and actors would come together, as they have done in the past, and form companies. The director would then be reduced to benevolently hovering over a bookshelf, checking the actors' queries, and knowing which shelf to go to in order to look up what Tudor underpants were like.

In contrast to this fact-finder of a director, I think it is essential that the director feels provoked by the text rather than responsible for it. I hope that when this happens I do not react eccentrically, or see things that it would be perverse to say existed in the text. I like to provide the cast with a series of very approximate frames in which we can work. I am articulate but not, as it is often assumed, a terrifyingly intellectual director who daunts the cast. In fact, most of the people who have worked with me are struck by my permissiveness, in that my advice and recommendations are not dictations with regard to large-scale portraiture but little suggestions of gesture and nuance which, if acknowledged and possessed, the actors will find have implications beyond the play in question. The aim is that, without having to be further prompted, the cast will then continue to generate more performances that are consistent with these suggestions. The director is, in short, the creator of intuitive insights at moments where rehearsal might otherwise grind to a halt.

Complementary to the suggestion that only in the process of subjectively living the lines in performance will their full range of possible meanings come to light, there are certain aspects of the lines that can be brought to life *only* by some outside, objective judgement as to how the words sound when they are spoken in a particular way. The co-existence of the two – objective and subjective – is essential to the progress of the work as a whole. The lines must be lived actively and subjectively by the only person who is privileged to speak them, the actor, but, on the other hand, some of their meanings and implications are apparent only to someone who stands outside, and who will never enjoy the privilege of speaking them, the director. After all, this is what happens in our ordinary life. A person may speak the lines of their life without quite knowing what it is he or she means by them. Friends, and bystanders, are often in a better position to see what is meant than the person who is speaking to them.

In some ways the relationship of a director to an actor is, or should be, comparable to the relationship of any instructor to a learner. Obviously, learners can acquire a complex motor skill, like riding a bicycle, only if they take the risk of trying initially without adequate skill, and endure the possible humiliation and danger, of falling before they succeed. A director can give broad instructions but cannot ensure success. Ultimately what must happen is that, like the child who has to taste the improbable experience of sitting upright on a machine whose base is not very easy to balance, the actor has to take a chance. In the end, no amount of explicit instruction will result in someone riding a bicycle. But discovering how to perform a play is much more complicated than riding a bicycle, and I think that most actors would bear witness to the fact that a friendly, accommodating, and tactful adviser is a useful presence.

As with learning a motor skill, there is an element of mystery. I often find that the skill is not acquired during the learning session, and when the day ends both teacher and learner, or actor and director, go home tired and depressed by their failure to bring any skill to light. Then a day passes in which there is no rehearsal, no practice of any sort, and on their return the actors enter into the text and speak it like angels. So too a child, after a miserable day of falling off the bike in the park, despite instruction and encouragement, may find three days later that he or she simply rides off. How this happens I can only conjecture, but it is as if, in that interim without practice, all the results of practice are rehearsed in some internal representation. This mysterious process might be compared to a computer simulation based on all the information that has been garnered during the apparently futile practice period. The information has been fed into the database and, without having to go through the tiresome procedure of enactment, a simulated diagrammatic practice is performed by the machine internally. When we then encounter the real apparatus it is as if the computer simulation has eliminated all the boshed shots, and nine-tenths of the work has been realized and become very familiar.

There is a great deal of sentimental dogma about the length of time necessary for rehearsal to allow the possibility of some kind of strange alchemy to take place. It can simply become self-indulgent, and an opportunity for all sorts of silliness. Rehearsal is rather like painting, you sketch things in rapidly, and can soon see what is acceptable. Then the director can erase, and adjust in much the same way as an artist. My usual rehearsal period is four to five weeks – it becomes very boring if it stretches to six weeks. People could argue that this is because I have pre-empted the alternatives too early, and not allowed the play to be productively unstable for long enough. I can only say that I have never regretted any decision reached early on in rehearsal, and have often sent actors home after four or five weeks to rest for a couple of days rather than drag on with unnecessary rehearsal.

I find it very hard to describe what I mean by a good actor. More often than not, it is someone who looks rather unpromising, humdrum and obscure when you meet them offstage. They are the people who are transfigured by the process of becoming someone else. The best actors are rather like very good saboteurs, or espionage agents, whose cover would be blown if they were recognizable as spies. You can easily pass them in the street without recognition, but they bring to their roles a peculiar density of detail. On stage, every action they make strikes the audience as being a real characteristic of the person they are supposed to be, without the need for an easy or sentimental cliché. They can induce a shock of recognition from the spectator because there is a weight of detail to their work that is both accurate and, often, surprising.

I have many misgivings about the formal training that actors receive in England. They have the advantage over Americans whose training is grossly inadequate since, with the notable exception of places like the Yale Drama School, very few schools expose young actors to the classics. This problem is exacerbated as there is no network of theatres in which the classics are in constant repertoire, where actors can simply exercise themselves in these roles. Usually American actors glean their experience by making small appearances in television series like *Hill Street Blues*, and although they may be wonderful (and *Hill Street Blues* is wonderful) it is not a very good training ground for playing Malcolm in *Macbeth* — unless you envisage Malcolm as an LA gumshoe wearing Tudor costume. But while the English schools expose students to verse-speaking, and technical skills, they tend to preserve many traditional clichés and encourage an attitude that is easily summarized in the phrase 'actor laddies'. Many young actors leave drama school with a sentimental view of their profession, a desire to be a lovable, handsome and amiable figure on the stage, without adequate, or effective, training in the classics. Actors who come straight out of Oxford or Cambridge, after simply performing in one university production after another, have the rough edges knocked off them in practice, and are ultimately just as well trained as those who have been explicitly drilled in the techniques of acting. But the university actor is often rather affected and arrogant. Many of them enter the theatre with a highly self-satisfied style of performance which is partly reinforced by their sense of themselves as graduates.

I often hear the phrase 'stage charisma', but this is a value that is usually associated with reputation rather than ability. Charisma arises from the fact that the person is famous, and that whatever he or she does strikes the audience as being remarkable, increasing his or her reputation until he or she occupies a space so large in the public imagination that it cannot possibly be filled. If we adapt the concept of specific gravity, which provides a ratio between weight and volume, the charismatic actor is often someone whose volume is much larger than is justified by the weight he or she brings to the performance. There are, of course, exceptions, like Laurence Olivier who occupies a very large space in the public imagination but also brings an enormous amount of detail and weight to the performance. There are few actors who have this ability. I suppose Ralph Richardson had it, and John Gielgud acquired it more recently in his portrayals of crusty old curmudgeons. But I find that I admire actors like Colin Blakely or Tony Rohr, who works with the Joint Stock Company, performers who are rarely referred to as charismatic. Julie Covington is another example of an actress who brings such detail, such accuracy of observation and accomplished mimicry to a role that there is an almost disturbing sense of familiarity every time you see such performers on stage. The audience then forgets that it is an actor on stage but this is rare, and actors too frequently give performances of being an actor rather than of the character they are representing.

It is strange that even when actors find what they are asking for in a director, they often resist it in favour of rather vulgar intuitions. When actors complain, in many instances, it is because they would prefer to follow intuitions that are clichés. There are performers who will ignore the production as a whole, and come on with their performance as though, like Lear, they are telling us all: 'Blow production, crack your cheeks, I will endure.' When a young director comes in with an idea that is usually described as 'too clever by half' he or she is very likely to meet a wall of sullen hostility. Sullen, because for the social reasons of the stage the actors *have* to obey; hostile, because they have a far longer and wider experience of the stage. After twenty years, I like to think that actors approach my rehearsals with eager curiosity, participating in the ideas and finding themselves liberated to produce something new which is consistent with the genre of the work.

There are very great performers who are too shrewd to overlook the setting in which the director has put them, and they will adapt their performance. When, as a young director, I worked with Olivier and we put on *The Merchant of Venice* in a late nineteenth-century setting, he took note of the production. While he could have given *his* performance regardless, he realized that either he or the production could then have looked absurd. He recognized that there was something interesting in the format of the production that was consistent with the work, adapted himself, and gave a performance of a nineteenth-century character, rather than a barnstorming, Irvingish performance of what he thought the traditional Shylock should be like.

If I were to direct *The Merchant of Venice* now I would not dream of setting it in the nineteenth century but, in 1970, when Olivier offered me the job at the Old Vic it seemed appropriate. It is difficult to explain precisely why I chose that setting, and it certainly did not start with the thought of how interesting it would be to move the play to that century.

*Count de Primoli, Fruit Seller in Venice at the end of August, 1889*

*Shortly before I was asked to direct* The Merchant of Venice *for the National Theatre, I came across photographs of Venice and Trieste taken at the end of the nineteenth century by the Count de Primoli. The traditional lines of the play now spoke to me in a setting that could not possibly have been visualized by Shakespeare himself. But the drama seemed interestingly consistent with this new context, and transposed into this late nineteenth-century world, the play unavoidably delivered meanings that had been inaudible to me before.*

*Laurence Olivier as Shylock, in* The
Merchant of Venice, *The Old Vic, 1970*

*Confronted by the possibility of visualizing
Shylock as a nineteenth-century banker,
Olivier remade the character in a way which
is comparable to the transformation that
Michelangelo inflicted upon Marcus
Aurelius. But this version does not pre-empt
the possibility of rediscovering the character
in his traditional guise. Shylock is a
hypothetical monster with an unfinished
history that remains to be played again.*

I think it came out of my hearing certain speeches, in my mind's ear, delivered in a way that was incompatible with a sixteenth-century setting. As a director I often respond negatively to a precedent and, in this case, I recoiled from the sentimental radiance that actresses bring to Portia's famous mercy speech. I could imagine the speech being delivered in a much more argumentative and impatient way, in response to the apparent stupidity of Shylock's enquiry when he asks, '*On what compulsion must I? tell me that*' In my mind's eye I saw Portia leaning impatiently across the table to say, '*The quality of mercy is not* strained' as if having laboriously to explain what should have been self-evident to someone too stupid to understand. This dispute was too ugly to be argued out in public. The courtroom disappeared and was replaced in my mind by a rather drab Justice's Chambers. When I reached this point, I began to realize that it would be an impossible location for the sixteenth century, but I did not want to set it in a modern era where all the twentieth-century notions of anti-Semitism would overwhelm the play.

I began, then, to think about other themes of the play which might themselves suggest an appropriate setting. The relationship between Bassanio and Antonio made me think of the relationship between Oscar Wilde and Bosie where a sad old queen regrets the opportunistic hetero-sexual love of a person whom he adored. Again, this echo of a relationship seemed appropriate to the nineteenth century. But the production had to acknowledge Venice as its location, and so I looked at late nineteenth-century photographs of that city taken by the Count de Primoli who also recorded Trieste, and the trading cities of northern Italy. I imagined the rather dull, Adriatic mercantile life that Italo Svevo re-creates in his novels, and the footling young men who frequented the waterside cafés. By this time, I felt that I had the beginnings of a totally new way of staging *The Merchant of Venice*, which could bring the speeches to life in a completely different context, and yet remain consistent with Shakespeare's play. The costumes and designs were all influenced by the Count de Primoli's photographs. In many ways I regret making the production quite so richly pictorial. I would have preferred to make it resemble Svevo's Italy, and set it in a rather boring, unscenic, un-Venetian world of the kind that you find in Trieste.

It was in relation to this that Olivier adjusted his performance. He began with the idea of being a grotesque, ornamentally Jewish figure and bought himself very expensive dentures, a big hook nose and ringlets. I think he had a George Arliss view of himself, but gradually he realized the possible advantage in making himself look much more like everyone else, as it is this crucial question of difference that lies at the heart of the play. With the exception of the teeth, in which he had invested such a large amount of money that I did not feel justified in asking him to surrender them, he gradually lost the other excrescences, partly because

I suspect that he could see that the production could have made him appear like a ridiculous pantomime dame in the midst of the rather ordinary nineteenth-century set. As a director, I was able to supply him with bits of business that made him feel secure enough to abandon the Arliss look. When I suggested that Shylock might enter with Jessica's dress in his arms, I simply pointed out that when she leaves the house wearing men's costume she would have left her dress behind her – like a snake shedding its skin – for Shylock to find in her absence. Shylock coming in with the dress draped in his arms has a wonderful overtone of Lear carrying Cordelia. In *King Lear*, as in *The Merchant of Venice*, a daughter who betrays her father seems, in his eyes, to die when she denies him her love. Holding the empty dress, Olivier appeared to be carrying the corpse of the departed daughter, as Shylock wishes when he says, '*I would my daughter were dead at my foot, and the jewels in her ear! would she were hearsed at my foot, and the ducats in her coffin!*'

There was another little gesture that pleased Olivier. At the moment when Tubal tells Shylock that Antonio's ships have gone down there is a pause for some memorable and exotic gesture. I asked Olivier if he recalled the newsreel showing Hitler in the railway carriage, at Compiègne, at the surrender of France. Suddenly, the Führer was seen dancing a funny little jig of triumph, and I suggested that Olivier follow it. He was delighted with the unpredictable peculiarity of this gesture, and felt he had enough in these details to make the part stand out without needing false noses.

# II: iii

When a director approaches a play like *Hamlet* or *The Merchant of Venice*, the initial reaction is, in many instances, not determined by a positive view of a particular character but a desire to overthrow a tired interpretation. The role of precedent is very strong, and there is a tendency for performances to clone. Actors, and directors, like to preserve their originality and would feel very offended if anyone accused them of going by prototype, but I think there is a conspiracy in the theatre to perpetuate certain prototypes in the belief that they contain the secret truth of the characters in question. This collusion between actors and directors is broken only by successful innovation which interrupts the prevailing mode. Often, what exerts a peculiar and disabling influence over our imagination is not the precedent of the distant past, the original Tudor production, but of the recent past, which comes to assume the status of a canonical performance, although it (like its predecessors) is an interpretation of the play in question. The problem is that audiences who object to what they regard as frivolous departures from the prototype mistakenly take one particular, and favourite, production as their standard by which all subsequent performances stand or fall. This means that those who grew up on the Olivier/Gielgud tradition, at the Old Vic in the 1930s, tend to think the more recent interpretations of Shakespeare's plays are deplorable departures from what he meant and intended. They do not realize that these are merely different from the one production that they have seen. This alarmed response is always magnified in the case of Shakespeare.

I came into the theatre in the wake of directors like Peter Brook and Peter Hall, and as a consequence I was less aware of precedent than they might have been. But in the case of *Hamlet*, which I have directed three times, I was very anxious to escape from prototypes. The gloomy, young Dane; the monstrous, slobbering villain, Claudius, and the blowzy Gertrude were all familiar caricatures, which struck me as tiresome and unsupportable by any textual evidence. As I have said, the idea for a production does not begin, as so many critics and audiences assume, with the director's comprehensive plan. I have often found that it grows from a peculiar view of one particular character, which may lead me, with the cast, to develop certain inferences and implications that were barely visible when we began rehearsal. My approach is very similar to that of the palaeontologist Cuvier, who believed that you could reconstruct the entire body of a fossilized mammal by a careful and intelligent series of deductions made from a very small, and apparently unrepresentative, fragment. By looking at the toe, or the shape of a tooth, he might discover what sort of terrain it walked on, or the kind of diet the creature had. From such odd fragments he could infer all sorts of details, and eventually build up a picture of the complete animal.

As Hamlet is the part in which so many performers have made their mark, and that every young actor wants to play, it is tempting to think that his character must be the starting point for any serious production. Now, I would be a fool if I did not apply great thought and imagination to his character but that is not *necessarily* where I begin. Pieces of the play often occur to me in the same way that fossils occur in cliffs — metaphorically it is as if a piece of an elbow sticks out and strikes me as interesting. I have always been struck by the skeletal pieces of Claudius' elbow that stick out of the chalk, and have refashioned his character in several different ways. This does not mean that I deliberately neglect Hamlet, Gertrude or Ophelia, it is merely the *beginning* of my approach to the play that may look at some apparently peripheral character or speech.

In my first production of *Hamlet*, in 1970 with the Oxford and Cambridge Shakespeare Company, I overlooked entirely any sense of lechery in Claudius' character. I felt licensed to do so by a principle that I have always upheld, that one should note, but never altogether believe, what one character says about another in the play. Hamlet tells us that Claudius is a filthy, lascivious monster but *we* do not know about the '*incestuous sheets*' or the '*enseamed bed*'. The fact that Hamlet uses such crude language may tell us more about him than it does about Claudius. I thought that it would be interesting to see what happens if Claudius is made into someone who, admittedly, murdered his brother but was not necessarily prompted by lust, rather, as a hard expedient politician he married Gertrude simply to secure power and prevent opposition. A wife cannot give evidence against her husband.

With this in mind I cast someone who would play Claudius as a sort of Prussian *Junker*. Many actors are delighted to be given a model on which they can build a character, and when a director does this it is intended, and often received, as a gift and not a tyranny intended to constrain the performer. You may object to this idea of Claudius and think it absurd that Gertrude should have married him but there is another play of Shakespeare's in which an even more villainous person manages, through the power of his ambition, to persuade someone to sleep with him. You have only to think of *Richard III*, Act I scene ii, where Anne is wooed by the future king. This was my initial model of Claudius, and at the first rehearsal I discussed one or two general ideas, and the motifs we might explore. This interpretation of Claudius meant that we had to reconsider Gertrude. Instead of the voluptuous, busty Queen who is always having her *décolletage* interfered with by her lascivious brother-in-law and husband she became a rather frightened, timid woman, ignored by Claudius and totally obedient. In the course of the rehearsals we explored her desperate appeals to Hamlet in the light of this reading. When she is shown not to be culpable at the level that Hamlet assumes, Gertrude's self-justifications and pleading became all the more pathetic and moving.

With the character of Hamlet, prototypes are very crude and pressing, the well-worn clichés affect dress and even posture, having cast him as an attractive, gloomy and knowing cynic. I have always been interested in the idea of Hamlet as a rather unattractive character, a tiresome, clever, destructive boy who is very intelligent but volatile, dirty-minded and immature. This interpretation does not subvert the intelligence of the speeches even though we are usually given the noble Dane as a philosophical and restrained character whose reluctance to avenge is prompted by a fastidious refusal to indulge in bloody and inelegant actions. It may well be that he is also a childish creature full of tantrums and resentments who, in a purely Freudian way, is reluctant to kill the object that he seems to hate because by keeping Claudius, the object of his hatred, alive he can ignore the person he might have loathed even more – his father. This is, of course, a very modern interpretation, but again it raises the question as to whether we have to take literally what Hamlet says about another character – his noble father. There are many ways in which people go through elaborate incantations of admiration which conceal extremely intense hatred. As long as the murderous villain of his imagination is alive, all adverse feelings can be projected on to the living villainous father by law and Hamlet can then indulge in self-deluding fantasies of affection for the dead father.

Hamlet's soliloquies are so well known as poetry that stands out without appearing in the play, this can create a great problem for the actor. This leads to a state of anxious tension in a performer who knows that the audience expects something new and feels he has to search for a way of raising the nap on a speech that has become threadbare. But actors should not be so damn noble with Hamlet's soliloquies and must perform them as speeches that *cannot* be spoken in isolation. They have to be re-immersed in the play so that they can be heard coming quite inevitably and consecutively from the action on the stage.

If we take '*Oh what a rogue and peasant slave am I*', the speech that comes immediately after Hamlet's meeting with the players, there is absolutely no point in having the stage suddenly clear with the sense of anticipation for these oft-quoted lines. It should follow, and come out of, the players' ability to produce crocodile tears. In each production I found that I required Hamlet to give a dismissive, rather desperate laugh at the beginning of the speech as if to say: 'God – absurd. What is happening, here's this ridiculous fellow who can do all this, and I can't do a fucking thing . . .' It should be an appeal to the audience to recognize how absurd his predicament seems beside the players' tragic performance.

In the case of *Hamlet*, I have never been tempted to modernize it, or to set it in anything other than a vaguely Tudor period. While I think it would be rather perverse diligently and specifically to set it in a completely different period, I am not in favour of a pedantically accurate

In Hamlet and his other plays, Shakespeare created a Necker cube – an unimaginable range of possible figures for each character. None of these are inconsistent with the lines that he wrote, but many are completely inconsistent with one another. Sometimes, these characterizations precede casting and determine it, but at other times casting determines how one sees the character. By giving the part to this or that actor, one automatically begins to invest the lines with meanings that had previously been inaudible. In some cases, the subsequent production of a play as famous as Hamlet is dictated by the determination to eliminate, or at least escape from, what one has previously seen in the past as a result of a striking performance given by a famous actor such as Olivier. His brooding Dane monopolized the imagination of the mid-twentieth-century audiences and made it difficult to see any alternative figures in the part. The performance was so insistent and so charismatic that, like the inscription on the duck/rabbit figure which says 'see a duck', it may become impossible to see the equal and opposite claims for it to be a rabbit. When I cast Peter Eyre as Hamlet however, an alternative figure did emerge. His 'duck' Hamlet supplanted the perception of Olivier's 'rabbit'. When Anton Lesser then played the part, in another subsequent performance, a third figure emerged from the author's composition.

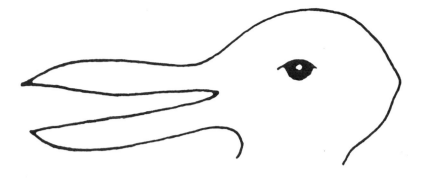

*Duck/rabbit drawing from* Seeing *by* John P. Frisby

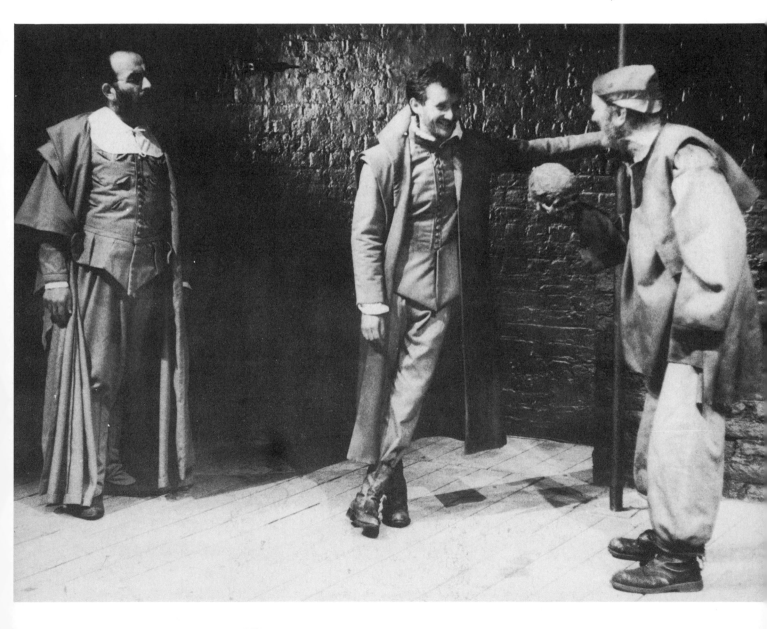

Tudor setting either. I prefer it to appear fairly nondescript with a Tudor flavour. In all three productions of the play, my direction has almost entirely been a matter of reconsidering the motives of the various characters, and trying to redesign the people so that the same words appear to mean something really quite different on each occasion.

Several years later, in 1974, I directed *Hamlet* again, this time at the Greenwich Theatre with Robert Stephens as Claudius. It is impossible *not* to use a certain fleshly quality in Stephens, and I found myself going back to some aspects of Claudius' character that I had previously repudiated. Since Irene Worth was playing Gertrude it was not feasible to make her a timid creature, and instead she was a forceful, rather violent woman whose lust was central to the action. On the whole, I was less satisfied with that more traditional production.

In the subsequent *Hamlet*, eight years later in 1982 at the Donmar Warehouse, I was struck again by one of the little fossil-like knucklebones that stick out of the text. In rehearsal we brushed up against this strange fragment of a speech that Claudius makes to Laertes in an attempt to explain why he has not taken action against Hamlet. He talks very curiously about his relationship to Gertrude when he says:

> *The queen his mother*
> *Lives almost by his looks, and for myself,—*
> *My virtue or my plague, be it either which,—*
> *She's so conjunctive to my life and soul,*
> *That, as the star moves not but in his sphere,*
> *I could not but by her.*
> (Act IV, scene vii)

We found ourselves puzzling over these words. There is something strangely appealing and vulnerable in these lines which convey the sense that Claudius is being moved by *love* and not by lust. As a result of this fragment John Shrapnel, as Claudius, did not stress the villainy of the character but played a person who was a practical administrator and had a genuine passionate love for his brother's wife. We backtracked then and redesigned the character so that he knew from the very beginning of the play that he had committed a terrible crime for a love, which was in itself virtuous. From scene one he was caught in the coils of his crime, and this Claudius did not need the play to have his pain and guilty love revealed. In Act III scene i he recoils at Polonius' words to Ophelia when he says:

> *How smart a lash that speech doth give my conscience!*
> *The harlot's cheek, beautied with plastering art,*
> *Is not more ugly to the thing that helps it*
> *Than is my deed to my most painted word:*
> *O heavy burden!*

Vulnerable, agonized and hating himself for what he does, Claudius is totally incapable of escaping from the one thing he felt he had to have – Gertrude's love. One of the many consequences that flowed from concentrating initially on those odd lines to Laertes was that we developed an interesting conclusion to the play in the light of Claudius' prayer:

> *Whereto serves mercy*
> *But to confront the visage of offence?*
> *And what's in prayer but this two-fold force,*
> *To be forestalled, ere we come to fall,*
> *Or pardon'd, being down? Then, I'll look up;*
> *My fault is past. But, O! what form of prayer*
> *Can serve my turn? 'Forgive me my foul murder'?*
> *That cannot be; since I am still possess'd*
> *Of those effects for which I did the murder,*
> *My crown, mine own ambition, and my queen.*
> (Act III, scene iii)

When we came to the final scene and Hamlet commands Claudius to '*Drink off this potion; – Is thy union here?/Follow my mother*', far from having to be forced to drink the poison, he accepted the cup as if it were a welcome chalice. Having lost Gertrude, which meant everything, he suddenly knelt, his prayers flying spontaneously and generously upward. He had finally been relieved of the tyranny of possession. No longer holding any of the prizes for which he had committed the original crime, Hamlet is denied his revenge.

In all three productions, I wanted to take Ophelia's lunacy seriously. Three very different actors played the part distinctively but the character changed less dramatically than Claudius' in the successive productions. I was always impressed by the fact that people do not go mad as a result of grief. In fact, it is by grieving successfully that we overcome the possibility of madness. Grief is what enables us to lose our attachment to the lost, loved object. I found myself asking why, then, does Ophelia go mad? The only way in which I could answer this question, as a director, was by suggesting that from the beginning of the play she is already more vulnerable than might be explained by her tender age alone. I began to think of her as someone who has never known the love and support of a mother. She is surrounded by hectoring, bullying men who supply her with a self-image, and her character is a reaction to their advice as to what she might or ought to be. Laertes gives her a long didactic speech about female sexuality, suggesting that if she merely exposes herself to the moon she might fall:

> *Fear it, Ophelia, fear it, my dear sister;*
> *And keep you in the rear of your affection,*
> *Out of the shot and danger of desire.*
> *The chariest maid is prodigal enough*
> *If she unmask her beauty to the moon;*
> *Virtue herself 'scapes not calumnious strokes;*
> *The canker galls the infants of the spring*
> *Too oft before their buttons be disclos'd,*
> *And in the morn and liquid dew of youth*
> *Contagious blastments are most imminent.*
> *Be wary then; best safety lies in fear:*
> *Youth to itself rebels, though none else near.*
> (Act I, scene iii)

Polonius repeats these warnings, '*Marry, I'll teach you; think yourself a baby*', as does Hamlet with the admonition: '*Get thee to a nunnery: why wouldst thou be a breeder of sinners?*'

Gradually these portrait painters leave her; they vanish one by one, and Ophelia is suddenly alone with an empty frame in which the painting had been provided by others. It is then that she goes mad and in her talk plays back a garbled version, as if she had a tape recording in her mind, of all the images of herself and all the advice she has received in the first half of the play: '*By cock they are to blame*'. It is the incongruity of the picture she re-creates that is so grotesque and not the state of madness in the abstract.

My approach to Ophelia has been influenced by the work of R. D. Laing, and it was not until I worked with the very abrupt and nervously brilliant performer Kathryn Pogson in 1982 that I was able to realize the full effect of this kind of schizophrenia on stage. I gave her a lot of clinical information but also simply reminded her of behaviour and mannerisms while she was constantly on the look out for characteristics she could use on stage. One afternoon, on a train journey, she saw a girl talking to herself with all the angry, knowing quality that schizophrenics have as if they alone are privy to a secret. She re-created that easy distractibility, and exaggeration of movement on stage. Kathryn was, for me, an *objet trouvé*, but then she came bearing her own discoveries and observations. The collaborativeness of the work was clear, and rather than being tyrannized by my directing, I think she was released into a performance that was both startling and harrowing in stark contrast to the usually charming figure of the mad Ophelia prettily handing round flowers to the rest of the cast. I brought my knowledge from the medical world to bear and it was accurate. Kathryn's strange stereotypic movements and curious anorectic gestures as she forced her finger down her throat in an attempt to vomit alarmed the audience.

Once again, it was a funny little knucklebone of a sentence that provoked this performance, and from which we reconstructed the whole of her character. In Act I scene iii she replies to Polonius' question as to what she should think with a tiny phrase: '*I do not know, my lord, what I should think.*' This seems to epitomize her character – she does not know what to think. Subsequently, she responds to Hamlet's similar question as to her thoughts, '*I think nothing, my lord.*' All her actions are responses to what other people think for, and of, her before they disappear and all her support is removed. There is a very touching moment in Act III scene i when Gertrude shows a strangely intimate sympathy for Ophelia, and in that split-second there is a suggestion that Ophelia could have been rescued if only that kind of affection had been available to her before.

In that same production, I can remember a gesture that evolved from the actor Philip Locke's ideas about Hamlet's '*Speak the speech, I pray you*' speech to the Players. This scene (Act III scene ii) is usually performed as if the emphasis should fall on Hamlet giving this marvellous advice to the troupe. Now, although the advice is good, it is totally gratuitous as far as the Players are concerned. We worked on the idea of what it is like to be a professional actor when some university hooray comes backstage with a lot of Leavisite ideas. Philip suggested that as the Player he should be making up. He broke a mirror and appeared with a tiny fragment, a shard, wearing his braces dangling loose over a singlet, and painting his face while listening impatiently to Hamlet as if he was thinking 'Yes, yes. I'm on in five minutes!' This left the actor playing Hamlet dodging around eagerly telling this old pro how to conduct himself. It was a slightly different, less reverent, and more amusing way of performing the scene which did not diminish Hamlet's speech.

While I know what surprises might affect the audience on a first night, and watch for them, I am often pleased to find new aspects that the actors might develop once the play is in performance. I hope that by the first night a performance has emerged that has the possibilities of an enormous amount of spontaneous growth and amplification. Some directors feel a tremendous proprietary pedantry about that, and if the merest detail departs from what was done in rehearsal they will go backstage after the show to give all sorts of reproving notes. My general feeling is that if you have directed well, and have given an extremely elastic direction, the play will almost inevitably improve in unexpected ways, all of which remain consistent with the original design. I am delighted whenever I see the cast enrich the production by their own imaginative work because the process of playing is the only way to find out what the full implications of any script might be. If the production is bad, however, and the rehearsal has been a miserable and wretched period, the actors will use subsequent performances to repudiate the director's work. I have been fairly lucky and, with one or two exceptions, subsequent performances of plays I have directed have been a confirmation rather than a rejection of all that has grown out of the rehearsal period. The production is inevitably a provisional sketch, a promissory note, and it is only when the play or opera is well into its run that it reaches its climax.

The other day, I went to see the English National Opera's *Rigoletto* in something like its fiftieth performance. As I watched the opening party on stage, members of the cast were doing things that I had never seen before and never asked them to do. But all the new gestures were absolutely consistent with what I *had* asked them to do in rehearsal. The scene was *filled* with rich incidents, movements and expressions that had emerged as the actors and singers had occupied *their* party. They were living the party that we had created in rehearsal, and had grown into new but consistent moves. Whenever I have gone back to watch *Rigoletto* I have been delighted to find that it is a truly emergent production.

The director has an enormously ample domain in which to suggest, guide and prompt a particular performance. In a way it is comparable to what the linguist Noam Chomsky has said about language – there are an infinite series of sentences, all of whose *surface structures* are different but that can nevertheless express the same *deep structure*. If the cast is provided with the *generative grammar* for a performance, it can then go on to generate an infinite series of novelties, all of which are consistent with that deep grammar. The mark of a good director is that he or she lays down, at a fairly early stage, an extremely productive generative grammar for the character's performance, so that an enormous variety of actual performances are generated by this single competence. If the director provides the brainwork for this competence the production will be both stable and potentially variable. But too many directors feel that their authority and creative mandate are in some way jeopardized by any variation from the surface structure of the performance. You may meet an opera director, for example, who goes into a tantrum if a *hand* gesture does not occur on the bar when he dictated that it should. I have never asked performers to move in music to the bar, or given them actual gestures. What I usually do is to provide something that is in fact specified *below the level* of actual performance that can then generate, on any evening, an infinite variety of actual performances, all of which can be traced back to the deep structure that we have agreed on at the start.

The *deep structure* generates in the actors an understanding of character and motivation. The question then is whether the director is accommodating enough to accept a range of alternative meanings that are faithful, if not identical, to the ones he directed. In the same way that we expect the script to be able to generate alternative meanings, the director must be capable of being as generous about his own production as he expects the author to be about his original text when it enters its afterlife.

# II: iv

As a director I have modernized both Shakespeare and opera, but I think that there are dangers when people talk about 'contemporary' Shakespeare, or the 'timelessness' of the classics. While the idea of the afterlife challenges arguments about 'the authenticity' of a production, and releases a play or an opera for interpretation, it does not mean that we can justify the survival of any work *only* by making it address what is happening today. The notion of making Shakespeare relevant is often taken as a licence for quite absurd and literal transpositions into contemporary time, and assumes that no one is capable of adjusting his or her imagination to any political period other than the present. This is a form of historical provincialism, aptly described by T. S. Eliot as an overvaluing of our own times – a belief that the past is on probation, and has to prove itself by its capacity to accommodate current interests.

We cannot act or see Shakespeare today as the Elizabethans and the author did but we can take into account that our perception is a modern one without rewriting the plays to make them contemporary. Unable to re-create, or revisit the past as Elizabethans, we can establish a relationship to that past if we allow for differences, but this does not mean that we have to make the play's concerns identical with our own. By accepting how different the world referred to at the time of writing is from our own, similarities, in views and emotional experience, become much more striking. The plays are products of their time, and I hope that even when I have directed Shakespeare in modern or nineteenth-century dress, I have not lost sight entirely of the play's antiquity in my interpretation.

The best example of this overvaluing of our own time is shown in the American approach to Shakespeare; here I am thinking of directors like Joseph Papp. The American vice is seen most clearly in plays like *The Taming of the Shrew* which suddenly become a test case for feminism. Petruchio is portrayed as a typical male chauvinist pig, and Katharina as a bullied victim who then has to deliver her last speech, which seems to be so abjectly submissive, in a way that implies to the audience both that she is not defeated and that her submission to Petruchio is very ironic. This is sad because it demonstrates the belief that a work from the past can be performed in its afterlife only if it is made to conform to the values of the present.

In contrast, I think that one of the advantages of directing a play like *The Taming of the Shrew* is that it invites us to look at it on its own terms, and to see that the past is a foreign country with different customs and values from our own. The play at least offers us the opportunity to try to understand what is now the radically unvisitable past. Unlike Papp's approach to the play, my own enthusiastically recognizes Tudor social ideas of the function of the woman in the household without agreeing

with them. When I tried to modernize the play, it was not in the sense of setting it in the present but of looking much more carefully, through contemporary eyes, at what it was expressing in the past. Conventional English productions of *The Taming of the Shrew* have had their own type of modernity, which now appears to be rather mandarin, and portrays the entire play as a mischievous and inoffensive wrong in which Petruchio becomes a moustachio-twirling cavalier.

My interpretation was very influenced by a book by Michael Waltzer. In *The Revolution of the Saints* he wrote about ideas prevalent among the Marian exiles, the Puritans who returned to England after exile under Mary Tudor. He stresses that for the Puritan — and by the time Shakespeare was writing, there was a substantial Puritan squirarchy— the Calvinistic view was of the world as a fallen place in which we had all inherited the sin of Adam congenitally. On this potentially unruly and unmanageable earth, sovereign authority was needed in order for there to be some kind of control. For the Puritans, there were two magistrates deputed by God to supervise order in an otherwise fallen world: in the family it was the husband and father, and in the state it was the king. The woman was required to obey, not simply because it flattered the vanity of man but because some authority had to be invested in one unquestionable person, whether or not he was necessarily qualified for this responsibility. In other plays, Shakespeare obviously makes us question whether certain officers *are* fit to occupy office. Lear is one example, a rash, foolish old man who occupies the position of the sovereign and is evidently unqualified to exercise the authority that he seems to abdicate wilfully. But in *The Taming of the Shrew*, we have an instance of Shakespeare writing about the need for order, and here is a play in which we have tuition exercised by a man and not, as is so often the case in Shakespeare, by a woman. What we see is not the bullying and subordination of an otherwise high-spirited girl, but a course of tuition as a result of which Kate learns the necessity of obedience. If you represent Petruchio as a serious man, you can take and develop the implications of lines such as '*To me she's married, not unto my clothes*' and '*'tis the mind that makes the body rich*' and see how consistent these are with a Puritan view. The alternative is to present Petruchio as a flamboyant bully.

When I directed *The Taming of the Shrew* for television, John Cleese took the part. I was interested in the irritability he showed in the character of Basil Fawlty but there are also strange sympathetic depths in the man that I thought could be usefully applied to the character of Petruchio. The attention that Petruchio pays to the tuition of Katharina can be portrayed much more sympathetically than it is in most productions. Unlike so many of the other suitors, he is not put off by her tantrums and there is a sense in which he is seen as a more caring character. He identifies Kate as someone worth spending time with, and sees that much of her difficulty is due to her self-image – she thinks of herself as unloved and unlovable, rejected by her father and not so favourably regarded as her sister. By suddenly becoming the subject of such detailed and apparently bullying tuition, Kate realizes that somebody has bothered to look beyond her unruly appearance and see her for the first time. It is as though she has become spiritually and morally visible in a way that she was not when simply perceived as a scold. Petruchio has recognized in her shrewish behaviour symptoms of unhappiness and, by behaving badly himself, he gives Kate back an image of herself.

Their first encounter, when Kate tries to attack Petruchio, is usually presented as a tremendous rough and tumble on stage. During the course of rehearsing the scene when Kate slaps Petruchio, something very interesting emerged. Instead of Petruchio suddenly throwing himself violently on her, John Cleese leant considerately towards her and simply went 'Hm, mm.' as if this was an interesting move on her part which had to be considered. He then said very quietly, *'I swear I'll cuff you if you strike again.'* This is a disconcerting move for which the character of Kate is unprepared, and it forces her to visualize her behaviour in a way that she would not have time to do if Petruchio had responded immediately with some comparable loud and violent move. The very fact that Kate might be ruffled by such a gesture is interesting. She looks at him then, perhaps for the first time, and sees that he is not quite like the other suitors as he is neither frightened, nor is he simply provoked into a display of rumbustious bad temper. By unpredictable behaviour in that moment he gives her back a self-image that she can evaluate. Kate begins to realize that someone who is prepared to devote so much time to her must be prompted by affection rather than by a selfish determination to have his own authority observed. But even with this slightly more subtle performance of Petruchio, his absolute commitment to the idea that there must be rule in a household can be seen throughout the play underlying the humour and sympathy.

We no longer share this view of domesticity, which is framed by theological dogma, but as a director, approaching these plays from the past, I must recognize and accommodate the production to those theological assumptions. The alternative is to frog-march Shakespeare into the twentieth century and make the plays address *our* problems, and literally identify with our values. The language then seems wrong and artificial. If, however, you allow such differences in attitudes to be visible in the production, the play comes alive and Kate's final speech is rather moving as it is an agreement to abide by the rules within a framework in which it is possible to enjoy a close affection. In contrast to Kate's rather graceful submission, the disagreeable behaviour of her sister Bianca becomes repugnant and you can then see that the real shrew is Bianca and not Katharina at all.

The problem of setting does not become acute in the plays that are set at the time when Shakespeare wrote them, but it poses a real dilemma in those in which he wrote about a period other than his own. It is quite clear that Shakespeare is not writing about a literal, historical past, and the more we learn about the Elizabethan period the more striking the discrepancy between what he writes and the supposed date of the play's action becomes. It may well be that an audience contemporary with Shakespeare, who did not visualize their own period as a visible artefact, took on trust that what they were watching was an accurate historical picture of the past. But our own distance from Shakespeare's time means that our perception is very different, and the plays have themselves become historical documents. The artefact of being a play by Shakespeare is just as visible as the past to which the plays nominally refer.

My general policy is that the Roman or Greek plays cannot be set literally in the period to which they refer. It is much better either to set them in some kind of sixteenth-century Renaissance limbo or any setting that makes allowance for the past. There are several ways of doing this. You can take a play like *Troilus and Cressida* and put it into an Elizabethan setting using Greek names. Alternatively, you can ask, as I did with *Antony and Cleopatra*, what happened to sixteenth-century painters who viewed antiquity without the benefit of archaeological knowledge? How did they represent antiquity? This led me to re-create a syncretic appearance showing fragments of antique dress, and figures in sixteenth-century armour alongside ordinary stage costumes reflecting the time at which the play was written. Many traditional productions of *Troilus and Cressida* have gone to quite extraordinary lengths visually to represent Troy. John Barton's production at the RSC made quite strenuous efforts to reproduce the appearance of the warriors so that they looked as if they had fallen off Greek vases. But the better the archaeological knowledge on display, the greater the discrepancy between appearance and sound on stage. The director has to decide how to balance the various elements that must be recognized in a production: the fact that the play nominally takes place in Troy, that it was written in the Elizabethan era, and that some reference must be made to the eternity of war.

When I was directing the play for television, I thought a great deal about how to resolve these problems. To begin with I had to decide how the characters should look, and this made me wonder about the origins of the Troilus and Cressida story. Without their tale being given in detail, Troilus and Cressida are referred to in Homer, but as a myth they are a creation of the Gothic Middle Ages and represented in the poetry of Henryson and, of course, Chaucer, long before Shakespeare's play. Initially I was prompted to find a setting that acknowledged that this same story had played such a prominent part in the iconography of the Gothic Middle Ages. I remembered seeing the Trojan tapestries in the Norton

*Anton Lesser as Troilus and John Shrapnel as Hector in* Troilus and Cressida, *BBC production, 1981*

*One's image of a character is often determined by the performance of an actor in an altogether different part. I had seen Anton Lesser play Konstantin in a Royal Court production of* The Seagull, *and in the depths of his representation of that character I recognized features that were interestingly transferable to the personality of Troilus. Later, it was in his frustrated desperation as Troilus that I saw the possibility of his playing Hamlet. In other words, parts can remake actors who in turn can reconstruct the characters that they play. Konstantin was reconstituted in the process of being replayed by Anton Lesser, but Lesser was redesigned by enacting Konstantin, and this made it possible to revisualize Troilus and eventually generated an alternative Hamlet. In a subsequent performance of Troilus produced by someone else, I suspect that his reincarnation was influenced, in some respects at least, by the Hamlet that I borrowed from my own production of Troilus.*

*Tony Steedman as Aeneas in the BBC 1981 production of* Troilus and Cressida

Simon Museum in Pasadena where the Greek heroes are represented in the costumes of the High Gothic and, with this in mind, I tried to find a setting that would (1) point towards Greece, (2) clearly embody the Renaissance and, perhaps, make reference to the Middle Ages as well as (3) give some indication that the problems and issue of an endless war are still with us today.

I looked at a very early Renaissance artist, one who was some eighty years older than Shakespeare and in whose work there were still traces of the Gothic in what are obviously the costumes of the European Renaissance – Cranach. I also referred to the German artists of the 1520s and 1530s – the woodcuts of Beham and Dürer. In those rather Gothic costumes with their puffed sleeves, knees and breeches, and strange spoon-shaped shoes, I saw something that would still have traces of the Gothic world of Chaucer but would also make references to Greece if I followed the examples of the Franco-Flemish tapestries and simply labelled them. This still left me wondering how I could suggest a war familiar to the modern audience without putting the play into modern time. To meet this requirement I chose costumes based on Cranach and Beham but instead of representing them in the colours of the period we made the silhouettes and details of the costumes in the style of the 1530s but out of khaki with visible identity tags worn around the neck. The effect was that the cast looked like officers out of *M.A.S.H.* in Gothic-style uniform. The Greek encampment was made by using canvas, also indistinguishable from *M.A.S.H.*, so that characters sat on upturned ammunition boxes. I even went to the extent of having pin-ups on the wall of Ajax's tent, and showed a large, very rubbed out pin-up photograph of Cranach's *Eve*. In Agamemnon's tent, there was a big easel showing the plan of fortifications of Troy, and a working drawing in the early stages of research and development of the horse.

Without literally modernizing it, I set *Troilus and Cressida* in a way that made reference by implication rather than by specific explication. I still had to find some sort of physical setting for the City of Troy and instead of having a literal Greek or Trojan setting, or the alternative of Greek columns, we simply made the town out of stock BBC plywood, but based the design on a series of Renaissance model drawings of exercises in perspective by Jan Vredeman de Vries, a Dutch artist of the 1600s. It was quite clearly an artificial stage limbo but it made references both old and new for the spectator to pick up.

If we take *Julius Caesar*, I do not think that modernizing and presenting it as a play about a totalitarian state is either justified or interesting except, perhaps, in a very particular political climate. When I directed it I attempted to reconcile in one format all the conflicting themes – Roman antiquity, the Renaissance and the faint implications of modern Italian Fascism which I did not want to make explicit but to hint at. The format

*Jan Vredeman de Vries, perspective drawing*

*In directing Shakespeare's Greek or Roman plays it is easy to fall into the trap of confusing 'use' with 'mention'. The fact that Shakespeare mentions a classical setting does not necessarily imply the literal use of the reference. On the contrary, to a modern audience the Renaissance significance of the play is much more important than the historical setting to which Shakespeare nominally refers. But since the Renaissance setting is itself somewhat notional, it is necessary to find some representational device which quotes the sixteenth-century context without literally depicting it. So, to create a dramatic Troy as opposed to an historical one, I plagiarized Jan Vredeman de Vries' seventeenth-century perspective exercises which gave the impression of a 'Trojan' palace invested at the same time with the atmosphere of an abstract Renaissance building. In the effort to confirm the artificiality of the whole enterprise, I asked the designer to make the whole edifice in raw plywood.*

that brought all this together – and highlighted that strange sense of surrealist premonition which runs throughout the language with its peculiar dream images and its stabbed bleeding statues – was given to me by the paintings of de' Chirico. The setting was based on his work, which is full of Roman piazzas, classical statues and long shadows, and enabled us to bring the surrealist ingredients of the play to life. In this framework, the hallucinogenic speeches no longer seemed contrived or too improbable.

In my mind's eye I have seen *Julius Caesar* in all sorts of settings, but never a modern one. One idea would be to set it in the Republican Rome as conceived by the French Revolution where they saw themselves as Romans and even re-numbered their years and calendar months in terms of Roman antiquity. They commissioned painters like David to depict numerous heroic scenes of Roman antiquity as a way of extolling the Republican virtues of the new state. It would be very interesting to stage *Julius Caesar* in a sort of Thermidorean world, or even have Napoleon offered the crown. Without slavishly mapping the play on to recognizable characters you can extract various figures of the Revolution who are consistent with those who appear in the play. In the discontented, malcontent figure of Cassius, you could very easily see a Marat-like figure, and in Brutus, a Girondist rather like Danton. Or alternatively the play could simply be set as an Elizabethan work looking at the Roman past.

*King Lear*, which I have directed three times, poses this problem again. In my first initiative with the play, I was prompted by a determination to avoid what struck me as the boring clichés of precedent, of which I think the most depressing one was the Druidical representation of the ancient, pre-Christian Lear – the long white beard surrounded by a retinue of figures swathed in savage leather. It is true that when I came to *Lear*, that tradition had already been very creatively overthrown by Peter Brook's production, where Scofield represented him as a sort of bullet-headed, impatient warrior. But where Brook was prompted much more by views of savage antiquity and, above all, by what Boass and Lovejoy refer to as 'hard primitivism', what struck me in reading the play was not the primitivism of the antique but the fact that so much of what happens and so many of its symbols are manipulated within the context of the period of its writing.

In every production I have avoided the hypothetical antiquity in which it is set in order to bring to light certain themes that seem to me to be absolutely contemporary with the play's writing. The Christianity that runs throughout *King Lear* is one example, despite its almost pedantic denial by reference to the gods. There is the pervasive and extraordinary apocalyptic imagery that clusters around the characters of Edmund and Edgar, whom I see as glosses upon Lucifer and Christ. The strange speech when Edgar, as Poor Tom, discusses a variety of devils is derived from the Book of Revelation, and the play's language is saturated with that

*Giorgio de' Chirico*, The Disquieting Muses

*The steeply raked stage of Giorgio de' Chirico's* Disquieting Muses *seems to be waiting for the entry of speaking characters. When I first directed* Julius Caesar *I was delighted to discover that the play could be revealingly accommodated in this ominous setting.*

book together with the imagery of the Gospel of St John. The play also explores the relationship between family and state, and in an earlier setting the concept of the state would be anachronistic. *King Lear* is a Stuart, not a Druid, play about statecraft and its breakdown when authority is removed. I chose to set it in the seventeenth century as I cannot see how these themes can make sense in the literal Druidical antiquity in which it is traditionally played.

One feature of the play that is difficult to ignore is its almost Hobbesian view of man and nature, and a very seventeenth-century sense of the reciprocal symbolism between family and state. Hobbes, writing after the Civil War, not only saw man in the state of nature as brutish but also implied that in order to redeem himself from such a solitary, savage, short life in nature, human society has to submit itself to the authority of sovereigns. The two systems of family – domestic and state – are related to one another in the mode of microcosm and macrocosm, and cast a light upon the late sixteenth-century and early seventeenth-century view of the nature of the body politic. There had to be a sovereign base, in both society and the family, and *King Lear* seems to show how families fall apart when parents abdicate their responsibility and their powers, and how the state similarly fragments if its symbolic head abdicates responsibility. This is a pervasive theme in Shakespeare's plays, with the notions of degree and chaos demonstrated again in *Troilus and Cressida*, but *King Lear* raises the following kind of questions that people must have asked themselves when the nature of sovereignty began to appear to be unstable. Sovereigns are indispensable if society is to be orderly but, given this fact, do we owe respect and loyalty to the crown or to the king? How must the officer live up to the office that he occupies when there is a frail skin between what medieval jurisprudence called the two bodies of the king? One of the problems of the play is that of the king's two bodies, which are so vividly shown as Lear's regal appearance disintegrates and he tears off his clothes. Finally, I think that the play asks a question that is never really settled: what do you do with an office without which society would disintegrate if the officer himself is disintegrating?

When I first staged the play in Nottingham in 1969, it was set in a period near to that of its writing – the Thirty Years War. This was a time of social chaos and upheaval, when men devoured one another like monsters of the deep, to borrow Albany's expression. I then looked for a painter who would bring this to life for me on stage, one who dealt both with the horrors of war and with the world of the seventeenth century and I found a French engraver, Jacques Callot. The costumes were based on Callot's illustrations, but I was also influenced by my memories of Brecht's *Mother Courage*, and we used an empty stage with the minimum number of props. It was an extremely bleak staging with nothing to be seen except the characters.

*Paul Scofield as King Lear in the Royal Shakespeare Company's 1962 production*

*Under the direction of Peter Brook, who was inspired in his turn by Jan Kott's essay on 'King Lear, or Endgame', the figure of King Lear underwent a radical transformation that marked a fundamental shift from the traditional representation of the old king. The druidical patriach gave way to a grizzled warrior.*

King Lear, *The Nottingham Playhouse, 1969*

*When I staged* King Lear *a few years after
Brook, I found myself reacting against the
romantic antiquity of traditional productions
and the rugged primitivism of his production.
As far as I was concerned the play's vaunted
timelessness was more plausibly delivered if it
was set in a social context nearer to the one
in which Shakespeare had written it. I was
struck by the overtones of Hobbes' arguments
about sovereignty, and Filmer's* Patriarcha.
*Looking at this picture now, however, I find
myself recoiling from its picturesque
appearance and I am convinced that it will
soon look just as old-fashioned as William
Poel's Tussaud production.*

*Although I have changed the look of the play in the two productions I have done since Nottingham, I found it difficult to get away from my original conception of Lear's relationship to his Fool. Even now, I see them both as old men — mirror images of folly, distinguished from one another only by their social station. A foolish old king shadowed by a wise old fool.*

Having directed the play twice since then, I find very minor differences between subsequent performances in which the same actor, Michael Hordern, played Lear. I think this is because I had a much more comprehensive vision of this particular play, which did not allow for very much change. The physical staging of *King Lear* is far less important than the emphasis that you put upon the characterizations, and the clustered relationships, in performance. So to Michael Hordern as Lear the recommendations that I made during the course of rehearsal emphasized neither the bullet-headed strength of Brook's warrior, nor the dignified ruin of the Druidical king of tradition, but simply the cantankerous, petulant, weak-willed foolish old man that Lear himself describes: '*I am a very foolish fond old man*'. I saw him as paranoic, depressive but vigilant, on the look-out for slights. Someone who starts in a mood of grudging depression knowing full well that Cordelia is going to disappoint him. I always have a strange impression that Lear sets up the ritual contest as a revengeful act to humiliate Cordelia, anticipating the rebuttal from the daughter he loves best and from whom he can never obtain enough expressions of love.

We reacted away from the traditionally fey representations both of the mad Lear and of the Fool, who is so often presented as a whinnying, falsetto boy. This clichéd rendition removes the force of the Fool's wisdom and pathos, and I have never been tempted to see the Fool as anything other than an old man, Lear's contemporary, and a broken-down rather insufferable clown. He comes closer to Lear than anyone and this is not because he is a young, charming, soft, capering goat but due to his age and performance, which is rather like an old music-hall comic – old Max Miller. The Fool rambles on and every now and again produces some quite wise remarks. I was prompted to think of him in this way by something I read about Louis XIV's bodyservant, Bontemps, who was the same age as his master and had grown up with him. Bontemps was the only person in court who was allowed to call Louis by name and be rude and familiar. A young person could never have had this kind of intimacy. They are simply two old men together, and it is through the curious, strange caprices of fate, that one old man should be a Fool while the other old man is a fool who happens to be King.

Rather than concentrating on irritating pieces of pedantic scholarship that tell us that the same actor played the Fool and Cordelia in Elizabethan productions, it is much more valuable to have a broad notion of character. This is why I became interested in the old men – Lear, Gloucester and the Fool – who are all old fools in different social roles. Again, when it came to the madness in Lear and the supposed lunacy of Poor Tom, I took this aspect very seriously. I drew heavily on my knowledge of geriatric lunatics for *Lear*. I gave Michael Hordern a model, a description and only wished that I could have taken him to an old people's home so that he could have incorporated a kind of ranting incontinence into the performance. I wanted to roughen the madness and restore its horribleness.

In the relationship of Edmund and Edgar, I also tried to avoid prototype, in a slightly negative sense to begin with. In the case of Edmund, in order to avoid the traditional representation of him as a rough, lecherous fellow, I took great pains to have him as an almost foppish figure, as Edgar says in the apocalyptic scenes on the heath, '*The prince of darkness is a gentleman*'. Instead of wrapping him in rough leathers or motorbike kit, I was struck by this idea of making him extravagantly courtly.

The passage of Edgar throughout *King Lear* has always struck me as being *analogous*, not identical, to the ministry of Christ. I find Edgar incomprehensible unless he is placed in a contrasted relationship with his ingenious, witty, jocular brother who is rather like Milton's Lucifer. Edgar in addition to having a Christian thrust towards self-annihilation, '*Edgar I nothing am*', voluntarily undertakes to become nothing so that he can then become something and discover who he might be. This, of course, parallels the nothingness that overtakes both Lear and Gloucester.

So many characters in *King Lear* move towards annihilation, down a moral perspective towards a vanishing point at which the self disappears, a point that is epitomized in the great image of vanishing points that Edgar creates on the clifftop with his blind father. Like so many of Shakespeare's images this imagined scene has metaphorical functions over and above the one that it serves at that particular moment in the plot. Its overt function, of course, is to prepare the blind Gloucester for his sham suicide by creating an imaginary space into which he can hurl himself. But it also epitomizes the perspective of social reality enjoyed by those in high places. It is only from the privileged heights occupied by those in robes and furred gowns that fishermen and all other common people can look like negligible mice. And only from such a height that great men, such as Gloucester and Lear, can overlook and fail to feel what wretches feel. Conversely, it is only after their fall having previously '*ta'en too little care of this*' that they can understand the realities of normal suffering. The scene bears a startling resemblance to that moment in *The Third Man* when Harry Lime takes Martins to the top of the ferris wheel and asks him to consider whether it would really matter to him if one or more of those little human dots were to stop moving.

Edgar reminded me of the figure of Dostoevsky's ecstatic, holy idiot and this presented me with interesting choices when it came to representing his appearance and behaviour in the guise of Poor Tom. I began by looking at his speeches about Bedlam beggars and his description of desolate wanderings between poor villages. This reminded me of a book I had read many years before, Norman Cohn's *Pursuit of a Millennium*. In this he discusses at length the peculiar trackless world,

*Michael Hordern as Lear and Ronald Pickup as Edgar, and* (right) *Michael Jayston as Edmund in the 1975 BBC production of* King Lear.

*As far as I can remember I had a somewhat Miltonic view of the bastard Edmund. An intelligent Lucifer set against the sacred idiocy of his Christ-like brother. It would have been hard to develop these typographical themes in a pre-Christian setting. In giving Edgar as Poor Tom his crown of thorns, I was not trying to imply that he was Christ, but like the vagrant madmen of the Middle Ages and Renaissance that he would have assumed the guise of a lunatic who tried to impersonate Christ. The waste lands of Northern Europe in the Middle Ages were roamed by self-appointed saviours like this, and in the role-playing which is one of the central concerns of the play, Edmund and Edgar almost vanish into the apocalyptic parts that they start by playing.*

beyond the towns and villages of medieval Europe where the outcast, the beggar and the lunatic wander. These listless, homeless figures inhabit a wilderness outside society and are annihilated in ways described in Michel Foucault's book, *Madness and Civilization*. It was from this reservoir of the restless, mad and impoverished vagrant that ecstatic, chiliastic leaders rose up; people claiming to be Christ, who often gave rise to huge apocalyptic movements. I thought of making Poor Tom represent himself not merely as a beggar, sticking sticks and thorns into his skin, but as a mad one who thinks of himself as Christ.

In the production he appeared naked, accept for a loin-cloth, his flesh covered with weals so that he almost seemed to have enacted the flagellation of Christ, and had fashioned for himself not merely thorns to stick into his palms but a crown of thorns to wrench across his forehead. Many people seeing the production seriously thought that I wanted them to think he *was* Christ! What I had hoped to convey was that Edgar, in thinking of himself as nothing, imagined a self-annihilation modelled on Christ's own when he made himself the subject of mockery and contempt. Edgar says that he sticks pins into himself, so what do you show? How would someone in the seventeenth century, visualizing himself as a poor Bedlam beggar, have used his pins to mutilate himself? He would have done it in the mode of the Christian ecstatic, with afflicted stigmata. The commanding image of the most exalted co-existing with the lowliest is that of Christ who endured mockery, flagellation and crucifixion but who returns as the Great Judge, which is exactly what Edgar does when the trumpet sounds.

What is so fascinating about *King Lear* is that, unlike *Hamlet*, it contains all kinds of fairy-tale elements. There are the three daughters, the three caskets or portions of love, the choices and the ugly sisters – the basic Cinderella story is there in another form. In this sense, I suppose that much of my thinking about the play was prompted by my reading of Vladimir Propp's book on *The Morphology of the Folk Tale*. Propp reminds us that, not withstanding the surface differences between characters, there are underlying structures that are the same. There are what he calls 'functions', which are performed by people who might be quite different in character – a woman and her son, a young prince, or a miller's daughter – but they are all figures to whom a gift is given which then confers upon them some sort of immunity, and there are always helpers to support them. *King Lear* can be parsed in this way if we disregard the superficial structure for a moment and consider the character of Edgar. If we look at the underlying structure, we can map it on to features that it has in common with the ministry of Christ. A young man goes into the wilderness, cures or, in this instance at least, assists a blind man and is a helper. He goes through a series of strange temptations as his rantings tell us; he wrestles with the devils tormenting him and then he disappears. But on the third trumpet sound he reappears, throws down his fallen brother and is revealed victorious. This kind of reading can be useful and, although I cannot point to specific recipes in detail, the general approach to a play that reveals structures deeper than its surface appearance is something that I took from Propp but is common to all the structuralists.

I want to pause over this point as very often critical objections to various productions utilize terms like *Freudian* or *structuralist* as forms of abuse. I have never directed a Freudian interpretation or a structuralist interpretation, but when I work I always have a toolbox which, as a child of the twentieth century, I have inherited from thinkers of the last eighty years or so. In this box are bits and pieces that can be used to unpick and unbolt the play to see how it works. I would feel very upset if someone were to think that my work was simply Freudian or structuralist although I admit that when working on a play I will sometimes take advantage of insights that the structuralists have provided, but these are ways of thinking about a play and not models for production. It is terribly hard to do *Hamlet* without taking Freud into consideration, but a slavishly Oedipal version of the play (in order to exhibit certain principles of Freud's ideas about sons and mothers) would be very tiresome. The point is that when you have a toolbox and you employ the tools no one should be able to tell from the reconstructed engine which tools you have used; they should not characterize and dominate the structure that emerges in the end.

Most critics simply think that because a production is modern it must be structuralist. Structuralism is not a dogma, although when misunderstood by a third-rate critic it appears dogmatic and an end in itself rather than a tool for comprehension. Structuralism is quite simply a useful way of thinking about a narrative, whether in dramatic form or in prose. There are certain things in *The Magic Flute*, for example, which, because it is very clearly a folk tale, you would be foolish to neglect when thinking about how to stage it. Let me explain. Here again is a common pattern with a hero, a young prince who is endangered when a monster threatens him. He is rescued by three helpers, the helpers give him a gift that confers immunity on him for any subsequent ordeal that he has to face. When he is attacked by Monostatos' slaves, they are charmed by the playing of the glockenspiel that has been given to Papageno. The structure informs the way you think about the opera as it is not just something that happens in this particular instance; it has features in common with all folk stories. Then we have to discover the common theme which allows us to think more clearly about the structure that lies deeper than all these specific incidents and characterizations: it is to do with the story of quests. This structure goes beyond even those things that Propp identified and enables you to ask 'What are these expressions of?'

They are expressions of something very fundamental in human life, the idea that we go through life subject to risks and dangers, and are periodically helped and land ourselves in debt. There are responsibilities and duties as well as privileges associated with these gifts, and if we misbehave, having been given the privilege of such gifts, they will be taken away *and* we will be penalized. This, of course, is what happens with the 'Soldier and the Tinder-box' when he abuses that gift. The same could happen with Tamino: if he does not obey the various injunctions that Sarastro lays upon him he will not get the benefits of his flute. You might see a relationship between this opera and *As You Like It*, which is Shakespeare's *Magic Flute*.

To return to *King Lear*, here is a play that starts with someone who seems to make, as if in Greek tragedy, 'a fatal mistake'. I found myself wondering at a psychological level as to the nature of Lear's mistake and what prompted it in the first place. Lear's action need not, and indeed cannot, be explained in historical terms; we have to look to something that is more continuous and permanent – the question of the sudden loss of confidence in love. Here is someone who – for reasons that are never fully explained but might perhaps be seen in terms of the depression that overtakes people in old age – is no longer certain of the love that he believes is his due, and so he tests it. It is fatal to make love explicit in terms of a mercantile relationship, and Lear asks his daughters not only to express but to *evaluate* their love.

In Cordelia, we have a rather Puritan character, someone who believes that she cannot *heave* her heart into her mouth, and refuses to join in the game. Her dumbness does not necessarily reflect a lack of love, '*Thy youngest daughter does not love thee least*', says Kent. In a way, what happens with Lear is that he makes a choice comparable to the false choice made by the first two suitors in *The Merchant of Venice* between the gold and silver caskets. In Lear's choice of the silver-tongued and golden-tongued elder daughters, he chooses the wrong ones. The silent lead, the silent Cordelia, contains the love that would be destroyed by being expressed. She is Cinderella, while Regan and Goneril are the two ugly sisters. They can be dazzlingly beautiful but their moral ugliness becomes apparent in contrast to silent Cinders/Cordelia who has to be sought for her true worth. Her valued love is identified by the King of France, but in contrast to Cinderella she is found and fitted with the slipper at the very beginning rather than at the end of the play. Rejected by her father, she is chosen by the King of France, '*Thee and thy virtues here I seize upon*'. It is her father's not her lover's love that she finally wins at the reconciliation near the end of the play when Lear recognizes her as the most loving child.

Cordelia is swept away, returning in search of her father after a curious and interesting absence, which is comparable to another pattern that recurs, not in folklore but in the Renaissance story of Astraea, the virgin who is taken up into the heavens and then, at the appointed time, returns to produce a redeeming reconciliation. I have always felt that Cordelia's return, far from being explained by the fact that the part was played by the same actor who played the Fool, is a much more exalted strategy on the part of Shakespeare. She, like Astraea, mysteriously and suddenly reappears after a long and charismatic absence, after the age of brass and steel has supervened upon the age of gold.

One of the pitfalls that exist when you are dealing with the three daughters is the traditional representation of Regan and Goneril as serpentine villainesses. This leads to clichéed performances in which they wear their villainy on their sleeves and are either treacherously beautiful or display some obvious sign of the venom expressed in their behaviour. One way to avoid this is to think more intelligently about their motives. If you treat them simply as exponents of some abstract principle of vileness, they inevitably become cartoon figures, which is inconsistent with the complexity of Shakespeare's imagination within the play. We cannot presume simplistically that they are monstrous women. Often interesting results are produced by deliberately going for a paradox of some sort. We traditionally assume that the behaviour of the daughters drives the father mad, but can we, for a moment, learn anything from a seemingly paradoxical conjecture about Lear having driven them mad? If you assume that there is something peculiarly weak, foolish, and hyperbolic about the selfishness of Lear's behaviour, as shown by his demand for love, which may not be the first of its kind, might it not be that this is simply the culmination of behaviour that they have been subjected to all their lives? This is a man who has made exorbitant demands upon explicit displays of love, and it might be that the behaviour of these women is explicable, although not excusable, in terms of the exposure that they have had to briberies of affection. One of the ways to stage this is *not* to present them speaking honeyed phrases as if they mean to be believed by Lear, but to show their deliberate irony as they glance slyly one to the other. As the first woman is invited to begin there are knowing and inquisitive looks between them, as if they are asking one another, 'Well, how are we going to put it, dear?' Once they slide into this helter-skelter, the terrible slippery spiral into which Lear's initial demand tips him and everyone else, their behaviour gradually becomes monstrous.

In the character of Cordelia the traditional representation is of someone who is too sweet for words, for whom butter would not melt in her mouth, and who certainly does not intend to produce buttered phrases of any sort. It is too easy to present her as intolerably virtuous. To escape from this cliché, it is quite interesting to represent her as someone rather obstinate, in fact we can go beyond mere obstinacy if we compare her with other 'tuitional' heroines in Shakespeare's plays.

\*

*Sarah Badel as Goneril and Penelope*
*Wilton as Regan in the 1975 BBC*
*production of* King Lear

*In my first television production of* King
Lear, *I borrowed costumes from Caravaggio*
*and de La Tour's treacherous harlots, but*
*this trick did not survive the glassy scrutiny*
*of modern photography and Goneril's costume*
*gives me the disturbing sense of having been*
*designed by Hartnell.*

Shakespeare repeats, from one play to the next, women characters who are either cast by events or who take it upon themselves to teach men how to love all the moral virtues that their stupidity, chauvinism or simple view of the world has denied them. Men are constantly shown to be blinkered, and have to be taught to see by women. In a world dominated by men, women can exercise this tutorial function only when they are in disguise. Cordelia as a woman, a visible daughter, who falls below par with regard to her expected answers is dismissed with the phrase '*Nothing will come of nothing*'. Her behaviour is regarded as a mere impudence but by her refusal to speak the words he wants to hear she teaches him. In this particular case it may be inadvertent, as Cordelia teaches by silence. Her tutorial function is exercised in her absence, as she disappears or acquires the most spectacular form of disguise that anyone can assume, that of invisibility. She simply goes away and comes back only when the lesson has been learnt. Lear has to be reduced to the lowest conceivable point, so that he is deprived not merely of his kingdom but also of his senses, he is 'nothing'. Only from this vanishing point can something come of nothing, and Cordelia return to forgive – Lear has learnt.

In other plays when women exercise tutorial functions, they can do so when physically present only by literally assuming a disguise. In *Twelfth Night* Viola can teach Orsino how to love only by presenting herself in the form of Cesario, and Rosalind can teach Orlando to love only when her femininity is concealed in the form of Ganymede. Portia, in the Court, can teach forgiveness, love and mercy only when she plays the part of Balthazar. It is not until the lessons have been learnt that they, like Cordelia, can return from exile and assume their women's weeds. The representation of these travesty roles, which in one respect allow women to exercise tutorial functions in drag, reminds me of the much older Platonic notions of love. In these curious male or invisible girls – Viola/Cesario; Rosalind/Ganymede; Portia/Balthazar; Cordelia/absent Cordelia – we have echoes of the personifications of Heavenly Love referred to in Diotima's great speech in Plato's Symposium. She speaks to Socrates of the status of love and describes it as neither male nor female but as a reconciling personality that prevents the parts of the world from falling into two halves. If we take that seriously, it allows us to represent these boy/girls as something other than thigh-thwacking, swaggering women, with big bottoms and barely concealed breasts who are pretending to be men with swords. I think it emphasizes their rather hermaphroditic function. They exercise their tutorial function as men in relation to the men to whom they speak, but to the audience they must be seen as neither male nor female. As representatives of this Platonist version of love they occupy an indeterminate space.

I have always seen in Viola/Cesario's arrival on the shore of Illyria a

curious echo of Botticelli's *Birth of Venus*, in which the figure of Venus is blown ashore naked and is clothed by the angels. In the same way, when Viola is blown ashore from the billows of the storm, she is clothed as a man in order to exercise her ministry in Illyria — a word that has overtones of disharmony and names the island where she comes to retune this jangled world by teaching not only Orsino but Olivia as well. In her great speeches when she teaches them how to love, she represents the figure of divine Aphrodite, or rather Hermaphrodite, as she speaks as neither man nor woman. When Orsino finally comes to his senses and sees that he has been in love all along not with Olivia but with Viola he falls in love with someone who has not changed his/her appearance and whom he has never seen in women's clothes. He asks her to change but he has acknowledged his love while she is still in the role of a boy. In a way what emerges is not that he has fallen in love with Viola, but that he has somehow seen the value of love which transcends gender.

In exactly the same way that woman can exercise a tutorial function only by temporarily sacrificing her visibility and undertaking the neutral role of Hermaphrodite or, for the men she teaches, the role of a man, which allows her to speak with an authority conventionally withheld from her, there are other figures who have a tutorial function in Shakespeare's plays because they are generally regarded as negligible or insignificant. It is the converse of the practice where someone is allowed to teach precisely because they have assumed an authoritative role. In the Fool we have a character who is allowed to teach because he has assumed the unauthoritative role of idiot, he is therefore provisionally negligible, and can speak in a way that in anyone else would be regarded as impudent. He who jokes must be clothed in some uniform that allows the wisdom of his words to be listened to without the impertinence of his phrases needing to be rejected as offensive. The ministry of fools and madmen is given licence, but what does it mean to confer licence on these characters?

Licence is granted either to an equal or to someone regarded as being so lowly that they are of little or no account. They are non-persons who can exercise a tutorial function because they cannot either assume or presume to be rude. A fool must be a blank whose words of wisdom can be extracted without their being taken to be offensive although they must, in many cases, be offensive in order to be effective. They are listened to because they are from nowhere. As Edgar says, '*Edgar I nothing am*'. In medieval literature, the Fool is visualized as a living vacancy, someone in whom sexuality has either been destroyed or is lacking. In this state of annihilation they have the licence to utter whatever words they want, and once again something emerges from nothing. The talk of fools is immune, its offence cancelled, as if they had crossed their fingers whilst speaking. But it is nature that has figuratively crossed their fingers

*Georges de La Tour*, Job in Prison

*In the three versions of* King Lear *that I have directed, both the character and the appearance of Cordelia have changed more than any other part in the play. At some level, I have always visualized her as an austere Cinderella, but by the time I came to the second production I became interested in her role as one of Shakespeare's tutoria — tuitional heroines who patiently endure contempt and rejection — as she exercises her mission of teaching a father the proper offices of love. Shortly before this production I had seen Georges de La Tour's picture of Job in prison and the pastoral tenderness of the woman who gazes down at the humiliated old man prompted me to borrow her wimpled head-dress.*

*Angela Down as Cordelia in* King Lear, *1975*

for them, rendering them either a hunchback or a person with a hare-lip, or even an exile in the form of a gravedigger or a hangman. These are people who occupy the role that anthropologists might call *interstitial*. They slip between the main structural elements, and are therefore made socially invisible. This social invisibility is their disguise and because, not in spite, of this their moral audibility becomes salient.

∗

This brings me to the question of another generalized personality that appears in *King Lear*, and many other plays, who has elected affinities with the Fool but is quite different – the villain. So often, Shakespeare's villains are the most attractive figures in a play. If we take the two greatest villains, Iago in *Othello* and Edmund in *King Lear*, they appear as the wittiest, most ironic and sarcastic figures who question and challenge the moral assumptions by which everyone else in the play operates. Unlike fools, these characters do not have licence, but what gives them the motive to challenge and offend is that, like the fools, they occupy an interstitial position.

Iago is an unpromoted officer who could never aspire to promotion because his class rules him out; he is a masterless man. Edmund is a bastard; he is illegitimate, '*Fine word, "illegitimate"*!' Fine word indeed for him, because it is this that, while it disqualifies him from inheritance, qualifies him to see more clearly the values of all those who are legitimate. He is not one of the principal weight-bearing members of society, he can neither inherit, nor can he command. In this position of exclusion, Edmund and Iago can look at society askance. In that word we have the suggestion of *ask*-ance – that by looking at the world askance you are in a position to exercise inquiry and irony.

In *King Lear*, Act I scene ii, for example, where Gloucester talks of the late eclipses of the sun and moon which '*portend no good*', he expresses the traditional views of the relationship between society and the cosmos. As soon as Gloucester exits, Edmund, looking askance and asking, declares how absurd these views are: '*This is the excellent foppery of the world*'. By these cosmic principles, he says mockingly, '*it follows I am rough and lecherous. 'Sfoot! I should have been that I am had the maidenliest star in the firmament twinkled on my bastardizing.*' This sentiment is also expressed by Cassius, the malcontent, when he says '*The fault, dear Brutus, is not in our stars/But in ourselves*'.

These characteristics of jocularity and looking askance exist together in one emblematic image, which is found in the pack of playing cards. In the pack of cards the face cards of the court, the kings, the queens, and the jacks have the assigned values and suits to which they belong. So their identities and values are not changeable. There is, however, another face card in the pack – the Joker – which, as they say in poker, is wild. In other words, having been dealt the Joker of the pack, you can assign whatever value you like to it. The Joker can choose, and this is how he exercises his jocular function. As the card is unpredictable, he can actually throw the game into unexpected directions, and this is precisely what Edmund does in *King Lear*. We do not know, nor do any of the other characters, which side he will be on at any given moment. He is the wild card in the pack exercising the jocular ironic function in the play by commenting on the values of all those around him who must act according to the station allotted them by virtue of their birth. Edmund, by virtue of dubious birth, is not obliged to exercise any predictable function. Not only can his behaviour be wild but he is also in a position to exercise unpredictable judgements upon the society around him, and in this way he can be the source of creative, innovative visions about that society.

Let's think about Iago for a moment. As with many Shakespearean characters, that of Iago has been determined very largely by precedent, and has cloned from one production to the next as a silky, insinuating, persuasive villain. He is the personification of evil – but what does that mean? I cannot make any sense of the notion of evil in the abstract, or as a general principle that might be personified in a particular character. Instead I ask myself: what does this character do or mean? If we look at *Othello* it seems to be a play, like *The Merchant of Venice*, in which tragedy issues from the fatal impact between envy on the one hand and jealousy on the other – the propulsive force of the play is Iago's envious behaviour.

Iago is not merely the longest part in *Othello*, but the longest part in Shakespeare. The play's topic is not, in my view, Othello's jealousy but the drama that results from the interaction of Iago's envy and Othello's jealousy. When I directed the play I put considerably more emphasis upon Iago's character, and his motivating envy, than upon Othello's jealousy. I felt it was necessary to restore the balance and to bring back the two equal and opposite forces that constitute the play's dramatic engine. I began by asking about the nature of envy itself and found that there are several ways of approaching the question. At an almost psychoanalytic level you can ask what it is that makes people destructively envious. To find an answer I turned to the most revealing line that Iago speaks almost inadvertently, towards the end of the play, when he is waiting in the shadows for the murder of Cassio, and remarks '*He hath a daily beauty in his life/That makes me ugly*'. This seems to summarize for me the nature of envy. In thinking about Iago, I was guided and inspired by an essay by Melanie Klein on 'Envy and Gratitude'. She draws a picture of the envious person who, on their first ferocious and unsatisfying encounter with the breast, fails to receive the nourishment and hope that might reconcile him or her to the promises and opportunities of ordinary life. This defeat makes him or her unable to deal with the daily frustrations and results in someone who must pollute and destroy what he or she is

otherwise put in the humiliating position of having to admire. In this light, Iago is not *evil* but wickedly unsatisfiable and cannot tolerate the presence of anything beautiful, happy, or balanced. He can experience satisfaction only when everything around him that is possibly beautiful is made ugly, when something that is satisfied is made restless.

In casting Bob Hoskins as Iago there were two other important elements that I wanted to bring out in the character of Iago. One is the image of the Trickster, the person who conceals his identity like Rumpelstiltskin, and is destructively dangerous precisely because he does not divulge his personal character. Apparently amiable and honest, he is a monstrous dwarf – and in that sense takes us back to the most ancient myths of the Trickster, the subversive, disruptive, anti-creative force that must constantly be resisted because it threatens to subvert the very fabric of the social universe. By making Iago into a working-class sergeant I wanted to stress the idea of social frustration, and to think again about the Puritan element in Shakespeare's plays. What Iago's character reveals are certain themes and expressions that in any other person might be seen as admirable. He emphasizes self-reliance and ignores the notion of public reputation, in the belief that you should credit yourself only with those things you think are worth crediting to yourself, and should not depend upon the opinion of others. Iago rebukes Cassio for saying that he has lost that most valuable part of himself, his reputation, '*Reputation is an idle and most false imposition; oft got without merit, and lost without deserving: you have lost no reputation at all, unless you repute yourself such a loser*' (Act II scene iii). In order to place Iago in a socially *real* context, which makes him a historically credible character, you have to start asking more questions about the sources of his dissatisfaction, which extend beyond conjectures derived either from the play or from psychoanalysis.

Iago, Edmund, and Cassius in *Julius Caesar* are all malcontents who share qualities that in other contexts might appear commendable. They show an intelligent, meritorious self-reliance that makes them dispute the success of people who owe their rank to birth rather than personal virtues and merits, and are frustrated by their failure to have their merit recognized. In some respects, these villains are the expressions of personalities who were ultimately to find their fulfilment in the Puritan world that supervened once the Civil War was won. Iago might, for example, had he lived in the society that succeeded the one in which Shakespeare wrote, have been a Major General in Cromwell's New Model Army. His character was caught in a time-warp and circumscribed by a society bound by status rather than contract.

In thinking about this, I have been influenced by a model that comes from Henry Maine's *Ancient Law* where he talks about the transition between a society based on status and one based on contract. In traditional societies your role and identity were determined by your position and

*Bob Hoskins as Iago in the BBC production of* Othello, *1981*

*In casting the cockney actor Bob Hoskins as Iago several images came together in one person. The rough army sergeant, the puritan trooper at Naseby and the mischief-making fairy-tale dwarf – a primal trickster like Rumpelstiltskin.*

birth – as long as that birth was legitimate. Legitimacy did not merely determine your right of inheritance, but also assigned your duties in society so that you knew who you were by examining your position. In a world based upon commercial contract, identity was determined by the contracts you voluntarily undertook with others, and you were bound then by promises and not by status. In these jocular Shakespearean villains I think we see people who are caught half-way, and are moving towards a society which will ultimately be based not on status but on contract. As they are born into a society that is between two worlds, they are socially amphibious figures. In a society that has not yet undergone the complete evolution from status to contract, they have potentially very destructive and subversive roles as they dispute the general assumption that the world is governed by a single cohesive set of rules. When the emphasis shifts from birthright to contract, ingenuity and the exercise of personal merit together with the villain's inclination for expediency become the general rule for behaviour.

The marginal or interstitial characters in Shakespeare seem to be associated with subversion. As they look askance and question, they play the roles of mischief-makers both creating and destroying society around them. They put their energies into destruction and they themselves have to be destroyed. But without the exercise of their evil talents, society could not be re-made in the image of order that prevails at the end of the plays. There are, however, some mischievous figures who are not evil, and are purely benevolent, but they cannot exert this function of creative mischief-making unless they are marginal and interstitial. This is the position allotted to Shakespeare's tuitional heroines and, of course, to the epitome of marginality, the hermaphrodite.

In the same way, there are times of the year that could be called interstitial and associated with mischievous and subversive acts. Edmund Leap, in an essay entitled 'Of Time and False Noses', describes the regular sequence of daily business life as 'profane time' which has to be punctuated and broken up by parenthetic periods of sacred or magic time – these are periods of 'time out' in which whatever happens does not count. Like the interstitial characters these high days and holidays tend to become mischievously subversive and festive. Christopher Barber's book on *Shakespeare's Festive Comedies* points to this notion, but I think it has never been set in the larger anthropological context that links festivity, villainy and mischief with the interstitial, both with regard to people and to time.

At the end of the week we have the weekend which is neither this week nor next week but the period separating the two. These two days are the mortar binding the weeks together and the period of time that links them is in between, a port in which rest occurs. It is not merely a period of rest, but also a period of peculiar restlessness. The weekend is a holiday or holy day, a sacred time of black, as well as white, magic and a period of mischief-making which would be strictly culpable and liable were it to be enjoyed in 'profane time'. During these intervening times there is a kind of licence; liability is suspended as it is for a character like the fool. And there are, of course, fools' days or mischief days which, together with other festive occasions, whether Christmas or Saturnalia, mark the transitions from one time to another.

Shakespeare's *As You Like It* provides a perfect example of two kinds of time. In the court, profane time rules the prudential world of legality and mundane responsibility but beyond it in Arden, festive time takes over. In the forest, all kinds of subversion and inversion take place and in this parenthetic setting characters can abdicate their daily roles. Men can become women, women can become men, dukes become shepherds in just the same way that masters may be seen serving at table at Christmas, and a child or fool can be appointed the Lord of Misrule.

The world is turned upside-down and just as the shaking of the kaleidoscope between two successive configurations creates the possibility of a stable pattern on either side so the mischief-making disturbance of order between one stretch of profane time and the next guarantees the stability of the future period. This is why we call such periods recreational, and in a sense what seems to happen is that the prevailing order is called into question and ultimately re-created. These mischief-making times can only exist, and have any meaning, because profane time will return. The celebrants will resume their normal roles having been re-created in the intervening period.

This idea can apply to places as well as times. In *King Lear*, there is no period of time which is set aside specifically for the inversion and annihilation of roles but there is a place – the heath. On the heath Edgar has to annihilate himself as the legitimate inheritor of land and become nothing: '*Edgar I nothing am*'. By placing himself in a spatial limbo, he re-emerges more qualified to sustain the gored state. Only as an interstitial figure in an interstitial place is he able to exert a magical tuitional influence on his father. There are perhaps no two roles which better epitomize the notion of the interstitial than the inhabitant of Bedlam and the beggar. The beggar and the lunatic are nothing, both inhabit a place that is nowhere but where they may be able to make something from their annihilation. In *King Lear*, the King himself becomes a truant before he has escaped into the space allowed for truancy. By giving his house to his daughters, he confirms his undoing by fleeing into the place reserved for the socially invisible, the heath on which there are no rules and no hierarchy. It is as if his vision of the order of things is dulled and dim in profane time. It is only when stripped of legitimacy and rendered illegitimate that we, like Lear, are made to take care of those things of which we have taken too little care. Lear's mistake is summarized in his initial belief that nothing will come of nothing, when in fact *everything* comes from nothing.

This concept of the liminal, the interstitial or the marginal, is brought out in an essay written at the beginning of this century by Van Gennep. He describes the ceremonies created by society in order to dramatize the positions that occur between one office, or one status, and another. In the same way that we try to order the otherwise unbroken sequence of time, he points out that transitions in life are similarly made intelligible by having ritual enactments assigned to them. The foetus becomes a christened baby; the growing child becomes a mature adult; the spinster girl becomes bride and wife; the bachelor becomes the husband. In all these transitions, there are three successive phases: the rites of separation, where you are disassociated from your previous status or role; the liminal phase where you are separated but not yet reconnected; and this state of temporary annihilation which is followed by the rites of aggregation where having been nothing, you are then made into something else. So, for example, the woman who enters a convent, shaves her head to show the separation from her previous associations and role as fully gendered woman, and then abases herself in a rite of vigil and annihilation during which she is neither girl nor novice nun but a subject of mockery and abasement. She is then subject to the rites of aggregation which incorporate her into the company of the convent.

Rites, like confirmation, or bar mitzvah, can be analysed into these three components. In preparation for confirmation, the child enters a liminal state, casting off childish things and irresponsibilities. After a short period of preparation, he is formally aggregated and taken into the church as a fully responsible member of the congregation, a legitimate communicant. It is also possible to look at birth in these terms. The foetus enters the world in a liminal state, neither independent nor inside the mother, and lies panting on the table joined by a cord. When the cord is cut the child is separated, washed, cleaned and christened. By the rite of christening the child is incorporated not only into the body of the church but into the body of society which now recognizes him by virtue of his name. In death, we can see this process in reverse. The dying man is gradually separated by certain rites from the world of the living. When the corpse is laid out and the vigil begins, he goes through a period of annihilation. But the corpse cannot be laid into the ground straight away. It has to go through this liminal period of being nothing, just the body from which might arise the mischievous and mischief-making ghost. When it has been washed and dressed for the grave, and taken into the company of the dead, the body becomes an ancestor to whom all sorts of rites are due, such as prayers for the dead and chantries. If the body is allowed to remain in the liminal condition, not having undergone the formal rites of transition into the role of fully deceased ancestor, it becomes a vampire, the undead, an interstitial mischief-maker who is neither alive nor dead, but has a morbid vitality. Like Edmund or Iago, the vampire tries to recruit other people to his ranks.

These may seem extreme examples but I think that there is a parallel between these three stages that separate transitions in life and the interstitial periods that mark the transition from one kind of time to another. At the end of each year, for example, we pause to tear up old vows, throw away burdensome oaths and enjoy a period of vigil, or saturnalia and festivity, before the rites of aggregation when we assume new vows and responsibilities for the forthcoming period of order and legitimacy – the New Year.

While there is no one way of approaching a play, there are many techniques or keys with which you can begin to open a script to interpretation. Every director, and reader, of a play arrives at the text with a particular bunch of skeleton keys, and one of my keys, as I have mentioned before, is the structuralist one provided by Propp. I always hesitate to use the term, because I do not think that the technique needs to be dignified by a name that invites misunderstanding. All I mean by structuralism is that if you look at a play, and particularly a group of plays, you can see beneath the surface that totally different characters are exercising identical functions. Without necessarily having to think of yourself as exercising some distinct structuralist skill, this sort of approach allows you to discover a grammar of plot, a deep structure of relationships, which is relatively abstract and indifferent to the specific surface appearance of the particular characters. It is an extremely helpful way of bringing to life what happens in the depths of a play. A useful device for showing this is to superimpose two plays, and see how the structures that are common to both become visible.

This technique of interpretation by superimposition is one that I exercised quite deliberately at Greenwich Theatre in 1974 when I put together three plays in one season with the same actors playing corresponding roles from one night to the next. The programme was called 'Family Romances', which was an allusion – a witty one, I hope – to Freud's phrase, and the plays that I juxtaposed were *Hamlet*, Chekhov's *The Seagull* and Ibsen's *Ghosts*.

What came to light as a result of this superimposition was the following structure which was common to all three plays. In each play you have a young man who has a difficult moral and spiritual problem as a result of his mother either losing or overthrowing her husband and entering into a relationship with another man keenly resented by the young hero. This right-angled triangular relationship of the son, mother and lover, plus absent father means that the young man is prevented from realizing and fulfilling his proper erotic relationship to a lover of his own: Regina, in the case of *Ghosts*, Nina in the case of *The Seagull*, and Ophelia in the case of *Hamlet*. Now it may well be that as far as the audience was concerned the effects of the superimposition were not readily apparent in any one of the plays but if you saw all three together the salient structures common to each play were very prominent. Interpretation is a question of what becomes most visible in a particular production.

The juxtaposition of these three plays raises an important point in relation to the idea of the afterlife of works of art, and the legitimacy of interpretation. It brought out features in each that would not have been visibly present had they been performed on their own or in a repertoire with other plays. Similarly, what any work of art can be seen to exemplify depends on the context in which it is displayed, whether it is a play by Chekhov or Shakespeare or a painting in a gallery. If we looked at a still life exhibited alongside works by the same painter we would be aware of those features in the picture that were examples of his style. But if the same picture appeared alongside other still lifes the most prominent feature would be quite different and we might be struck by how odd it is that apples and pears should be represented in so many different ways.

This overthrows a traditional view of perception which assumes that we perceive whatever there is to be perceived. My point is that what is seen is determined by what it is that is supposed to be exemplified, and that depends very much on the context in which you view any object whether a play or a painting. The same is true of language, as the meaning of a sentence is not determined by the linguistic properties that it has in isolation. Although these are necessary features, they do not tell us what the speaker means by the sentence – that is determined by the context in which it is uttered.

This is why, in fact, one speaks of the indeterminacy of works of art and plays in particular. It is not that they are totally undetermined, or indeterminable, because there are certain things that are obviously determined – to a very large extent – by their actual linguistic structure. When Hamlet says '*To be or not to be*' it is quite clear that he is not talking about making raspberry jam. But the context in which he is saying it, and the fact that he is saying it to himself and to no one else is part of the meaning which cannot be extracted merely by inspecting the linguistic structure.

On this question of what shapes become visible in particular productions of Shakespeare, there are three plays that may provide useful examples. When I directed both *The Merchant of Venice* and *Othello*, I deliberately diminished the visibility of race in order to show other themes, which had become invisible by default – or at least by comparison to the unnatural prominence usually given to race, to blackness and Jewishness, in these plays. In the case of *The Tempest*, however, I made race more visible and I used it to bring out themes that had not been previously presented in relation to it.

In many respects *The Merchant of Venice* is an unavoidably offensive play, but by setting it in the nineteenth century, and allowing Shylock to appear as one among many businessmen, scarcely distinguishable from them, it made sense of his claim that, apart from his customs, a Jew is like everyone else. He has '*hands, organs, dimensions, senses, affections, passions*' and all the same vulnerabilities. As he points out himself in one of his most important speeches, '*I will buy with you, sell with you, talk with you, walk with you, and so following; but I will not eat with you, drink with you, nor pray with you.*' I felt that there was no need in a nineteenth-century setting to distinguish him except by the customs and rituals that he follows discreetly in his home. This highlights and emphasizes the absurdity of the racial prejudice, whereas, if I had set the play in a ghetto world of the sixteenth century, he would have had to appear to be noticeably different from his contemporaries.

What influenced my thoughts about the play was a sort of etymological intuition which came from surveying the extraordinary punning, repetition and play that Shakespeare exercises on the cognate concepts of kin, kindred, kind, kindness, generation, gender – all of which are derivatives of the same etymological root. Kin are of the same kind or kindred if they are engendered by the same parent. In other words, it is through affiliation and descent that we produce kin, children, *Kinder*, creatures who are of the same kind. The notion of kind and type is in fact a concept that is cognate with the notion of children and of descent.

Then there is this other word – kindness. As opposed to kind, the word kindness represents the feelings that you have for your own kind – the Gentile will grow gentle, he will grow kind. And so I began to recognize throughout the play an emphasis upon and scrutiny of notions of kinship, kindness and kin, type and class, showing both how different things are one from another and how similar things are one to another. Take Act III scene i where Salanio and Salarino attack Shylock who says '*I say my daughter is my flesh and blood*'. Salarino then replies: '*There is more difference between thy flesh and hers than between jet and ivory; more between your bloods than there is between red wine and Rhenish.*' Here is a daughter who is different from her father, in spite of the fact that she is kin. She is not simply a daughter who is unkind to her father, she is a daughter who has ceased to be kin to her father, and although a Jewess, she says '*Our house is hell*', so ceasing to identify with her father. Here is the paradox of a person who is the same kin ceasing to think of herself as the same kind, and therefore as a consequence ceasing to be kind to her father and showing unkindness. These phrases share a common root in the German 'kun', which comes from the Greek for womb, 'gynos', the site of generation, affiliation and descent. This notion of kinship and affinity, and of kindness as a sentiment that you feel in the face of those of the same kind, comes out in many different scenes in Shakespeare.

When Shylock recognizes his daughter, he does not realize that he has incubated a child that will not recognize him; their blindness is meta-phorical. In the extraordinary encounter between Launcelot Gobbo and his blind father in Act II scene ii, a meeting echoing the encounter between Gloucester and his son in *King Lear*, we hear that '*if you had your eyes, you might fail of the knowing me: it is a wise father that knows his own child*'. Here by a simple obstacle of losing his senses, the father fails to recognize his son in precisely the same way that the blind Gloucester mistakes his own son for a Bedlam beggar. Gobbo plays a game with his father, '*I will try confusions with him*' and before divulging his identity turns to the audience saying, '*Mark me now; now will I raise waters*' from blind eyes.

These points did not bring out anything specific I can point to in the performance, but influenced my thoughts and informed the emphasis in rehearsals. I kept on reminding the cast to highlight this tension between kin and kind, and that the play was a constant subliminal argument about the notions of difference and similarity, and the feelings of affinity that arise from them – differences between Jew and Christian, between child and parent, and simply between people; individual differences, cultural differences and family differences, all of which are bound up in these overlapping concepts of kin, kindness, kindred, *Kinder*, to produce the potentially dangerous *other*.

It is very interesting to follow the way in which the notion of gratitude is pursued right through to the very end of *The Merchant of Venice*. Up to the middle of the trial, we are led to believe that Bassanio, by virtue of his oath to Portia, will never lose the ring. But the possibility of some superordinate obligation that cancels out previous oaths *always* exists. Despite the oath Bassanio has made to his betrothed when Portia, in disguise, asks him to give her the ring as a reward for winning the case he withholds it until Antonio says, '*Let his deservings and my love withal/Be valu'd 'gainst your wife's commandment.*' We are led to the conclusion, as we are throughout many of Shakespeare's plays, that there are no unarguable moral axioms, and that the weight one gives to any principle can be redistributed from one occasion to the next. And that is really what the whole play reflects, as it raises questions about those to whom you owe debts of gratitude, of loyalty, whether filial, cultural, social or that of friendship, and shows the contradictory tensions that arise from the different pulling threads.

There is no single superordinate rule to which characters can refer so that they can say in any one situation 'This must take precedence over that.' Shakespeare constantly shows that loyalties are unstable and un-foreseeable. They are in fact *debatable* and the play reveals that it is in the nature of moral issues that they are problematic and require mature judgement and the capacity to evaluate competing claims upon resources – whether those resources are of love or of commodity. Having thought about the play for many years, I now believe that far from being a rather trivial and regrettable work, it is perhaps the most complex and interesting of them all.

In *Othello*, the issue of race has been too greatly emphasized, and in the most unfortunate way with the blacking up of white actors and the crude stereotype of the lithe black body, which reflects racism rather than race. This is distracting and it is quite possible to do the play with the minimum of emphasis on the racial distinction. As in *The Merchant of Venice*, the conflict is between two principles rather than between two

races. In just the same way that race has tended to overshadow more important issues that lie in the play, the issue of Othello's jealousy has tended to obscure the fact that the play is driven by the envy of Iago.

I considered doing the play in modern dress and setting it in Cyprus in 1954 with Othello as a Sandhurst-trained Indian officer who had been put in charge of the security forces at the time of the Eoka unrest, and with Iago as an army sergeant. The person I had in mind as a model for this Othello was King Hussein of Jordan who is Sandhurst-educated and rather well spoken with tightly cropped hair and a moustache – a Hashemite warrior, drilled in British Army manners who married a white woman. Othello forgets his racial difference, and this point is reinforced and made much more interesting if instead of stressing the extent to which he is exotically different the production reflects his yielding to the temptation to try to assimilate. The differences should be eclipsed by a large central area of similarity so that their visibility in performance is reduced to a thin line or a tiny crack. This came through in Anthony Hopkins' performance, although I think we probably allowed the make-up people to do too much to him. In another production I would like to shave away the last remaining differences. When Othello reverts to a violent despair, on discovering himself to be trapped in a world that hates him for his race, it becomes much more striking if, up to that point, he is seen to be very similar to everyone else. It is only Othello who fails to recognize his racial difference. If the play stresses the central visibility of his blackness, the audience anticipates a confrontation, whereas it should come as a terrible surprise and shock when disappointed rage ends in murder.

When I directed *The Tempest* at the Mermaid Theatre in 1970, we had Rudolph Walker as Caliban and Norman Beaton, another black actor, playing Ariel. In this production I brought race in and made it a much more central theme of the play in contrast to my treatment of *Othello* and *The Merchant of Venice*. In past productions of *The Tempest* the emphasis has been placed on the metaphysical distinctions that Prospero, the great magician, works with the dark phonic figure of Caliban, the earth monster, with Ariel representing air and fire, and ethereal beauty. I felt that it would be quite interesting and restorative to forget, for a moment, these almost alchemical themes of earth and fire in order to root the play in the secular social context of the seventeenth century. My approach to *The Tempest* was very largely guided by *Prospero and Caliban*, a book by O. Mannoni. He gave an anthropological interpretation of the Malagasy Revolt and emphasized the effect of the paternal white imperial conqueror on an indigenous native population. So, instead of making Caliban and Ariel personify natural principles, I simply made them into native people, the rightful inhabitants of the island. I was guided not only by this book, but also by reference to the imperial themes of the late sixteenth and seventeenth century and the notion of the New World. There are accounts of the journey that describe the behaviour of British sailors on the shore of Massachusetts making the Indians drunk. This made me want to see what would happen if I liberated Caliban from his fishy scales, and mythical monstrous identity, and made him monstrous simply in the eyes of those who arrive on the island. Caliban's servitude was a social one.

Then I wondered what would happen if Ariel was also presented as an indigenous figure rather than a metaphysical principle. In thinking about this I was guided by the recent history of Nigeria, in which the response to a paternal white European authority differed among the various tribal groups that fell under that jurisdiction. On the one hand, the Ibo tended to become deft, accomplished, westernized civil servants and, on the other, the Hausa tended to become totally demoralized and de-tribalized in servitude. Two apparently different black temperaments were to be seen in one nation. Ariel seemed in some way to be expressible as one kind of temperament and Caliban as the other. This allowed me to introduce the notion of difference in the face of what to Europeans would be racially identical figures. Norman Beaton played Ariel as a Patrice Lamumba figure, a French-speaking, Sorbonne-educated, fly-whisk-wielding, ironic, well-spoken figure, obedient rather than servile, who was constantly and ironically pressing for his liberty, and waiting only for the moment when the white master will disappear to take control himself. At the very end of the play, when Prospero breaks his staff and Caliban shuffles to the edge of the water to bid farewell to his master, we suggested that his future might be just as servile and impotent as his recent past. I wanted Ariel speculatively to pick up the broken staff and mend it in the knowledge that when the whites leave his tribe will in fact take control of the island with all the power, skill and wisdom that they have acquired.

But I want to return to the questions of kin, kind and kindness in Shakespeare's plays. The peculiar momentum and tendency of these plays to go on being reproduced in subsequent performances indicates that something in the work insists from one period to the next upon successive resurrections. Despite profound social changes, the plays provide references to features of our life that continue to exist. In Shakespeare's drama a complex, ironic imagination operates on emotional experiences that are common to the species regardless of when the individual members happen to live. People use a shorthand when referring to this common feature and talk about 'human nature' without bothering to parse it in more detail.

What is it about human nature that is the same? What institutions would have to change so that one would no longer recognize the living individuals as being exponents of something we can call human nature? I think what is common to both Shakespeare and our time, regardless of the massive technical, political and social changes that have overtaken us in the past 400 years, is simply the fact that we breed in the same way – we are born of woman and are reared by mothers and share our parents with others born in the same way: in other words, that we have parents and siblings, and share a grammar of relationships that is grounded in this particular method of reproduction.

What is peculiar to Shakespeare, of course, is that in some mysterious way, which no one has yet satisfactorily described or explained, the plays are open and sensitive to so many of the currents that are set up by this relationship that every subsequent performance constantly reminds us of the enormous complexity of moral and filial obligations. Shakespeare has a range of acknowledgements that supersedes and surpasses anyone who came either before or after. And he seems to me to be the great chronicler of the family that survives, and of a species that reproduces as we do.

One of the deep structures that persists throughout all Shakespeare's plays that deal with fathers and daughters is the almost pathological theme of fathers who are ultimately always betrayed by their daughters. They betray only in the sense that they have to teach their fathers that the filial love they owe is in fact divisible, and must in the end be assigned in part to another – a deserving competitor – in the form of a potential husband or lover. Men in Shakespeare seem to have exorbitant expectations of the love that is to be obtained from women – wives, daughters or lovers – and they become raging monsters when the possibility of a divided love appears, whether in the form of infidelity, when they are cuckolded by an unfaithful wife, or in the form of the legitimate infidelity of the daughter who finds that she must now allocate one half of her love to a deserving husband. These themes are explored in the figures of Desdemona in *Othello*, Cordelia in *King Lear* and Miranda in *The Tempest*.

The character of Miranda is much more interesting than she is usually made out to be; similarly Desdemona often suffers from being played as a faint, white flower, a scentless but beautiful camellia. Miranda becomes much more interesting if you consider the psychological consequences of an isolated child, imprisoned and subject to the love and scrutiny of a possessive father. She is, in some way, disabled by it. I imagined her a strangely withdrawn infant-adult and the reason why I asked Angela Pleasence to play her was that she reminded me of a statue by Epstein, called *The Visitation*. It shows a strange, hollow-chested girl accepting the role that divinity has thrust upon her. When I began working on the play I was struck by the strangely psychoanalytic character of the first scene between Prospero and Miranda as he encourages her to remember, and to look back into the dark abyss of time to re-create the past which the shipwreck has made her forget. It is almost as if he is psychoanalysing Miranda who has to learn to become a person, and this can happen only when she liberates herself from her father and recognizes, as so many of Shakespeare's daughters do, that 'I cannot love my father all.' In this, she is like Cordelia, '*Why have my sisters husbands, if they say/They love you all?/Haply, when I shall wed/That lord whose hand must take my plight shall carry/Half my love with him, half my care and duty/Sure I shall never marry like my sisters/To love my father all.*' No one can *be*, in the true plenary sense of the word, until they have reconstructed their memories and established connections with the past and their own previous biography. So at the beginning of the play, Miranda is not a person, she is infantilized by her father until he encourages her fatal development as an adult by provoking her into this act of creative reminiscence. It is almost as if he, Prospero, starts the very process that will destroy him, and then brings to the island the person who will conclude the story by dividing Miranda's love. Similarly Lear inadvertently procures a husband for Cordelia, whose rejection of him he both fears and allows to happen.

When Prospero inflicts the various ordeals on Ferdinand, it seems as if he is testing him, but there is also a sense of a sadistic and vindictive desire to destroy this competitor for his daughter's affection. Ferdinand is analogous to the King of France visiting Cordelia at the beginning of *King Lear*. I often thought that the island upon which Prospero maroons himself to be alone with his daughter is a desert version of the prison in which Lear decides to go with his Cordelia: '*Come, let's away to prison;/We two alone will sing like birds i' the cage.*'

All of us now recognize this kind of acute imaginative and psychological dramatic insight, even though so much else from the Elizabethan period seems foreign and unrecognizable today. And yet, this particular moment in history offers us the first real possibility that the process of reproduction, as we know it, may one day be superseded. If transplantation and fertilization outside the body enable us to reproduce as if in Huxley's *Brave New World* it may well be that the plays of Shakespeare will no longer have an afterlife. When the family structure and its clustered relationships become unintelligible so might the plays themselves.

*Sir Jacob Epstein*, The Visitation

The Tempest, *The Mermaid Theatre,
1970, with Angela Pleasence as Miranda*

*In fairy-tale versions of* The Tempest,
*Miranda is usually represented as a beautiful
princess who awaits the awakening kiss of her
chivalrous Ferdinand. But when I approached
the play for the first time, this image was
supplanted by disruptive questions about the
character of a child reared in isolation by a
brooding and possessive father. To my mind
she shared the peculiar, schizophrenic
reticence of Ophelia and I recalled Epstein's
almost abject virgin. Angela Pleasence laid
claim to the part and pre-empted any other
competitor.*

# II: vi

*At last, to the pleasure of us all, Anton Pavlovich sent the first act of the new play, still unnamed. Then there arrived the second act and the third. Only the last act was missing. Finally Chekhov came himself with the fourth act, and the reading of the play was arranged, with the author present. As was our custom, a large table was placed in the foyer of the theatre and covered with cloth, and we all sat around it, the author and the stage directors in the centre. The atmosphere was triumphant and uplifted. All the members of the company, the ushers, some of the stage hands and even a tailor or two were present. The author was apparently excited and felt out of place in the chairman's seat. Now and then he would leap from his chair and walk about, especially at those moments when the conversation, in his opinion, took a false or unpleasant direction. After the reading of the play some of us, in talking of our impressions of the play, called it a drama, and others even a tragedy, without noticing that these definitions amazed Chekhov.*

The unnamed play Stanislavsky refers to is *Three Sisters*. Chekhov was not only *'amazed'* but *'left the meeting'*. When Stanislavsky sought out the unhappy playwright, he discovered that the reason for his anger *'was that he had written a happy comedy, and all of us had considered the play a tragedy and even wept over it. Evidently Chekhov thought that the play had been misunderstood and that it was already a failure.'*

Although Chekhov is a very different playwright from Shakespeare, his work similarly enjoys an afterlife and shares some of the problems I have suggested in relation to works of art in general when they outlive their authors. This story, however, indicates that his intention was problematic even when he was alive and superintending a play reading. What has happened since Chekhov's demise? Initially his work was cared for by his widow who took on the dramatist's mantle and acted as the custodian to his intention. His plays have now become intricately connected with the slice-of-life realism and method of Stanislavsky. In England the misunderstanding of genre evident in Chekhov's time has been compounded by what I call the Keats' Grove genteel, well-mannered school of acting that flourished in the late 1930s and post-Second World War period. His plays have often been performed by the English theatrical Royal Family – with leading actresses like Peggy Ashcroft – and a certain style of acting has been so consistently associated with them that people begin to think of the melancholy, pausing version as the only permissible one. When another style is introduced, and Chekhov's work is played much more rapidly, casually, even shabbily, they think that a beautiful work has been violated. This seems to me to misunderstand what is remarkable about Chekhov – that his work takes such pleasure in what is un-beautiful and mundane about life. I have directed *The Seagull*, *Three Sisters* and *The Cherry Orchard* and in each case I reacted against the genteel approach, trying to make the work much coarser and more comic.

*Three Sisters* is a comedy in which someone is killed in a rather farcical and idiotic accident. Soliony has never struck me as a wonderful, sinister, duelling villain who with unerring aim kills Toozenbach. I've directed him as a rather drunken, resentful, solitary and harassed figure who was dangerous precisely because he was unexpected. Similarly, the sisters' failure to get to Moscow is *not* tragic; they simply have to continue having a dull suburban life – with an affair now and again – as time passes by. Chekhov says somewhere that in most of his plays people just have conversations and drink tea, and most of our lives are filled up doing that. In a sense, the feeling in the plays is rather like Beckett – it passed the time and it would have passed anyway. This element together with the comedy needs to be brought out. The plays float on a rather indolent tide of undirected chit-chat, and unless time in rehearsal is given to that, we find people trumpeting and elocuting the lines as if singing arias.

In the process of rehearsing *Three Sisters* we discovered the recurrent themes of time and memory. There are references to the passage of time and the impermanence of strong feelings on almost every page. Starting with the first speech when Olga says, '*It's exactly a year ago that Father died, isn't it? This very day, the fifth of May . . .*' we learn that Irena was prostrated with grief but that she is now radiant with happiness. The characters then attempt to date the significant moments in their lives '*your Saint's day, Irena*' and later Andrey asks Natasha when it was he first began to love her. '*Eleven years have gone by,*' says Olga, remembering when they left Moscow, '*yet I remember everything about it, as if we'd only left yesterday.*' For some of the characters the past seems vividly present but to others it seems lost altogether. When Vershinin is reintroduced to the sisters, he has to admit, '*I don't really remember you, you know, I only remember that there were three sisters.*' But he remembers their father, '*I remember your father, though, I remember him very well. All I need to do is to close my eyes and I can see him standing there as if he were alive.*' And the memory of Vershinin himself is incompletely distributed between the three girls. '*I don't remember you, at all,*' says Masha, and then a few speeches later she says, '*Do you remember, Olga, there was someone they used to call "the lovesick Major"?*' With the return of this memory she adds, '*Oh, dear, how much older you look! How much older!*' This raises the second issue with regard to time, and that is how things, especially people, are altered. '*Yes, I was still a young man in the days when they called me "the lovesick major",*' says Vershinin, '*I was in love then. It's different now.* Again in the opening lines, '*It's exactly a year ago that Father died . . . I felt then as if I should never survive his death . . . And now – a year's gone by, and we talk about it so easily.*' Even grief, it seems, will be forgotten, both those for whom we grieve and even the bereaved themselves: '*You know, I'm even beginning to forget what she looked like. I suppose people will lose all memory of us in just the same way. We'll all be forgotten.'* And then there is the effort to try and visualize what the oblivious future will be like, *'Let's try to imagine what life will be like after we're dead, say in two or three hundred years time.'* And although, of course, they will be forgotten and no one will remember who they were or what they were like, they all, as Vershinin points out, have a stake in the forgetful future, for each one of them will have contributed to everything that follows. They cannot experience the posterity they imagine, but it will not come into existence without their actions. The happiness that Vershinin confidently anticipates is brought into existence by the suffering that we have to endure. In other words, it does no good to suppose that one could enjoy future happiness by hibernating until it comes into existence of its own accord, since it is brought into existence only by the misery that has to be endured.

As in Proust, the metaphor of photography is used to emphasize the experience of time. A group photograph is taken at the end of the first act and at the beginning of the last – two moments enjoyed and perhaps remembered by the participants but whose visual record will be impenetrable and enigmatic to anyone looking at it hereafter. When they pose for the photograph, it provides a moment at which strange and unexpected smiles will be recorded, but they do not look like anyone's smile because they are half-way between, their lips caught either on the way up or on the way down. When I directed this scene, the characters applauded themselves when the photograph was taken as though they had just performed and would see themselves on camera later.

Another metaphor of time is provided by the spinning top that briefly silences the company at the end of Act I while each of them contemplates his or her mortality as it spins, slows, falls silent, wobbles and finally topples to a standstill. Suddenly the company see their lives winding down in miniature. The fact that things that seem so important at the time are soon forgotten pervades Chekhov's work. In *The Seagull*, there is a similar effect to that of the opening of *Three Sisters* when Dorn says, *'By the way – where is Zaryechnaia now?'* and the response, equally casual and throwaway, is *'I suppose she is alright.'* Things are soon forgotten, our lives pass with someone growing ill, having a stroke or dying. One of Trigorin's lines captures Chekhov's preoccupation with time: *'So we are going? More railway carriages, stations, refreshment bars, veal cutlets, conversations.'* That is the world of the plays – idle chatter, and the comic surface of social interaction.

While it is widely accepted now that genteel, pausing melancholy is not the way to perform Chekhov, I have always been very stringent about the amount of comedy that can be included in his work. Again, as with Shakespeare, the director has to be careful not to follow or fall into stereotypes. Those in Chekhov are much less famous than they are with a play like *Hamlet*, precisely because Chekhov's work has been with us for a much shorter time and it is not written on the heroic scale that attracts simple, prototypic outlines in performance. Even so, for years Trigorin has been played as a rather silvery, distinguished figure, reminiscent of a slightly disreputable English gynaecologist. Arkadina also invites stereotypes. She is usually played in a very English-actressy way whereas it would be rather interesting to show her as a rather pudgy little spitfire played by an actress like Prunella Scales. This would bring out a particular sort of raucous, Russian vulgarity which is usually neglected. There should be a lot more of the eruptive gaiety that is characteristic of Russians – floods of tears followed immediately by hysterical laughter. Masha is also a part that has fallen into a cliché by being seen as a star performance that should be played by a 'great actress'. In fact, Masha is a rather unlikeable provincial girl with ideas that would have suited the Bloomsbury set. She thinks she is much more sensitive and intelligent than she is – after all she falls in love with the most boring, dull cavalry officer.

Another example is little Irena in *Three Sisters*, a part that is often played as a sweet innocent child, as indeed she is described by Chebutykin who, as it happens, is a sentimental old fool. I have always imagined her as a very hard woman and discovered this was realizable on stage by redesigning the delivery of one short line at the end of the play. This came about in rehearsal with Angela Down playing Irena. Usually when the Doctor enters with the news that Toozenbach has been shot, there is a melancholy and sad surrendering '*I* knew *it, I knew it* . . .' Instead I had her suddenly bite and slam her fist down on the ground, spitting out the words as though shouting an expletive. This totally transformed the character and restrospectively we had to reconstruct her.

Chekhov is quite clearly more realistic than Shakespeare. The characters speak lines that are very like those that ordinary people speak when conversing with one another. There are ways of enhancing that sense of being in the presence of reality, and it is most important to attend to what are called 'the rules of conversation'. These have been identified only in the last twenty years or so by psycholinguists who are very interested in what is called 'turn-taking' in conversation. Conversation has a certain internal structure which is determined by rules that we all somehow know without understanding how we acquire this knowledge. There are rules of listening, of not speaking until the other person has finished, learning how to take your turn, and all sorts of mutually understood rules for establishing how to become the next speaker, and how floor space is allocated. If the actors pay great attention to this, the plays can possess a glittering sense of social reality. Otherwise the speeches simply follow one another and become stale because they do not reproduce the rhythm of ordinary speech. I found it essential to be more slipshod, and allow more hesitation and pauses of the kind you find in any ordinary conversation. It is also useful to allow for things that Chekhov has not written, by this I mean interruption, reduplication and overlap with people starting to talk when the previous speaker has not finished and then having to apologize. All these little characteristics of speech take a long time to re-create on stage but when the actors manage it the audience feels as if it is in the presence of a real conversation.

On the other hand, we have to recognize that there is a certain artificiality about the organization of the scenes in Chekhov's plays. Despite the fact that they are much nearer approximations to spoken conversation than Shakespeare, for example, they are still what we might call 'fourth-order approximations' and not real speech. In Chekhov's writing there is a hidden sonata structure. This draws your attention, as a director, to thematic recurrences and the shape of the plays. Certain themes are stated, developed, reduplicated, inverted and then returned again to the main theme. The sonata structure can still be preserved while encouraging the actors to speak in ways that are not written into the text. This is a rather complicated idea that needs some explanation.

When an author writes down a speech that he thinks of as being a genuine record of how people might speak, he inadvertently does something similar to what psychologists have recognized in perception and called 'regression to the real object'. This means that when we look at a scene we are not aware of the fact that the objects arranged in space create images on the retina that are very much smaller as they get more distant. All that we are aware of is that the objects appear as we know them to be. Similarly, in recording speech a naive draftsman writes down the speech as it is understood, its clear meaning, rather than its actual sound. On the page, we see the meaning of what is heard and not what is *actually* heard. So the speech appears to be much more grammatical than it would if it had been spoken, and lacks the hesitations, the incompletenesses and the overlaps you might find on a tape-recording of the conversation. In a strange way, if you want to make the speeches seem real you have to overlook the way in which they are written down and try to remember how people actually sound, recognizing that what you have on the page is something that has regressed to the real object.

In order to return Chekhov's over-clarified speeches to the state of real conversation it is necessary to break them up and pay very close attention to the processes involved in conversation. This means having to listen to all the verbal and non-verbal accompaniments of conversation that regulate the process of turn-taking. This can be captured only from memory and most actors do *not* remember. They remember what the speeches mean and everything else, which is so vital to the production and belongs to social exchange, is disregarded. Most people will reproduce what is on the page without realizing that the text provides only a clarified picture of what the characters mean. They forget that the lines do not convey how they might actively be spoken. In Shakespeare's play, we are not presented with this problem because writing in the particular verse form and rhetorical idioms that he did there was no need to pay attention to the dynamics of conversation. The verses follow one another with their metrical structure and we cannot insert hesitations and interruptions, nor can we have people mumbling and interjecting with agreements. Yet Chekhov invites these little details which have been rinsed out of the script because they are actually inaudible.

With great care and attention, these details must be consciously restored to the speeches, and when this happens successfully Chekhov's lines take off and become animated. It also means you can shorten the playing time by allowing for overlap. One of the reasons that Chekhov traditionally takes so much time is because pauses, instead of merely indicating lack of response, are self-indulgently wallowed in and given melancholy significance.

Chekhov's dramas are often family affairs and when silence falls in the home, it is not felt to be an enigmatic pause but simply a moment when no one speaks. In contrast, there is an unease about silence in a social situation such as the scene where Vershinin enters; everybody tries desperately to make conversation and feels tremendously relieved every time Vershinin says something, as it fills in the gap. In order to show that they are not being inhospitable, the family goes on reacting long beyond the need to respond to his remarks. Erving Goffman describes the very complicated requirements placed on each of us in a social scene. These not only require us to show ourselves in the best possible light, but to support other people involved in the exchange. What often happens in conversation is that if somebody rather rudely or abruptly interrupts, they then have to overcompensate and apologize to the speaker they have stopped by over-agreeing and denigrating what it is they actually want to say. The dynamic of conversation is not scripted in Chekhov so the director simply has to remind the actors that this is what happens. It can be very exciting when actors suddenly understand what you are asking them to do, and again it is an element that is very variable in performance.

By simply remembering what the idioms would be in a normal conversation, the actors have access to a generative grammar. It is not something you can learn rigidly line by line, what happens is that the cast understands the rules of conversation and generates the sequences accordingly. These rules, very loosely, are what Grice describes in his 'Rules of Conversation Relevance'. This means that whatever contribution somebody makes should be relevant and not redundant and should not overload the listener with information. These very simple understandings are built into any conversation. Similarly, there are rules of courtesy that require us not endlessly to interrupt other people unless we have extremely good reason to do so. Actors have to internalize these habits in a performance, and then they can generate these differently every night. It was an intuitive awareness that prompted me to rehearse Chekhov in this way. I have since read a great deal about the structure of conversation, and listened to yards of carefully analysed tapes made by specialists so that my hunch as a director was later informed by other more authoritative sources.

Far from imposing his or her will on the actors, the director should be simply reminding, and releasing performances that only the actors' competence can bring to life. Most of the points I am making about Chekhov are familiar to us all; we do these things unthinkingly when we behave according to rules of conversational decorum. Offstage we never go through conversations without, in fact, offering a constant barrage of remedies – apologies, excuses, glosses – for potential or actual offences.

I have already mentioned many points with regard to intonation and inflexion that are not written into the script, but there are also interstitial features that are not part of what is being said, but rather linguistic and paralinguistic performances that affect how something is being said. Again, this is usually done without thought but it affects the audience's perception and understanding of the various relationships – familial and social – in Chekhov's plays, which are so full of the comic surface of social interaction. Often actors become more sure of a character when they discover for themselves the sort of performances that their fictional part might give of these remedial actions. For example, they might find that one particular character violates turn-taking procedures more than another, and never apologizes for the violation, or does so in a way that heightens the offensiveness of his or her social behaviour. This aspect of performance is much more revealing than any produced by the archivist director who researches historical setting in minute detail. Obviously, certain details need to be checked to avoid anachronism, but Chekhov's short stories are probably the best prefaces to his plays. Descriptions of people's conduct and their mannerisms are conspicuous by their absence from the plays, and in reconstructing them it is very helpful to read the stories, which are full of accounts of gesture, and tiny physical detail. It is as if, confronted by a play script by Dickens, you found inspiration for details in its performance by looking at the novels, which are full of wonderful vignettes, like the one of Mr Pocket, Herbert Pocket's father, who is seen picking himself up by the hair. It is possible by looking at the stories to effect a kind of internal transfusion of personal mannerisms – those little touches that are rarely written down in plays. A playwright like Shaw does include such details but he is such a bad observer that his descriptions of personal mannerism are just as much regressions to the real objects as the conversations he writes down. Dickens and Chekhov both excel in providing unexpected oddnesses of behaviour, which, incorporated into a play, can be quite breathtaking. One detail that Chekhov does provide in *Three Sisters* is an odd description of Soliony, who is described as constantly dabbing his hands with cologne. It is an interesting and rare little foible in the script and a very odd gesture that he makes because he hates the smell of his own hands – rather a Dickensian oddity. What makes any Chekhov production lift off is this morbid sparkle of tiny subliminal details, idiosyncrasies that are curious but never extraordinary.

Another example of this occurs again in *Three Sisters* where, idling away an evening, they are sitting over the samovar and drinking tea, gossiping while Irena sits playing patience. Chebutykin says something as he turns over a book. '*Balsac's marriage took place at Berdichev.*' A moment later, Irena repeats this phrase to herself but she is not responding; she has not been listening attentively. There is no connection between the two speakers, they are merely talking alongside one another, but people often struggle to find some profound significance in this repetition. It is, in fact, what is called echolalia, and unless it is treated as such, the effect is lost. It is a masterly inclusion of something that gives the genuine rhythm of undirected speech. Irena is preoccupied with turning over a card and the phrase has simply gone in one ear, and she faintly repeats the sound. Chekhov's plays are simply concerned with showing the chronic coming and going of fairly undirected discourse. Often the so-called philosophical conversation suggested by characters is treated with too much reverence. When Vershinin says '*Let's do a bit of philosophizing,*' the response reads '*Yes, let's. What about? Well . . . let's try to imagine what life will be like after we're dead, say in two or three hundred years.*' This is usually played with pace, firm intention and ferocious academic enthusiasm but people rarely talk like this. It is a game and they are merely trying to fend off boredom and pass the time. The line might go: '*(yawn) What about? (pause) well (pause) let's – try to – imagine – what – life – will – be – like (yawn) – after we're dead, – say – in two – or three hundred years.*' Then there might be a long gap.

Chekhov has been performed too often by people trying to sing the lines. There are no arias in Chekhov – only a diminishing sonata that is written in very atonal music. Subsequently, the characters need to be fairly radically redesigned so that they are neither too romantic, nor too attractive, nor too melodramatic. The ordinariness must be emphasized with the humour, although I have allowed some eccentricity in casting when in one production of *The Seagull* we had Fenella Fielding playing Arkadina. In another production it was Irene Worth, who was very funny but perhaps too grand. Arkadina is, after all, rather vulgar. Chekhov's characters are very provincial, smalltown people, not really gentry, who while away the time playing lotto and going on uneventful journeys. Conversations and veal cutlets – that's all there is to life.

## II: vii

The idea of 'function' and the notion of deep structure helped me to
discover how to stage *The Magic Flute*. I came to *The Magic Flute*
comparatively late in my Mozart career and it had always been an opera
that wearied me on stage but moved me very much by its music. I could
hardly sit through productions where oases of beautiful music were
separated by acres of boring talk. The singers usually reminded me of
lungfish, floundering over the mud of awful dialogue, relieved when they
finally flopped into a beautiful, refreshing pool of familiar melody. This
was because I found the staging in the past too literal as it had simply
taken at its face value the setting that Schikaneder and Mozart had written.
It may well be that in the period when they were writing the genre of the
staging realized their intentions but I found that this genre was no longer
satisfactory. So I had to discover a setting that preserved what I felt was
the genre of the work, while abandoning the traditional setting. I began
by asking a series of questions: first of all, does the staging have to be so
heavily furnished with pyramids and sphinxes? Does it have to be this
rather tawdry fairy story in order to preserve Mozart and Schikaneder's
original idea? This led me to wonder about the deep structure that
generated that particular surface performance in the hope that I could
find an alternative setting that would be consistent with that deep
structure, although quite different in appearance.

There are several things I enjoy about working on Mozart; one is simply
the experience of listening to the music all day in rehearsal. Another
aspect is the sheer pleasure of restoring the tone, the mood of the
eighteenth century from which it came, and I feel that relocating it in
another period avoids what is both attractive and interesting about that
world. Directing opera gives me a chance both to acquaint myself with,
and to restore through contemporary eyes and ears, the past from which
it comes. This is important in the case of Mozart, where the period is
deeply built into the music in a way that I do not sense as strongly in the
music of the nineteenth century. Obviously, I cannot revisit the past to
experience the music and drama in the same way that the original audience
would have done. I revisit it as an object rather than as a subjective
experience. Then, over and above the themes that are particular to the
eighteenth century, there are certain psychological themes in Mozart's
work that are common to all periods. In *The Magic Flute* particularly,
there are themes that bring to light issues made familiar by the work
of another Viennese a hundred years later – Sigmund Freud. I do not
want to say that this is a Freudian piece, but it is extraordinary that the
opera anticipates a picture of the mind that Freud was to create in the
1890s. This pattern is visible only in terms of the deeper, underlying
structure.

The joint figures, male and female, of Tamino and Pamina are the centre of the piece and basically represent conscious Ego: the mind that confronts reality and tries to reconcile the demands of appetite with those of duty. Papageno and Papagena represent the world of appetite unconstrained by duty – the Id. In Papageno we have someone who is unable to postpone gratification; as soon as the food is set down in front of Papageno, he eats. In contrast, Tamino listens to the constraints of conscience and is able to wait. Sarastro can be seen as the embodiment of the Super-Ego, of conscience and duty, and of the demands of restraining appetite in the name of some greater reward in the future.

When I began work on *The Magic Flute* I found myself asking several questions. One was to do with the eighteenth century in general and the great Mozart operas in their eighteenth-century setting. A theme common to all of the Mozart operas, reflecting and embodying certain eighteenth-century preoccupations, is that of liberty, of reason, of nature, and of enlightenment. The reconciling of appetite with reason, appetite with beauty, and duty with liberty – all of these became central preoccupations from the middle of the eighteenth century onwards. *The Marriage of Figaro* presents the plight of a servant who chafes under the yoke of his master's right to enjoy his wife on his wedding night; and questions the right of a man who is master of a household to inflict the whims of his aristocratic appetite upon everyone who surrounds him – not merely servants, but his wife as well. And all of this is ultimately reconciled in that great moment at the end of the opera, the Perdono aria, when the Countess, having disappeared, returns to forgive and reconcile everyone.

*Così fan tutte* brings together the ideas of reason and nature. The figure of Despina embodies nature, which says 'Follow your appetites, be honest with yourself about what you want', and Alfonso represents the idea of 'Know yourself, do not be deluded by sentimental notions of fidelity; face up to the realities of moral life and then you can pursue your interests in what, after all, is the best of all possible worlds, but not very good.' *Don Giovanni* is about the reconciling of appetite with the demands of society; here is someone who recklessly pursues sexual appetite without regard to other people's interests and who must in the end suffer and go to Hell for doing so.

In *The Magic Flute* we have what is perhaps the most complex of all representations of this theme of reconciling appetite with duty, and of the gradual emergence of the self in a world where duty calls on the one hand and appetite calls on the other. But this central conflict is complicated by all sorts of other considerations related to the tyranny of ancient and obscurantist religion, as opposed to the world of enlightened deism, and it is set in a domain that is very special to the end of the eighteenth century, that of freemasonry. I had to find some sort of metaphor that would bring together all those moral concerns in the special setting of freemasonry.

In traditional productions of *The Magic Flute*, lip-service has been paid to freemasonry by representing the outward form, so that there are solemn, boring processions of people dressed in robes that make them look as if they're members of the Mormon Tabernacle Choir. I had been struck for many years by the work of some utopian architects at the end of the eighteenth century, who were themselves freemasons; one of them was a man called Etiene Louis Boullée and the other was Nicholas Ledoux. Both these men had conceived ideal cities where some sort of new regime could be established, that would not embody subservience to a tyrannical old religion.

Nicholas Ledoux built a curious utopian city around a salt works in the south of France. The workers lived there in happy, enlightened industry in dwellings arranged in a series of concentric semi-circles around the great central evaporating rooms where the brine was delivered through pipes and then dried out. At the centre stood the bureau of the director who was the supervisor of the salt works. This seemed to me to embody the world of Sarastro. I knew, of course, that I could not realize that on the stage because it is an outdoor setting, but I looked at other designs that Ledoux and Boullée had done separately. They were utopian designs for a library. This struck me as the epitome of the Enlightenment; the world of accumulated wisdom of the past, from which you could cull all sorts of principles, going right back to the Egyptian hermetic mysteries. Here the Egyptian themes could be embodied in an eighteenth-century setting, and so my designer and I decided to set the whole thing inside a vast masonic library loosely based on Boullée's designs for a Bibliothèque Nationale. Having done that, we automatically eliminated the world of pyramids and sand dunes.

This setting meant that the drama had to be some sort of dream. We began the opera with the curtain up as the audience came in, and as they sat and settled in their seats they saw a huge library with walls of books soaring into the flies on all three sides of the set. Half-way up there was a great gallery with reading desks at which bewigged masonic gentlemen sat, with their heads in their hands, poring over volumes. On the floor of this library were relics of antiquity, as in the Sir John Soane Museum, there were great plaster casts of Egyptian pyramids. Strolling around this library, talking to one another, could be seen eighteenth-century gentlemen moving amongst the antiquities of this lodge, making sketches of obelisks or sitting at neo-classical sphinx-legged, walnut tables.

As the lights went down, a young man appeared with books under his arm, and he set them on one of the tables downstage, then went through his file cards and fetched various books from the shelves. As he sat at the table, the overture began, and he settled down for reading. Gradually

*Etiene Boullée, Bibliothèque Nationale,*
*Latitudinal section*

*Like many other modern producers and*
*directors, I recoil from putting nature on*
*stage and in the effort to avoid the outdoor*
*landscape with which* The Magic Flute
*begins, I tried to find an artificial enclosure*
*within which the theme of quest and*
*pilgrimage could be realized without having*
*to put artificial trees on stage. The eighteenth-*
*century architect Etiene Boullée provided*
*an ideal setting in the form of a Masonic*
*library within which Tamino could dream*
*his Rosicrucian enlightenment.*

The Magic Flute *at the Theatre Royal,*
*Glasgow, 1983*

*The library setting allowed me to escape*
*from the literal representation of Egyptian*
*pyramids. This is an eighteenth-century world*
*of Masonic scholars where the artefacts of*
*hermetic antiquity are represented by plaster*
*replicas and by Thomas Hope furniture, which*
*includes Egyptian motifs in its neoclassical*
*designs.*

people began to leave the library, lights were doused, and here was someone working in the stacks at night. As he read, and the overture progressed, he began to drowse over his books until, by the time the overture was half-way through, he had fallen asleep.

Once again, a little fragment of a picture I remembered suggested something in my mind's eye – the tiny engraving by Goya of *The Sleep of Reason brings forth Monsters*. As Tamino slept at the table and the overture came to a conclusion, that picture helped me to bring the serpent to life. I had always been struck by the arbitrariness and the abruptness with which the serpent appears. Here, the serpent was generated from the depths of Tamino's sleeping imagination, and out of the pyramid a sort of succubus appeared, a beautiful eighteenth-century woman, bare-breasted, with a huge boa constrictor coiled around her. She approached him wielding the creature with an enigmatic, seductive smile. When Tamino awoke within his dream to this sight he fainted. Then the Three Ladies came on presented as three Habsburg dowagers.

When it came to the Queen of Night I was able to escape from the awful tradition where she appears as if at Aztec Night at the Copacabana, trapped in an ornamental sunburst amidst the clatter of moving walls, and then vanishing. What does she represent? Perhaps the Queen of Night is intelligible only held against the figure of Sarastro. And thinking in terms of the eighteenth century again, I wanted to make her representative of that world of obscurantist Jesuitical Catholicism without having her literally embody the Empress Maria-Theresa. At the moment when the Three Ladies say '*she comes, she comes*', a strange morbid light appeared in one of the back corridors out of the stacks and, preceded by her archbishops, her confessors and her Jesuits, a sunny little Queen Victoria, reminiscent of Maria-Theresa, appeared and set Tamino on his quest.

In this production Sarastro was no longer a berobed bore but a bewigged eighteenth-century gentleman, an aristocratic mason. In contrast to the ecclesiastical retinue of the Queen, with altar boys and confessors and archbishops, the retinue of Sarastro became masonic, but not in the traditional Grand Order of Buffaloes style. I was very much prompted by John Trumbull's picture of the signatories of the Declaration of Independence, where the eighteenth-century rationalist gentlemen meeting in Philadelphia are leaning forward in discussion – most of the signatories were masons. They represented the rational world of a revolution based on the principles of John Locke – not the revolutions of 1848, still less those of 1917, but the world of the property-owning bourgeoisie taking possession of the world of the *ancien régime*. So now I had two opposed groups, two retinues: one representing the world of altars, cathedrals, and monasteries on the Danube, set against the world of the enlightened despotism of Joseph the Second and his masons.

Joseph the Second was in fact the Grand Master of one of the more enlightened Lodges in Vienna.

Once I reached this point, I could emancipate the absurd figure of Papageno, who is so often represented as Tweety-Pie – dressed in blue feathers, walking with his toes turned out and pretending to be a bird. If you look at the original drawings of the Schikaneder production Papageno is, in fact, fledged in feathers but this is compatible only with the popular theatre of that time. I wanted something that would be readable to a modern audience as a bird-catcher and compatible with the notion of a sort of Rousseau figure – the Man of Nature. What better than a gamekeeper? I went back and looked at eighteenth-century Meissenware pieces. There are hundreds of eighteenth-century ceramic figurines of bird-catchers, in breeches and gaiters with a little willow cage on their back. As this was our model for Papageno, Papagena then became a peasant girl.

*Meissenware ceramic figurine of a bird-catcher*

*Fledged with canary feathers, Papageno usually comes on like Tweety-Pie and it is difficult to identify him as Rousseau's natural man. In the image provided by this Meissenware bird-catcher, he is humanized and dignified.*

*John Trumbull*, The Declaration of Independence (below)

*The operatic representation of Freemasons is repulsively ritualistic and usually requires the chorus to wear costumes of Amy Sempel McPherson's choir. I saw them instead as enlightened gentlemen seeking a reasonable and constitutional solution to the problems of social order. Many of the signatories to the American Declaration of Independence were Freemasons and it was through the network of Illuminated Lodges that many of the ideas of the French Revolution took root.*

*Goya*, The Sleep of Reason brings forth Monsters (left)

*The appearance of the serpent at the beginning of* The Magic Flute *creates considerable difficulties for a producer. How can it be done without the embarrassment of creating something that looks like a street fair celebrating the Chinese New Year? By allowing Tamino to drowse over his Masonic manuscripts, I could let the sleep of reason bring forth monsters, and the serpent becomes a succubus.*

*Velázquez*, L'Infanta Maria Theresa (right)

*The Queen of Night usually makes her entrance in a production number that looks as if Yma Sumac is making a personal appearance in* Aztec Night at the Copacabana. *When the opera is restored to its eighteenth-century setting, she can revert to the role of Habsburg empress followed by an entourage of archbishops, confessors and altar boys.*

I looked next at the character of Monostatos, who is often made into a golliwog. I wanted him to convey an eighteenth-century view of the black, and there are some excellent paintings from the period of the Red Indian. Working from these I tried to make him someone who represents his race, but who has already been embedded in the revolutions of 1800. I used the painted figure of Toussaint L'Ouverture, haughtily dressed in almost Napoleonic garb, as the basis for the costume.

At rehearsal I began by explaining these ideas and showing the models and paintings I had used. I showed the cast pictures of the Empress Maria-Theresa, and of the signatories of the Declaration of Independence, Toussaint and the Sir John Soane Museum, hoping then that my ideas would appear reasonable. In the final scene I was inspired by the work of Jean Starobinski. His book, *Les Emblèmes de les Raisons*, is a study of the eighteenth-century symbols of Enlightenment in which the sun represents reason, and the night obscurantism. Instead of having a terrible procession of dowdy surburban Buffaloes I based the final chorus on some of the great festivals of the first two years of the Revolution which were staged for, and commissioned by, the Revolution, and executed by the painter David, who organized a festival – a Fête – to the Supreme Being.

The end of the opera is a great celebration of self-realization, and of Man reaching his highest fulfilment when he has conceded the natural rights that had previously been taken away from him by the world of the *ancien régime*. This is the world of the Revolution just before it went wrong. *The Magic Flute* was written in 1791 when the Bastille had already fallen, before the Terror had shown that revolution could introduce a tyranny just as great as the tyranny it had overthrown. But there was the moment described by Wordsworth '*Bliss was it in that dawn, to be alive*', and it was that dawn, which drives away the darkness of night with the sun.

It is often said that Mozart took no account of the events in France, and although there is nothing in his letters to indicate that he was even interested in it, *we* by hindsight cannot neglect the fact that this work was conceived at about the time of the Revolution. Of course you can go too far, and some Marxist interpretations look as if they are pointing towards the Revolution. A production need not appear to take account of the Revolution but it cannot ignore the spirit and climate that gave rise to it.

I did not feel tempted to relocate *The Magic Flute* in time, as I did *Rigoletto*, which, like some of Shakespeare's plays, is another example of a work written at one time about another period. It does not pose a problem of representing antiquity like *Aida*, but it presents us with a composer writing in 1850 about something that takes place in the 1550s. As we recede from the 1850s, there is a much more audible discrepancy between the style of nineteenth-century music and the visual appearance of the literal setting. In the case of *Rigoletto* this is made all the more startling by the fact that there is a great big brass band pumping away at the beginning and playing what is supposedly a dance in the Court of the Gonzagas. The inconsistency, the dissonance, between the appearance and the sound is so striking as to be distracting. As we grow better at re-creating the sixteenth century this seems more absurd, and highly anachronistic.

In the first production of *Rigoletto* that I directed, in 1975, I tried to eliminate that discrepancy by simply setting it in the period of its composition, and had a nineteenth-century version. The dissonance was eliminated, but at the same time I noticed how consistent the plot was with something that could have taken place in another Italian community where people have absolute power of life and death over others, namely the world of the Godfather and the Italian Mafia. Since the music of the nineteenth century continues to be played, and is influential in the Italian communities of the twentieth century, it seemed much less anachronistic, and a perfectly obvious and effortless transposition.

In all of these interpretations I have worked by a principle comparable to the mathematical one of mapping. You take two sets and see whether in fact they map without undue force being applied. Here the social world of the original court mapped completely, without any of the points having to be dislocated, on to the social world of the Mafia. Having done a theoretical mapping in my mind I was fairly sure that it would work, and as rehearsals went on even the chorus became convinced by the production. When we started they were obstinately opposed to it asking me, 'Why mess around with a perfectly good traditional format?' But as they began to see that it was a consistent interpretation they would come up to me during rehearsals and say with surprise: 'It works, doesn't it!' In moving the opera from a vaguely historical past to a recognizable modern setting consistency would have required an alteration in language.

I was tempted to recommend the use of recognizably American idioms, but the conductor resisted these changes in the belief that they would clash with Verdi's music. In the end we agreed to disagree and seeing the production after several revivals I still have serious misgivings about this discrepancy. *Rigoletto* was, however, an enormous success, and in one way this has proved rather inconvenient because people now ask me what I am going to do next to *Don Giovanni* – as if I have now found a formula and will automatically use it with all operas. But this cannot be done to any opera, let alone to Mozart. I feel the same sort of reluctance to shift the period of Mozart's operas as I do with much of Shakespeare.

When I consider the possible settings for any opera, I find that most nineteenth-century composers, between about 1830 and 1880, dealt rather carelessly with the past as they transposed opera into almost any period. In fact, you can hardly think of a century in the distant past that has not been ransacked, used and exploited for the setting of operas, and yet this

*Patrick Robertson's and Rosemary*
*Vercoe's set for* Rigoletto,
*English National Opera, 1982*
(below)

*Edward Hopper,* Nighthawks, *1942*
(right)

*In the flight from an improbable Renaissance*
*Mantua, I arrived in the world of mid-*
*twentieth-century Manhattan. Hopper's*
*midnight diner replaced the colourful*
*riverside tavern of tradition.*

has no significant influence upon the music. You cannot tell from listening to the music that it was the period of the Sicilian Vespers, as opposed to the Gonzaga period in *Rigoletto*. I feel justified in transposing these operas if it strikes me as a consistent interpretation. This amiably slipshod use of the past on the part of the nineteenth-century composers stands in strong contrast to earlier composers like Mozart, for example, who are either working right in their own period, as with *Così fan tutte* or *The Marriage of Figaro*, which take place in the period of composition; or in remote antiquity, as with Gluck's *Orfeo ed Euridice*, or Roman antiquity as in the case of Mozart's *La Clemenza di Tito*. The intervening years simply do not exist as places in which to set operas, and there is a sense of decorum about the setting in antiquity. Now this does not mean that you *have* to set the works in antiquity. I tend to think that they are better brought up to the date of their composition but never beyond that. For example, I believe that *La Clemenza di Tito* could be done very intelligently if set in the period for which it was written and even the occasion for which it was written – the coronation of Leopold the Second. Or, alternatively, it could be staged in a way that allows us ironic reference to the antique past by having costumes reflecting the eighteenth-century view of the past.

# II: viii

Introducing the idea of the afterlife, I took up Nelson Goodman's idea that although an unperformed play has a literary existence it remains a very forlorn object, whereas an unperformed opera is much more problematic – it is an inconceivable entity. Opera is half-way between a play, for which you could conceive an existence on the library shelf but is best performed, and a piece of music, which in fact has no existence unless it is performed.

It is a hybrid that is much nearer to the condition of pure music. An opera that is unperformed is just as forlorn as a symphony that is unperformed. You might argue that the equivalent of a play in book form is opera on record, but this is only so by default. Those critics who prefer opera on record are deploring either the ghastly old-fashioned type of opera, or the equally dreadful over-imaginative production that simply quotes the work in the midst of a large floridly self-emoting thesis invented by the director. In an attempt to make opera as relevant as people have sometimes attempted to make Shakespeare contemporary, many directors have gone to absurd lengths. You find examples of this in Germany where there are many opera houses and directors are in keen competition with one another. The attempt to raise the ante as regards novelty is such that almost every production in German opera houses has some sort of spectacular and bizarre effect so that it becomes very difficult to tell what is happening on the stage, and the story is smothered in the event of the staging. Novelty for its own sake in an opera production can appear to be simply philistine, and a director must be as careful as possible about identifying the deep structure of each opera. In this way, I approach opera as I do stage plays, applying the same questions as to how to stage a work when it has entered its afterlife.

Initially I approached opera with what might be seen as very serious disabilities. I can neither read nor perform music, and although I think I have a good ear and I know what music means dramatically, I may appear to have come to opera with practically no qualifications to stage it. But I think that one can be musically dyslexic and still musically literate and that is what I am, in the same way that someone who is ordinarily dyslexic can still understand what a play is and how it works. The most important function of musical notation, like a script as notation, is to enable it to be performed from one production to the next.

So, although I approached opera with a certain amount of reticence, admitting when I came into the first rehearsal that I could not read what the score meant, I came to it as a stage director who believes – and this has strengthened with experience – that 90 per cent of the dramatic diction in the work of composers like Mozart and Verdi, for example, is musical. If you are sensitive to music and allow for the existence of this extra dimension, which is lacking entirely in drama, opera is simply another play, in which there are very distinctive peculiarities of expression and tremendous artificiality because everything is bound by the tempo of the music. There are very spectacular overlappings, for example sextets in which six people sing at the same time, that do not happen in conversation. Once you have accepted that particular idiom of utterance, you recognize that this is simply another way of having a play. There is no other difference at all, and the artificiality of opera is no more difficult for a director than the now almost unnoticed artificiality of Shakespeare. We know perfectly well that no one speaks like the characters in Shakespeare, the artificiality of Shakespeare becomes apparent only if you misguidedly present him in a very realistic setting – which is why film and television versions of Shakespeare that go to the named locations and put people out in the open air with genuine scenery seem absurd. It is essential to match the artificiality of the verse with the artificiality of the stage setting, and the same applies to opera. A very explicit and self-conscious allowance must be made for the fact that opera's diction is as artificial as the speeches and pentameters of Shakespearean verse, and must have consistent actuality in performance.

It is because we are not as accustomed to opera as we are to Shakespeare that we have to acclimatize, but once we have it is suddenly very releasing. You can express a whole world that is inexpressible in language. That is what makes the opera so exciting and why, when the full integration is achieved, the experience of a great dramatic operatic work is almost transcendental, in ways in which it very rarely is with a straight play. It is as if you have found a system that can express the autonomic nerves rather than just the voluntary nervous system.

Opera seems to have been a very privileged art form for many years and even now, as its popularity increases, it is still associated in the public imagination with the idea of privilege, wealth and the kind of inattentive audiences that glitter in boxes. But this has been changing in the last ten years, both in England and in America. The exotic and imaginative side of opera seems to have superseded the appeal of the straight theatre, so that small companies like the Kent Opera in England, or Opera 80, and small provincial opera companies in America have become astoundingly successful. Television has broadcast more and more opera and it might seem that this has helped popularize opera but I doubt that any television company would have dreamt of putting it on if there had not been a noticeable change in public appetite. People go to the opera, and discuss it much more freely and with greater excitement than they did ten or fifteen years ago. It now takes up a large amount of space in newspaper reports and weekend arts pages – opera looms large.

For many years opera was isolated from the mainstream of drama, ruled by conductors and musicologists who had a very limited sense of the dramatic. It has been associated for too long with an expensive night out and gala events, and with lavish centres of excellence like Covent Garden. Making opera a good dramatic occasion was of secondary importance. What has happened in the last few years, corresponds to the revolution that was identified and deplored by Helen Gardner in relation to Shakespeare – the appearance, once again, of the interpretative director. Most people, unless they are very obstinate and conservative, would concede that opera has become a more widely available dramatic experience. What makes opera attractive now is that the music seems to be expressing something that is consistent with the libretto. But it is still perfectly true that there are very many operas that are nothing more than concerts in frocks, with very beautiful songs and orchestration, for which the story is negligible. As a director you have to work overtime to try and make such works come to life as a drama. For anyone who is as interested in the theatre as I am, there are probably only about thirty or forty operas that are worth staging – the rest you simply sit through and endure in order to listen to the music, and they probably are more enjoyable on record. Those are the works that are best kept in the original language because once you understood the words, you would be outraged. With the exception of those operas whose improbable plots and absurdities make them untransformable in dramatic terms, opera now seems to offer theatre directors great opportunity for creative reinterpretation.

The cloning of operatic styles of presentation, in which large and rather improbable figures sang in rather gaudy frocks before studiously realistic and heavy sets, is on the wane. Some of the revolutions that have occurred in staging in the ordinary theatre have now extended themselves into the operatic theatre. Audiences, producers and directors no longer accept rhetorical gestures, or ludicrous physiques, they treat the works simply as another form of theatre. Certainly my own approach to opera is indistinguishable from my approach to a production of Shakespeare. Opera is merely another form of theatrical diction. In the past when opera was accepted as a dramatic work it was for an audience whose sensibility was so different from our own that we cannot accept the way in which it appealed to them. In order for it to reassert itself as first-class music and drama it has to be emancipated from the formal presentation in which it may have been conceived but has now been imprisoned. Opera, like any other art form, has to undergo an afterlife. The same questions as to the legitimacy of interpretation and of genre occur in opera and Shakespeare.

On a practical level I approach an opera rehearsal in the same way as a play rehearsal by discussing the central ideas and setting. Many very fine

**Poussin**, Orpheus and Eurydice

*Refracted through the medium of a
seventeenth-century pictorial imagination,
mythical antiquity assumes a stoic calm that
cannot be realized by any effort to represent
a realistic Thrace. Poussin's noble composure
allowed me to realize the themes that are
expressed in Monteverdi's courtly composition.*

singing actors would flounder like seals on dry land if they were deprived of their music, but they act like angels when immersed in their natural medium of singing. There are some extremely bad singing actors who have wonderful voices but the experience of vocalizing does not penetrate them dramatically. But they are rare today as more young singers have the ability to act through the medium of singing.

The person who is directly concerned bar by bar, note by note, with phraseology, intonation, pace and tempo is the conductor. He is the musical mechanic who supervises the way the music is articulated on the level of its construction, and it would be a very bold director who dared to intervene more than occasionally. I consult with the conductor and we talk through how to reconcile the strictly musical constraints with dramatic demands. This is a negotiable area, and consultation with the conductor is absolutely essential. The conductor can learn a lot from the director, who hears something dramatic in the music that he may not have heard. Conversely, it would be very rash for a director who was not intensely musical to ignore a conductor, who might draw attention to a change in key, for example, reflecting a change of mood or intonation in the musical structure which required expression in the staging. There is and should be a reciprocal obligation between the director and conductor.

Conductors, like choruses, tend to be fantastically conservative, and some find a change in approach very difficult, but collaboration between the stage director and the musical conductor is essential for the hybrid form to work to its fullest and most powerful effect. Some conductors asked to face a rather different kind of spectacle from the pit feel that you have done something comparable to asking them to rescore the work for a Moog synthesizer and brass band. It is then up to the director to convince the conductor that the spectacle he is going to have to face every night as the curtain goes up is not irresponsibly inconsistent with the music that he is working to realize.

*La Favola d'Orfeo*, written in 1605 by Monteverdi, is an opera that epitomizes both the contraints I feel with regard to setting in operas of the Baroque period, and the problem of the afterlife. Here is a work that we can regard as the first opera, originally presented, or so it seems, in the Ducal apartments at Mantua, probably without scenery and with a relatively small orchestra. Subsequent performances were given on a much grander scale for a wider public, and then it seems to have gone out of commission altogether. Performances of Monteverdi's madrigals were revived by Nadia Boulanger in the 1930s. They were recorded, but no stage performance of his operas took place until about 1937, and there was no full-scale performance of *La Favola d'Orfeo* until after the Second World War. For the best part of three hundred years Monteverdi's work died, and by the time it was revived the problem of what sort of afterlife it was to have became very acute indeed. While Shakespeare's works have had a continuous, developing and evolving afterlife, in hundreds of subsequent performances, Monteverdi's work had undergone the equivalent of what in evolution is called 'a sudden, abrupt, quantum change in character'. When the opera was finally rediscovered it was rather like a statue that had been lost for a long time and was then totally appropriated by the period that at last reclaimed it.

When I first approached *La Favola d'Orfeo* I did so with an intuitive understanding that there were relatively tight constraints upon works of the Baroque period. There seemed to me to be three choices. I could either set it in something that was archaeologically orthodox, in other words put it in the setting to which Monteverdi refers – Thracian antiquity – and with all the archaeological resources that we now have at our disposal, which Monteverdi did not, I could in fact have a Greek Orfeo. The second possibility was to put it in Renaissance costume and to stage it as if it were a court masque that *referred* to classical antiquity. And the third one, which I finally adopted, was to find some sort of resolution of the problem of the representation of the antique within the idioms of the period in which the opera was conceived.

What sort of visual resources would I use in order to satisfy that decision? I had to think of a painter or painters from the same period who represented the antique. Poussin was the artist who came to mind although he had not begun painting at the time when *La Favola d'Orfeo* was written.

In his overall genre Poussin is, *par excellence*, a classicist. Quite apart from his subject matter, the actual idiom of his representation is classical and extremely formal in its arrangements. In the subsequent century Poussinism was opposed to Rubenism. Where Poussin represented austere, lucid and clearly defined volumes arranged *en plein air*, Rubenism exhibited turbulent, florid, deeply structured arrangements representing the height of the Baroque. The formal idioms of Poussin's work seem in some way to reflect the formal idioms of Monteverdi. Both use very restrained and formal structures to express a preference for a passionate stoicism. I was also encouraged to make this choice by the knowledge that Poussin himself had conceived the arrangements of physical figures in space as being analogous in some respects to the intervals that separated the notes of the classical Greek musical modes.

In Poussin I had chosen someone whose idioms reflected not merely the moral character of a work but also affected certain formal characteristics to be found in the music. In addition, the narrative content of much of Poussin's painting is classical. His painting *Orpheus and Eurydice* provided a starting point for discussions with a designer. We had to work out something that would express, and embody, Poussinism within a stage setting. There is no point in simply slavishly copying the landscape to be

191

*Poussin*, The Dance to the Music of Time

*In addition to his role as a scenic artist,*
*Poussin also rendered invaluable service as a*
*choreographer, and enabled me to develop*
*dances that were consistent with Monteverdi's*
*orchestral interludes.*

found in a Poussin picture if you then put living figures in front of it to obstruct the view. After a long series of discussions we decided to give each of the five acts in the opera a distinct Poussin landscape. Instead of simply copying each one on to a backcloth, I wanted Poussin's landscape to be presented on stage in a way that would distance the reproduction from the original. I asked Daniel Lang, a distinguished American landscape painter, to copy Poussin as closely as possible, knowing perfectly well that someone as original and creative as Lang would automatically introduce his own perspective in a twentieth-century rendition of Poussin. I could see from his landscape painting that in his own work Lang reacted to some of the mysterious qualities of blocks and volumes, and of cloud and vegetation. He made five small and valuable canvases.

I then began to do something comparable to a process I enjoy, which is to take a picture, photograph it, and then photocopy it repeatedly so that it acquires the curious physical characteristics of the reproductive process. If you copy the copy of a copy, strange edges begin to appear and the mechanical line becomes clearly visible. Instead of literally putting Lang's work through a copying machine, I set up a human copying chain. First, the scene painters copied Daniel Lang's pictures. This meant that they were going through a second stage of representation. The scene painters scaled it up and treated it like a cartoon – in a cartoon you prick holes along the contours of a figure and 'pounce' graphite through the holes on to the prepared surface of the wall. Lang's canvases were now reproduced as a full backdrop, but I did not want a simple uninterrupted cloth that would arrest the gaze at the back of the stage. I asked the scene painters to cut up the canvas vertically so that it could hang in strips. Arranged on a plane, the vertical strips were separated by about two or three feet, enough to admit a person coming through from the darkness at the back of the stage and moving into the foreground. This made the landscape penetrable and allowed for the free flow of the singers moving back and forth on stage.

To prevent these strips hanging like venetian blinds turned at right-angles, I had to find a way for them to alternate freely from one scene to the next, so that the scene change would be mysterious and minimal. The next step was to ask my scene designer to take the reproductions of Lang's Poussin landscape and to stick them on to the surfaces of a column made in triangular sections. This meant that all the components of each picture were on the same side, and when we wanted to change the scene the column was simply revolved through to the next landscape. It was rather like those advertisements you see on huge billboards or in the Tube, and produced a magical transformation. This effect enabled me to make a very theatrical rather than an explicit reference to Poussin.

We dressed the performers in Greek peplums, as if in a Poussin painting, and asked them to study carefully the strangely characteristic gestures shown by Poussin's figures – the way, for example, the hand is held. There are long symphonias in *La Favola d'Orfeo* which represent a choreographic challenge when it comes to staging them. Again the choice is: do you have Renaissance dances, or do you have dances that come from Greece? As we know very little about dances from Greece, and we had a Renaissance setting, I decided to go back to Poussin for my choreography. Every movement, down to the last detail, was choreographed on the basis of his pictures. There are two famous canvases in which dances are represented: one of them is *The Dance to the Music of Time*, where you see a ring of dancers with their backs to one another, arms linked in a circle. They are off-balance with feet raised and this means that there is only one position of stability to which they could return in order to restore balance so the next step is automatically given. We worked out the position they must have been in to reach the one shown. By having those three steps we had the basis of a dance to work from. And then we looked at those strange garlands of dancers in *The Worship of the Golden Calf* and repeated the process.

In the rehearsal rooms we kept a copy of Anthony Blunt's *Catalogue Raisonnée* or, as we learned to call it after his arrest, the *Catalogue Traisonnée*. The singers consulted it and found themselves falling into these postures, so much so that they assumed them instinctively and would greet each other in Poussin gestures as they got on buses or met in the street. I carefully grouped people in order to satisfy those requirements for *contrapposto* which existed in Renaissance paintings. If a figure was facing in one direction, the person adjacent to them had to face in the opposite direction; this meant that there was always a balance of backs with the arms in reciprocal positions. Then, from these positions we derived a choreography for the actions, even when there was no explicit dance. To begin with the cast were rather baffled by the idea, but they soon found it useful as it gave them a framework and a physical metre for their movements. The rehearsal period took four weeks and the final effect on stage was very beautiful.

*Così fan tutte* is another eighteenth-century opera where I followed a similar zig-zag course of exploration to find a formula for both the setting and the look of the characters. Here again there is a traditional precedent, a canonical version of the opera, which involves a lot of panniered dresses, trellis work, and maples. This opera is now taken more seriously than it would have been thirty years ago, when it was regarded as a delicious, artificial romp, but the change in attitude has not gone far enough. I returned to the period of composition to discover what the opera might have been expressing at a rather deeper level in eighteenth-century thought. I had always been struck by the similarity between certain scenes in *Così* and ones found in Jane Austen's novels – themes of sense and sensibility, of sentiment and sentimentality. The device of dressing

*John Stephens as Don Alfonso in the St Louis Festival Opera's 1982 production of* Così fan tutte

*Don Alfonso's eighteenth-century rationalism is usually overshadowed by a waggish misogyny. But if one takes his role as philosopher seriously he can exercise a much more prudent and dignified function in the opera. But after three productions of the work, I am shocked to find that I have overlooked a meddlesome cruelty in the character, comparable in some ways to the Duke of Dark Corners in* Measure for Measure. *How will he come out in my fourth subsequent performance?*

Così fan tutte *at the Kent Opera in 1975*

*In my first production of* Così fan tutte, *the staging was determined by Robert Rosenblum's insistence that late eighteenth-century artists squashed the action into a shallow rectangle that lay parallel to the picture plane. Critics missed the pictorial appearance of the Bay of Naples and claimed that Mozart's music demanded this alluring backdrop. Until my third production of the opera, I resisted this demand and it was only when I put the opera on television that a realistic Vesuvius first made its delayed appearance. Not because I had come to my senses by then but because the photographic realism of the medium now made such a landscape inevitable.*

up in order to discover an identity that emerges only with masquerade appears both in *Così* and *Mansfield Park*. There was an august seriousness about this link that I thought made it worth explaining, but to do so I had to look for the figure in the carpet, the diagram, which would solve my problems. *Così* must have struck many people as a work of great dramatic symmetry, and too often this has been represented merely ornamentally in order to arrive at a staging. But the symmetry is much more than a designer's aid, it is part of the moral purpose of the work. What emerges in the opera is a symmetrical format with two couples disposed around an axis. The latter is provided by two opposing figures, Don Alfonso representing Reason, and Despina representing Nature. The two couples revolve around this axis, and the men discover themselves by going through the process of pretending to be someone else.

Recently, women in particular have objected to the opera because it seems to disparage the two girls and make them into fools. This view overlooks the extent to which the young men are made to look foolish. In spite of the fact that they seem to be the active protagonists in the masquerade they are not in control. When assuming disguise they do not realize the extent to which this will release aspects of their characters that are never acknowledged in their official guises. The men are caught up and caught out by the metamorphosis, and in the second act, there is a strange development. While pretending to make love in disguise to their opposite partners, Ferrando and Guglielmo begin to discover the uncontrollable and unforeseen fact that they are in love with the partner they have chosen to dupe and have themselves become victims. They grow jealous in relation to the partner who they discover to be betraying them, and also feel love for the partner to whom they have decided to appear to pretend to make love. They are just as much the dupes of Don Alfonso's experiment as the two women who act in ignorance of the wager.

Too often, the notion of an 'old philosopher' is taken at its face value and Alfonso is made into a waggish, lorgnette-wielding figure who simply sets up the wager as an old cynic. I have always seen him as a genuine eighteenth-century philosopher, a mixture of Diderot and Voltaire, and this means that the opera then becomes an experiment with human nature. In the first scene, to show him as a philosopher and not a joker, I had him appear at a table covered with books and classical references – the drawings of Sir William Hamilton's Neapolitan Collections, some of Galvani's early experiments on animal electricity, and there might be a mesmeric tub in his room. He is interested in all these scientific and intellectual developments of the Enlightenment. The view that ultimately all human beings are the same because all individuals partake in the nature of Man is an eighteenth-century idea. It follows that if there is any escape from a basic human nature it is achieved only by acknowledging those parts of oneself that cannot be altered. If we behave as if we are in total control of ourselves, we are always deluded. I have always imagined Alfonso as having the mind of a psychoanalyst and an eighteenth-century experimental scientist – the action of the opera is, in his eyes, a serious rational experiment.

I took the mesmeric sequence at the end of Act One very seriously although it is usually played as comedy using magnets and tricks. Mesmerism itself was performed with serious intention using a bucket, or tub, into which iron bars were set while the participants sat around as if at a seance. In some strange way the mesmerism has a curious magical significance in the opera. It is nearly always played as farce, a trick used by the young men to engage the sympathies of the girls so that they can pursue their suit more effectively. But the mesmerism itself can be seen as a symbol of renewal, and the mesmeric tub assumes an almost baptismal significance – it is as if those involved experience not only a remedy but a regeneration. There is a sense in which the participants of the mesmeric seance undergo a secular baptism and re-birth, both the young men and the young women are transformed by it and everything that then occurs is magic. It is a pivotal moment as all four characters start to change their views, but its power and drama can be conveyed only if mesmerism is taken seriously. There are very good engravings of the practice from which the scene can be reconstructed. It is interesting that Mozart had his first opera sponsored by Mesmer when he was nine. *Bastien und Bastienne* was performed in Mesmer's garden. This evidently left an impression, and here is a back-handed tribute to his original sponsor that must be treated seriously if it is not to become an excuse for a lot of facetious theatrical horseplay.

There is always the question of where *Così* takes place. On the stage it is traditionally set near the Bay of Naples. But the drama on the stage does not literally occur anywhere – it takes effect only in the dramatic space assigned to it by the work. In deciding on the shape and size of the stage space, I was prompted by the work of Robert Rosenblum. In his book *Transformations in Late Eighteenth Century Art* he discusses the peculiarities of the neo-classical space – the space that began to assert itself in pictures after about 1770. This first appears in Vien's famous picture *The Seller of Cupids* and culminates in the paintings of David, in which there is a gradual foreshortening of the depth of picture. Whereas Baroque space is characteristically deep, dramatic and turbulent, and Rococo space is voluminous and filled with swirling, unintelligible draperies, the Neo-Classical space quietens the movement, narrowing the fore and aft so that most of the action is confined to a rectangular platform that lies parallel to the picture plane. On stage we created a back wall similar to those curtained-off back walls you find in the paintings of David, where the eyeline is arrested before it reaches these intelligible

The Magnetism *drawn by Sergent*

*Mesmer had abandoned magnets long before he became famous as the founder of medical hypnotism, and ten years before Mozart wrote* Così fan tutte *he was already famous for using the magnetic bucket which I introduced on to the stage for the first time in my St Louis production of the opera.*

THE MAGNETISM.

depths at the back, and the action is confined to a well-lit platform in the foreground. I used a wall pierced by two classical doorways, which again emphasized the symmetries of the entrances and exits so that it was almost as if the characters were coming and going like figures in a weather vane.

The cast played in a frieze-like space, which I suppose reached its ultimate reduction in art with the space of Jasper Ware by Wedgwood, where white classical figures are set against a Jasper background. Too often *Così* is cast in a Rococo form when in fact it is already Neo-Classical. These ideas for one setting enabled me to emphasize the curious and otherwise unbelievable artificiality of the piece; by doing so I was no longer constrained by attempting realism.

Directing *Così* for television introduces special problems as the medium demands a kind of realism that jars with opera's recognizable artificiality. Even when *Rigoletto* was given a rather realistic twentieth-century setting on stage it had a sharply curtailed realism. I would have found it very difficult to have gone into the streets of New York to direct *Rigoletto*. In a realistic setting, the absurdity, not so much of the plot but of what people say to one another, becomes apparent. That sort of realism is inappropriate even to something that is written in its own period. *West Side Story*, for example, is wonderful on the stage, but does not succeed as a film. In the theatre we see it as a realistic reminder whereas the film attempts a slavish re-creation of actuality. In television, it is rather more difficult to represent a flattened Neo-Classical space because you cannot keep your camera still looking down the mid-line at right-angles to a fixed space. Once there is a camera, it is almost always required to move, and this destroys the necessity of viewing from a fixed point on which Neo-Classical format depends. Directing *Così* for television I found myself forced to introduce the realism on which film insists whether showing Shakespeare or Mozart.

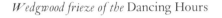

*Wedgwood frieze of the* Dancing Hours

*Some day I would like to take Rosenblum's ideas about reducing the dramatic depth of the stage to its logical conclusion and produce Gluck's* Orfeo, *perhaps in the two-dimensional format suggested by a Wedgwood frieze.*

## II: ix

At the end of Part I, I suggested that the act of removing a work from the medium for which it was written – the stage – and transplanting it into another presents impossible problems for the director. Televising Shakespeare or opera is not a natural extension of their afterlife but an exercise in media cross-dressing that forces the director into a curious compromise. This happens because film demands and enforces a more realistic representation than in the theatre. Television or cinema requires a replete realistic image, and the director has to represent details that could be overlooked in the theatre.

To begin to understand why this happens I want to examine again how watching a theatrical spectacle on a screen, whether large or small, differs from the experience and the understood code of representation employed in live theatre. I have already pointed out how in any representation there are rules of correspondence between the thing that is doing the representing and the world that is being represented. The reader, spectator or viewer has to be introduced to the conventions so that he or she recognizes different levels of representation – which features are to be seen as actively and literally representing and which are not. Let me explain by imagining for a moment a card-sized photograph. We know perfectly well that the one thing that is not pictorial about it is the size. No one pretends that a 3 by 4 inch colour transparency is a picture of a 3 by 4 inch view. Yet in practically every other respect – colour, tone and proportion – it is faithful. If there are variations in colour in any stretch of two or three millimetres, up or down, then we read that as being a representation of a corresponding variation in colour up and down with the seam. The picture is consistent from top to bottom and from left to right. But if we now move into an art gallery we will see paintings in which this consistency is not observed.

In the Frankfurt Gallery, there is a picture by Mantegna showing the Good Thief watched by two spectators at the Crucifixion. The pictoriality of the body of the thief, the loin cloth and the timber of the cross, is almost perfect – like a photograph. If there is a variation in the tone across the shin, we are expected to read it as a fairly faithful representation of the variation in tone of the shin of the thief. But the cross, the thief and the spectators are displayed against a background of burnished gold foil. Quite suddenly, as we look beyond the contours of the thief and his cross, we see gold, which we are not expected to read as being a representation of a gold background. Nor, within the variations of the gold foil, are we meant to read some corresponding variations in the sky beyond. Here is a rule of representation that says that certain objects are representatively displayed while others, the sky for example, are not, and are shown in purely diagrammatic form.

This happens in the theatre when there is what is misleadingly called abstract scenery. On seeing a very beautifully carved doorframe suspended in space, we do not assume that there is no wall. We accept that the set is being pictorial with regard to the proportions of the door frame but not with regard to the wall surfaces. The audience does not read it as a house with a very peculiar type of furnishing in which window frames hang in space. But in what sense can stage scenery be said to represent? Perhaps I can begin to answer this by giving an example from a production of *Measure for Measure* in which the scenery consisted of a row of doors nailed together without any stretches of wall to separate them. This row of doors did *not* represent a row of doors. At the moment when any one door in the façade was doing the job of representing a door, none of the others was doing so. On the contrary, for door A to represent a door successfully all the others had to sacrifice any claim to be representing doors. If they had not, it would have made nonsense of the door-representing claims of door A.

It is important to realize, and perhaps unnecessary to say, that representing a door is nothing that the scenic door does itself. It is an identity that the spectator assigns to the door. He or she sets it up as a door representation, and in doing so withholds door-representing recognition from all the other doors, extending 'blank wall' representing status to them instead. When any given door is doing the job of representing one, it does so by virtue of its detailed resemblance to an actual door. So its hinges, its locks and handles are all meant to be taken as hinges, locks and handles. But, when the same door is later doing its representational duty as a section of blank wall, the spectator is required to overlook the same features and to disregard them. How odd it seems, that features that were exerting detailed representational functions at one moment appear to stand down from representational duty ready to resume it again when the door of which they are a part resumes its duty of representing a door.

An object can represent something else but in doing so it may have difficulties. These arise (a) because of having too few features or properties that correspond to the features or properties of what it is that it is representing, or (b) because it has too many features of its own that the spectator may have some difficulty in disregarding. This raises another question. If we say that it is necessary to disregard certain features of a representation in order to let it function as one, there must nevertheless be some aspect of its appearance to which we attend when conferring the status of representation upon it. So, for example, when each of the other doors is participating in the representation of the blank wall, we must disregard each of their handles and hinges whilst attending to their collective height and width. In this case, the representation is *ad hoc* in the sense that we are forced to take it as we find it, and when it changes its representational role, from being a door to being a stretch of wall, the

**Measure for Measure,** *the National Theatre, 1974*

*Due to budgetary restrictions I had to improvise the set for* Measure for Measure *using doors taken from a building site. Although this setting was representational in that the various doors referred to the entrance and exits mentioned in the text, the overall style was dictated by the now fashionable idiom of an empty space within which an action could occur without having to be slavishly pictorial.*

spectators have to do the work of agreeing to disregard those features of its appearance that now contradict its claim. In most cases, of course, the representing item is custom built to fulfil its representational role. It is designed to include some, but not necessarily all of the features that resemble what it represents, and conversely that exclude some, though not necessarily all of the features for which there is no corresponding feature in the represented object. In some representations there is a clear and completely intelligible distinction between those properties which have representational status, and those which do not. In the example of a scale model of a building made out of boxwood, it is clearly understood that the relationship between the dimensions is mappable on to the relationship between the corresponding dimensions of the building. The absolute size of the model is to be disregarded, as is the colour and the texture of its wooden surface. But, in some representations the segregation is not so readily legible.

In Trevor Nunn's production of *Nicholas Nickleby*, for example, men sometimes doubled as women – as minor characters anyway – but no attempt was made to eliminate, or even diminish, those features which visibly contradicted their representation. The faces of the actors were often bearded and, unless one made the improbable assumption that these actors were representing bearded women, one had to disregard the beards and attend instead to the skirts and bonnets by virtue of which they were resembling, presumably, unbearded women. But it is over-simplifying the situation to say that the beards were simply disregarded while the skirts and bonnets took precedence. The aesthetic assumption of this type of theatrical representation depends, to some extent, on taking note of the discrepancy between the bearded actors and the unbearded women that they are representing. This is the theatrical equivalent of Wollheim's two-fold thesis *vis-à-vis* the type of scene that he insists is appropriate to representations. The spectator is not expected altogether to disregard those aspects of the representing medium for which there is no counterpart in the represented object. On the contrary, he is also expected to see and register the medium's non-representational, and even contradictory, properties. In some cases of pictorial representation, the representational properties of the format may be spatially separated from the less representational ones. So, a room may be represented somewhat patchily, with furniture represented by actual chairs and tables, whereas the walls and even the doors are represented in a more relaxed fashion simply by panels of gauze. These will represent the relevant surfaces simply by virtue of their dimensions and as much colour and texture as is needed to represent the fact that something prevents the gaze from seeing beyond. The viewer takes these noncommittal areas as walls, without 'seeing' walls in them, instead he fills in the missing features for himself.

There are stage representations in which there is so little visible resemblance between the so-called scenery and the represented scene that one might overlook its representational quality altogether and say that it was non-representational. But, of course, there is no such thing as totally non-representational scenery. There is always some respect in which the scenery represents the scene, only it may, as Stephen Palmer points out in his essay 'On Representation', not be quite straightforward and can even be illegible unless one is introduced to the convention. An example is this: on the Elizabethan stage, there is nothing that even remotely represents scenery. What you have is standing architecture ready to do representational service as long as the spectator agrees to disregard the positive features that conflict, and to fill in what is conspicuous by its absence. As far as scenery goes, the most reduced form of representation is one in which there is no visual information about background at all, so that the back wall represents neither a wall nor a mountain, nor infinite space and is to be taken as the back wall of the stage. Nevertheless, in this radically, or rather systematically, non-representational format there are still traces of legible representationality. On the Elizabethan stage the fact that someone is placed above the other actors in the balcony means no more than the fact that the character is higher, and the spectator is not expected to be able to read the actual height from the scenic height. When Richard advises Bolingbroke to come down to the base court he would, on the Elizabethan stage, be no more than three or four feet above Bolingbroke. The same dramatic effect could have been achieved by a much smaller difference in scenic height. Children can achieve just the same effect by standing on a bench and shouting, 'I'm the king of the castle', and as Palmer remarks, the predicate above could just as well be represented by being scenically below – as long as you understood the conventions. What matters in a representational system is the rule that determines the mapping from the representing world to the represented one. There is no such thing as a representation, only a representational system that relates one world to another by a function or mapping.

As in photography, film is traditionally pictorial from top to bottom and from side to side. It does not suddenly lapse into pictoriality when it shows one particular type of object, and as a film director you are forced to represent everything. When there are hyper-realistic stage settings, as in Chekhov where the stage scenery is often a reproduction of a real room, this differs from film in that it is shown inside an architectural framework that belongs to a theatre, whereas the architectural framework of the screen is overlooked. A television or film screen provides a window on to a world that is supposed to extend beyond the visible screen, and has the optics of reality. The audience sitting in a theatre knows perfectly well that however realistic the world on the stage appears to be it does not extend beyond the proscenium arch.

I want to return briefly to the distinction I drew between the theatre and screen in Part I where I wrote that in the theatre the frame separating the audience from the action is shared by actor and spectator – it is common to both. In contrast, the edge of a television screen is an arbitrary frame that excludes the spectator and separates us from the acting space of the performance. The screen is an extremely awkward interface between the viewer and the spectacle on screen from which he is conspicuously absent. While a theatre audience is part of the performance, in a television or cinema production the audience is strangely annihilated by being reduced to a pair of eyes.

A movie screen has no features, it is simply where the picture stops and darkness takes over. The audience is made up of disembodied spectators looking through a rectangular hole at a world that extends beyond the frame. In the theatre the spectator is part of an *embodied* audience whose attention can move from one part of the stage to another while remaining aware of the panoramic spectacle. When the eye shifts to one side of the stage we are fully conscious visually of the part of the stage that our gaze has left, and that we can return our eyes to it. In film our gaze is usurped by the eye of the camera, and the successive cuts and sample of the scene the film-maker has decided to present. This is not necessarily frustrating, and when cinema is *not* being parasitic on a work that has had a previous existence in another medium, it is the best possible way of telling a story. But when something has been written for the stage this coercion has certain regrettable features, as the director is often forced to give unrepresentative samplings of what is happening.

In the case of Shakespeare, and above all of Chekhov, the behaviour of everyone, even the silent listeners, is just as much part of the drama as the behaviour of the speaker. Psychologists talk of the uptake of understanding, and this means that the behaviour of the listener, as he or she begins to understand what is being spoken, is an essential part of the action. In film, the director has to take little polls of opinion about the speaker's speech by doing reaction shots. These sample what the listeners are thinking but like a poll that is said to be representative, this device provides only a rough sample. We are not allowed to see the continuous uptake of understanding on the part of the listener who is shown only at certain crucial moments. When something particularly shocking or revealing is said, the director cuts back to the look of surprise, or shock, or affection on the face of the listening character. In this way, an enormous amount of the dramatic tension is lost, although it allows the camera to move closer both to the speaker and the listener, so heightening the intimacy between characters, or between the audience and an actor speaking a soliloquy. This affects opera and Shakespeare, on the large or small screen, in slightly different ways.

Opera on television is afflicted by very peculiar drawbacks of its own, and the end result is often an uneven mixture – neither fish nor fowl nor good red herring. The television camera is, in effect, making a series of optical boreholes through the theatrical event in shots that eliminate the periphery and may concentrate on two people singing. In some strange way this diminishes, and often destroys completely, the peculiar theatrical quality that is written into and constitutive of the work. If the cameras are pulled back in an attempt to restore the panoramic spectacle to the screen, the viewer is distanced and senses this alienating remoteness as the image decreases in size. The experience always makes me feel as though I am looking at a theatrical spectacle through the wrong end of a telescope. The television director is caught between two equally unconvivial formats: the remote and distant Lilliputian image of a wide shot; and the unrepresentative and unrealistic close shot, which also exposes quite repulsive detail of dental fillings and wobbling tongues.

When I directed *The Beggar's Opera* for television I had to make various adjustments which I felt were more legitimate with a work that was written as an anti-opera, an attack on the prevailing Italian opera of that time. It is a play in which people break briefly and rapidly into snatches of song and is quite unlike any other opera. Rather than filming a stage version, I staged a version in a studio but even so I do not think it was successful. *The Beggar's Opera* is undoubtedly at its best when staged in its rightful environment, the theatre, and although I have recently worked on a production of *Così fan tutte* for television I already have misgivings.

Having directed *Così* twice for the stage I feel much more constrained in a television production for several reasons. It is very hard to settle the level of realism which is (a) appropriate to the television and (b) appropriate to the artificial art form of opera. There are also the very complicated problems of what I can show when more than one person is singing. It is quite easy to film single arias, as long as you do not get too close to the face and give a dental shot of the mouth. Similarly duets present little difficulty, but with quartets and, in the case of Mozart, sextets, it is extremely hard to angle the camera in a way that does justice to the fact that everyone is singing at the same time. In order to include six people you have to pull the camera so far back that the size of the figures is very unfavourable and dissipates the dramatic tension.

*Così fan tutte* is a highly contrived, rather diagrammatic plot, and although it is said to take place in Naples, the representation of place is very artificial. On stage you might have a painted backcloth where no attempt is made to delude the audience into thinking that it is anything other than a very realistic piece of scenery. The audience is never tempted to think that it is looking at Naples and this is neither a drawback nor a criticism of the scenery. In the case of *Così* for television I thought there might be a way of representing the artificiality by the choice of materials. My starting point for the production had to be an overall decision about the extent to which what is shown on the screen is or is not representative of what there might be in reality. Most of the action occurs in a house, and if you slavishly re-create all the textures of an actual room you are, by that token, forced to represent the Bay of Naples as seen through the window very realistically. To try to avoid this incongruity I made a series of signs to set the level at which the realism and the artificiality were to be established throughout the work, and from back to front of each scene – this at least was my aim. The room was made entirely out of polished plywood: all the mouldings, all the details and architectural features, were made out of very deeply grained wood, so that it looked rather like the details of the Farnese Theatre in Parma where everything is made out of unpainted wood. Then through the french windows and beyond the balcony was the Bay of Naples made out of blue gauze, which extended out to the sky-cloth. Set into it were marquetry representations of the mountains and bays so that the image resembled a piece of exploded marquetry. The set created a timber world from back to front – quite literally a wooden frame for the action. And yet through the eye of the camera my efforts to set the level of artificiality were soon revealed to be fruitless. The effect of the wooden frame on screen, with the help of remarkable lighting, is extremely realistic, and in watching the production take shape in the studio I realized very quickly that the end result would have to take into account the realism of the image. When I watch this production I begin to believe that it was shot on location the effect is so startlingly convincing.

In the cinema, films like Losey's *Don Giovanni* and the recent Rosi version of *Carmen* are in a strange way absurd despite – or perhaps because of – their apparent success as pieces of very attractive and seductive realism. Cinema distorts opera in all sorts of subtle ways. One vital element is removed, the visible presence of the orchestra. In the opera house the faint glow from the pit, and the occasional waving of the conductor's arm, intervenes between the audience and the spectacle to act as a horizon stabilizing the level of artificiality the audience is asked to accept. It is also a constant reminder that we are in the presence of an orchestral performance. In a film when music is simply on the track, it suddenly sounds like *Mozak* and is reduced to existing as a musical accompaniment to the drama. The orchestra, conspicuous by its absence, becomes very audible as we wonder where it is hiding. At the same time the viewer becomes aware of omissions that make the incongruous sight of opera singers acting in realistic settings, and the open air, even more disturbing. There are glaring omissions in the acoustics of outdoors, for example. In order to make the sound musically orthodox it has to be given the sound balances appropriate to a concert hall. This means that it has a volume that is totally inconsistent with the acoustic that should prevail in the visible scene. We know perfectly well that if someone was singing in a piazza their sound would be strangely and thinly dispersed as it dissipates in the open air. Similarly if someone moves to the back of the square, or the top of a hill, their voice should diminish, but there is no diminution, the voices remain equally near, loud and clear. As the music – both the singing and the orchestra – is recorded afterwards, we are aware that the singers are miming. The result is that although there is almost synchrony, and lip-synch is preserved, there is a strangely almost visible contraceptive membrane between the audience watching and the sound of the singing. The lips are moving in time to the music but do not seem to be producing the sound. It is almost as if the faces are afflicted with a strange sort of dental anaesthetic, and as a spectator I have the sense that they are not feeling the buzz of their lips as they sing. Similarly the physical effort of singing is not visible because they are not in full voice on the set. The result is that the strain of singing – which is, after all, part of the drama and intensity of opera – is lost. If we cannot see the blood rising in the neck and the physical effects of singing we are subliminally aware of an awkward discrepancy. Film cannot avoid this, and the result is a concert performance of the opera accompanied by a synchronous spectacle. Synchrony may be a necessary condition but it is by no means a sufficient one, because there are certain very small but consistent signs of simultaneity that are lacking, even with synchrony. Although the sound and the actions appear to correspond, certain significant things are conspicuous by their absence if not synchronized at the time of recording.

Drama, particularly Shakespeare, which I have directed many times for television, presents the director with an equally unrealistic task. When I directed *King Lear*, I soon discovered that a bare setting, which is intelligible in a theatre, is not as readable on television. Setting it in darkness, which I did, does not solve the problem as I still had to intimate architecture in order to make clear the distinction between civilization and nature. In both the first and second television versions the painter I turned to for inspiration was Caravaggio. His work has a turbulent, dramatic lighting where flesh and clothes are suddenly and fitfully illuminated. His painting *The Calling of St Matthew* shows figures seated at a table suddenly arrested by the light cast by Jesus pointing his hand towards Matthew. The light just catches the edge of the window sill, which tells you that it is an interior scene. Looking at his work enabled me to find a way to preserve darkness while at the same time allowing myself the luxury of some representation of architectural placing by suggestion and light.

Representing nature and the open air is extremely difficult, and in the storm scene I found myself forced to realize the actual meteorology. Just as we can look at a painting without being disturbed by a gold-foil background so a theatre audience will accept the acoustic equivalent of

*Caravaggio*, The Calling of St Matthew

*In order to satisfy the technical demands of shooting with
several cameras at the same time, television lighting tends to
be frontal and monotonous. As soon as you begin to dramatize
the illumination, as Caravaggio did, the lighting demands of
one camera are frustrated by those of the other and vice versa.
So the luxury of making a scene look dramatic by throwing
light in from one direction is purchased at the time-consuming
expense of shooting the scene with separate lighting set-ups for
each angle.*

the foil standing in for the sky — a thunder sheet visibly shaken on stage as it was in Peter Brook's production. There can be no equivalent on television and I managed only by fitful emulation of lightning flashes in the darkness. The morning after the storm also presents problems as the landscape must be shown in daylight. On a stage the audience will realize that a brightly lit blank space represents outside daylight but because the television audience is not present, and is looking into a possible world, any shortfalls in that world's reality become unacceptable. This is a crucial problem for any director filming a stage production.

As in opera one of the most frustrating problems was how to present fairly large groups of people. Encounters between two people are much easier, and I shoot them so that both heads are visible rather than focusing on one face and then cutting away to the listener. In a two-shot the development of the listener's understanding is just as visible as the development of the speaker's thesis. With rhetorical verse, it is a great disadvantage if you have to cut the actor off from the subliminal flow of reaction given by the live audience in the theatre. Shakespeare's plays, and operas, are designed for embodied audiences. The kind of distortions and problems I have outlined are unavoidable when film simply adopts such works, and becomes an eavesdropper and invisible eye on a theatrical event. It is only by actively adapting such works to the point of transformation that some of these problems can be avoided by the film director.

## II: x

*Never, as long as I live, shall I allow anyone to illustrate me, because: the most beautiful literary description is eaten up by the most wretched drawing. As soon as a figure is fixed by the pencil, it loses that character of generality, that harmony with a thousand known objects which makes the reader say: 'I've seen that' or 'That must be so'. A woman in a drawing looks like one woman, that's all. The idea is closed, complete, and every sentence becomes useless, whereas a written woman makes one dream of a thousand women. Therefore, since this is a question of aesthetics, I absolutely refuse any kind of illustration.*

Gustave Flaubert

*Anything that relieves responsible prose of the duty of being, while placed before us, good enough, interesting enough and, if the question be of picture, pictorial enough,* above all *in itself, does it the worst of services, and may well inspire in the lover of literature certain lively questions as to the future of that institution.*

Henry James

It is difficult to decide whether Henry James actually approved of the illustrations that his publisher persuaded him to accept for the complete edition of his works. As the creator of figures and scenes that 'are as nought from the moment they fail to become visible appearances', he was reassured 'to see such powers as he possessed approved and registered by the springing of such fruit from his seed'. At the same time, he regarded illustration as a dangerously competitive process, and as the author of a text 'putting forward illustrative claims by its own intrinsic virtue' he was reluctant to share the responsibility for reducing his reader to a state of hallucination with an illustrator. He accepted pictures, therefore, on the understanding 'that they would be expressions of no particular thing in the text' and, since he ruled out any attempt to keep dramatic step with the events represented in the text, the illustrations were to remain 'at most small pictures of our "set" stage with the actors left out'.

With the invention of cinematography it is no longer possible for a novelist to secure an agreement of this sort. It would be nonsensical to leave the actors out of a film, and the idea of a movie that failed to keep some sort of dramatic step with its suggested matter is a contradiction in terms. Instead of supplementing the text, moving pictures threaten to replace them altogether, and unless the author forbids the adaptation of his own work the best he can hope for is the right to veto anything that gets it wrong. But this, of course, is not the point at issue. When James objected to illustration it was not because he thought that the artist would get it wrong but because he recognized that there was no conceivable way a pictorial representation could *get it right*. Apart from the fact that language can express meanings that are inexpressible in any other medium, there is an important sense in which even its visual effects are distinctive. If we leave aside the peculiar resources of tense, metaphor, irony and indirect speech, for which, as I hope to show, there are no conceivable counterparts in illustration, the experience of *visualizing* something, as the result of reading a *description* of it, is altogether different from *seeing* it in the form of an actual picture.

Unfortunately this distinction is not always given the credit it deserves. On the contrary, we consistently blur it by thinking of the imagination as if it were a display of internal pictures. As Gilbert Ryle points out, when someone says that he is visualizing something, his nursery perhaps, 'We are tempted to construe his remark to mean that he is somehow contemplating not his nursery, but another visible object, namely a picture of his nursery, only not a photograph or an oil painting, but some counterpart to a photograph, one made of a different sort of stuff.' The reason why we think like this is as follows. The verb *to see* is transitive, which is another way of saying that we cannot *see* without seeing *something*. We *see* our nursery, or Helvelyn, and as long as the nursery, or Helvelyn, are out there to *be* seen there is no difficulty. But when we *visualize* something or, as we say, 'see' it, there is nothing out there to intercept our gaze. But since we assume that 'seeing' in inverted commas has the same transitive requirements as *seeing*, without them, we find ourselves stipulating the existence of a substitute, something that resembles the absent object without actually being it. Hence *mental* pictures seen not by the real eye but by the mind's eye.

The invention of movies and television allowed us to extend this pictorial metaphor so that when someone claims to be visualizing the scenes that are represented in a novel we are also tempted to assume that he is running a film or some counterpart to a film in the privacy of his own head. The problem is that if we do subscribe to the theory that visualizing a description is another way of looking at a film version of it, then a real film ought to do just as well, if not better, and the acceptability of any particular version would boil down to a straightforward question of whether it had *got it right*. But there is more to it than that. As Ryle points out, the fact that the cognate concepts of picturing, visualizing or 'seeing' are both useful and intelligible does not entail the existence of internal images which we look at. In fact there are many good reasons for rejecting the idea of internal images.

The most obvious distinction between pictures in front of the mind's eye and pictures in front of the real eye is brought out, indirectly, by Richard Wollheim in an essay he appended to the new edition of *Art and its Objects*. Although he does not explicitly address himself to the nature of mental images, the argument that he develops about physical representation inescapably draws our attention to the peculiarities of mental ones.

He recognizes that there is a form of seeing that is appropriate to representation, and identifies a requirement that he calls the two-fold thesis. This can be applied to representational objects, such as paintings, drawings, photos and, of course, movies, but is interestingly inapplicable to the pictorial experiences of the mind's eye. What the two-fold thesis says, in short, is that when I look at a physical representation, a picture for example, my attention must be distributed between two things: the medium that affords or sustains the representation and whatever it is that the representation shows. So that in looking at Rembrandt's *Polish Rider* for example, there are two intentional objects. I can see the young horseman, but I can also see Rembrandt's paintwork. This disjunction is analogous to the one previously pointed out by Gombrich, when he distinguished between seeing canvas on the one hand and nature on the other. According to Gombrich, however, the seeing of one actually precluded the possibility of seeing the other. To reinforce this claim he draws an analogy with the ambiguous figures, such as the famous duck/rabbit illustration, in which the seeing of one aspect requires the complete extinction of the alternative. Wollheim argues that Gombrich has given us an inappropriate and misleading analogy because, while we would all acknowledge that seeing the duck rules out the possibility of seeing the rabbit, the proper appreciation of a painting requires the two aspects to interpenetrate rather than alternate. In Wollheim's view, the painterly virtues of an artist such as Manet would be unrecognizable if, in looking at his pictures, we had to alternate visual attention between the material features on the painting and the object that the painting was representing.

In one sense this disagreement between Wollheim and Gombrich does not really influence my argument, although the question of optical illusions is relevant and I will return to it later. Wollheim's two-fold thesis reveals a distinction with regard to vision that seems hard, perhaps impossible, to apply to mental images. It is impossible to attach any significant meaning to the idea of switching one's attention from the object of one's imaginings to the medium that affords them their visibility.

It may seem unfair to compare mental images with paintings in which the brushwork is such a conspicuous part of the medium. After all, we would hardly expect mental pictures to betray visible signs of handiwork. A more reasonable comparison might be made with paintings in which the artist has systematically effaced all sign of his brushwork and by means of liquid glazes provides the viewer with an apparently unmediated view of the object itself. Yet Wollheim's disjunction still holds true, because close examination almost immediately reveals the inherent properties of the medium no matter how inconspicuous the artist tries to make it. Impalpable and invisible though the painted surface might seem, there is always some point at which the visible artefact hosting the illusion becomes self-evident to the spectator. Even when the representation is made vanishingly diaphanous, as it is in the case of a faithful colour transparency, there is always some perceptual procedure capable of driving a wedge between the picture and the objects that are to be seen *in* it. The most diaphanous representation shows non-pictorial properties in ways that are inconceivable in the case of mental images. Apart from the blemishes that one learns to overlook in a photograph for example, it has a determinate size which is an inescapably visible property of the format but lacks the slightest pictorial significance.

We may see Helvelyn in a 3 by 4 inch snapshot just as clearly as if it was shown in a huge 15 by 20 foot projection. The Helvelyn that we are seeing has not changed size. While it makes perfectly good sense to ask how large the *picture* is, such a question is completely meaningless when it comes to picturing Helvelyn in our mind's eye. We cannot ask the question: how large does the picture look? We can ask only the question: how large does Helvelyn seem?

To summarize these points: although mental images and photos are like one another in that they afford us visions of things that are not literally *there*, they differ in an important respect. The intentional objects that we see in a picture are afforded by something that *is* literally present, an intermediate physical object with all sorts of determinate properties of its own. Some of these properties enable it to fly under a flag of pictorial convenience, and not necessarily one flag. They may be such that they afford mutually exclusive visions. Three intersecting lines can host the image of the inside corner of a room or the outside corner of a cube. A symmetrical pattern of black and white patches can yield the impression of a white vase seen against a black background or two black profiles facing one another against a white background. What makes these visual experiences so striking is the fact that the alternation of aspects is visibly afforded by something that is neither, but merely a series of patches on the page. And even when the visible properties of the hosting format are used up so that they vanish without perceptual residue into one another, the viewer is still left with the subliminal assurance that there is a non-pictorial substrate shared in turn by each of his alternate visions.

For obvious reasons the visibility of the hosting medium is inversely proportional to the number of properties that it lends to each or any of the visions it affords us. In the case of a natural object such as a cloud only a few of its visible properties are on loan to alternative appearances since most of them are tied up in representing the cloud in its official capacity. This is the reason why Hamlet has such an uphill struggle persuading Polonius to see whales, weasels and camels. Admittedly Polonius has more urgent things on his mind at that moment, but if we compare that scene with the one in *King Lear* when Edgar, in the guise of Poor Tom, persuades his blind father to see the view from a non-existent clifftop, we

*When this format is presented to the physical eye, vases and faces mysteriously alternate with one another but the mind's eye cannot accommodate this optical illusion. One merely sees the intentional object of one's imagining.*

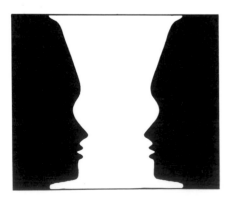

immediately recognize that seeing absent things with the naked eye, even in such an amorphous and unpromising candidate as a cloud, is quite unlike seeing absent things with the mind's eye where there is nothing, formed or unformed, in which to entertain the vision.

If Edgar's commentary works – and Gloucester's absurd behaviour a moment later shows that it must have done because he falls flat on his face on the grass – it seems reasonable, although not necessary, to assume that he has in some way seen the cliff or at least the vertiginous view. It is not necessary to assume that he has visualized the view because it is possible to grasp the point of a visual account without having to go through the labour of envisioning it. In fact, when Francis Galton asked his friends to recall the appearance of their breakfast table, he was surprised to find that some of them could itemize and list everything that was on the table, but refused to concede that they had a visual image of what they were listing. I will return to this issue because it has obvious relevance to the problem of how a novel is represented in the reader's imagination and whether in fact it is visualized at all.

Meanwhile let us assume that Gloucester does co-operatively visualize the scene, which it seems reasonable to assume that Edgar himself has to do in order to create such a vivid, visual description of it. This last consideration was the reason why on the three occasions I have staged *King Lear*, I have always asked the actor playing Edgar to close his eyes on the line '*How fearful/And dizzy 'tis to cast one's eyes so low*' to emphasize the helpfulness of extinguishing the vision of present things when trying to visualize the appearance of absent ones. This is reinforced when Edgar can be seen to open his eyes again with the words '*I'll look no more.*' If our own reaction to Edgar's speech is anything to go by, the vista in his mind's eye is very vivid. I was going to say it springs into existence, and yet that is the very thing that it cannot do because the description is inescapably consecutive.

What sort of visibilia occupied the as yet undescribed parts of the picture? In fact the question of what one imagines half-way through a vivid description is no less problematic than the question of what one sees when it is finished. If mental images are as pictorial as our language about them implies they might be, it should be possible to say something at least about the visible properties of the as yet unmentioned features. If, as we often say, it is left rather vague, why should we be at a loss when it comes to say what the vagueness itself looks like? After all, this is not a problem in the case of real pictures. There are many ways in which pictorial information can be represented vaguely in a picture, and yet it is impossible to equate any of these forms of pictorial vagueness with the so-called vagueness of mental images. Perhaps I can explain this by analysing some of the ways in which real physical pictures can show vagueness.

There is a controversy surrounding one of the most talked-about

paintings in the Royal Academy's 1983 Venetian exhibition – Titian's *Flaying of Marsyas*. It is claimed that the canvas was unfinished, although some experts insist that as far as the idea of finish or conclusion could usefully be applied to Titian's late work the painting is to all intents and purposes complete. In their view it is no less complete than other works of the same period which he was happy to relinquish to his patron, and yet for modern spectators unfamiliar with, or unfriendly to, Titian's later style, it seems incomplete, slapdash and vague, as it is not easy to see all that it supposedly represents. I am not referring to iconographic problems, since these arise in paintings that are more self-evidently finished and detailed, but to the crude perceptual problem of how much visual information you can glean about the various objects that Titian tries to represent. We have to take it on trust, for instance, that Apollo is using a knife rather than a blunt twig to skin the impudent victim, and it is only by referring to Winternitz's essay on the iconography of musical instruments that we can infer just how many strings the viol in the other corner of the picture might have. In other words, the painting is indeterminate with respect to certain features of the objects it represents. And yet the smudginess of the canvas, which seems perceptually hospitable to some and maddeningly noncommittal to others, is at least visible in its own right, as it is, a determinate property of the painted surface. This is something that I cannot imagine in the case of the mental image which does not owe its vagueness to smudginess but to its unmentioned features.

Since I began by raising the question of an unfinished description, perhaps it would be fairer to compare the incipient mental image with a painting that is unarguably incomplete. There is a small panel by Michelangelo in which several figures remain to be painted. They are recognizably blocked in terre-verte and, although it is impossible to say for certain what these expectant silhouettes would have looked like if Michelangelo had finished them, the picture preserves the spatial relationship of both the existing figures and the forthcoming ones in a way that mental images conspicuously do not. A comparable principle applies to mutilated pictures where the absconded fragment is conspicuous by its absence, and the visible properties of the non-pictorial repair afford the viewer a reminder of what might have been. Perceptual excuses like this simply cannot be applied to the supposed vagueness or incompleteness of mental images. It is not a question of poor resolution because although the identity of objects may be lost in a blurred physical picture their spatial relationships are preserved. In the case of mental images it is usually the other way round. On cross examination subjects can often list the items of a scene they have imagined and still make serious mistakes about their relative positions. When items are omitted from the report there is no mention, or indeed experience, of a visibly vacant slot. These findings are so inconsistent with the rules of material

*Michelangelo*, Madonna and Child with the Infant Baptist and Angels

*In conjuring up the image of a remembered scene someone may fail to recall the presence of this or that. But there is no gap in the mental picture. When something is left out of a picture the space that awaits its presence is readily visible.*

images that some people have been led to argue that mental images or mental representations have much more in common with language than pictures. In fact, since the early 1970s when the controversy about mental images became a major issue in the psychological community, a line has been drawn between those who uphold the so-called *imagist* position and those who argue that our mental representations are essentially *propositional* rather than pictorial.

To see exactly what is at stake in this conflict, we have to understand just what the opponents mean when they refer to images and propositions. It is claimed, for example, that images represent objects analogically. This is another way of saying that the structural relationships between their parts correspond to the visible relationships between the parts of the object represented. It is, in other words, a relationship based on visible resemblance, though not necessarily a perfect one. This means that there may be visible discrepancies some of which are intended, and some not. Here are some intentional ones. An architect builds a scale model of a new site and as long as the client makes an intelligent allowance for scale he can identify a visible relationship between the proportions of the model buildings and the proportions of the buildings that will eventually spring up on that site. When the enterprise is complete, he will recognize the model as an image of it by virtue of the fact that there is a one-to-one mapping from points on the model to points on the completed building. In other words, there is a visible resemblance between the two entities. Apart from the question of scale, there may be an equally intelligible discrepancy with respect to colour and texture. The architect may have to persuade the client by showing him a small sample of the textured concrete with which he intends to clad the surface. The image of the projected building may have to be provided in instalments, and it is up to the client to integrate these in his imagination. All the same, both the model and the sample are canonical instances of visual images in the sense that a subset of their visible properties physically resembles a subset of the properties that they are understood to represent.

The upholders of the imagist position insist that mental images represent by virtue of the same principle. And although they laugh off the suggestion that they are sponsoring a theory of pictures in the head, it is rather hard to see exactly why they are not. The experimental evidence that has recently been adduced in favour of the imagist position makes fascinating reading, despite the fact that it is not easy to gain a complete conceptual grasp of the result. As opponents of mental imagery imply, it is possible to explain many of the results without having to rely on the logically embarrassing assumption that the mind's eye is scanning pictorial representations of reality.

Apart from the purely introspective experience of imagery there is evidence that seems to imply that the imagination is visual as it seems to compete for the psychological resources that would otherwise be employed in processing real vision. It has been shown several times that when subjects are asked to retrieve and report certain features of an imagined scene their eyes move as if they were scanning a physical image. We cannot pretend that they are scanning a mental image with their physical eyes, that would be nonsense, but there is, perhaps, a coherent analogy to be made with the conjugate movements of the physical eyes. Everyone knows that the eyes are yoked together to make up a coherent gaze when following a moving object. It is less well known that the synchrony is not the result of both eyes seeing the same object and therefore following it synchronously. If it were, you would expect one eye to stay still as soon as you closed it, whereas of course the movements of both eyes are more or less unimpaired even when one is closed and the other eye is following the object. The blind eye seems to behave as if it were tracking an invisible object, or an object in front of its mental eye. Now it is tempting to argue that something analogous is happening in the case of the eye movements that accompany imagination. (I say analogous because I am not suggesting that the physical eyeballs are synchronized to the paired movements of non-existent eyeballs.) The evidence is not inconsistent with the idea that real sight and mind sight share the same spatially organized system, and that the nervous activity of scanning activates the functional movement of the real eyeball.

Other evidence in favour of this view comes from a famous experiment at the start of the century when a researcher with the charmingly appropriate name of Perky found that subjects facing an illuminated screen often confused things that they were imagining with faint images thrown, unknown to them, on to the screen by the experimenter. What happened was that they faced a ground-glass screen, and were then asked to imagine a banana while a real banana was thrown unpredictably on to the screen. They then found it difficult to discriminate between the image that they were putting in front of their mind's eye, and the one that was being supplied in front of their real eyes. This research has been extended and sophisticated by two American investigators, Segal and Fusella, who showed that when subjects were asked to visualize something while facing an illuminated screen, their capacity to detect a visual stimulus on the screen – a little flash for example – was recognizably impaired, whereas their efficiency in detecting an auditory stimulus at the same time was affected much less. This must have meant that visual resources were being used up while employing the mind's eye.

These experiments have implications that are comparable to ones discovered by Lee Brookes of McMaster University in 1968. Brookes showed that when subjects were asked to recall certain specified features of a geometrical figure, their response was much faster when they reported the items verbally than when they had to identify these features visually by pointing to the alternatives on a wall chart. Now apart from the fact that both the results of these experiments and the conclusions drawn from them have been disputed, they do not by any means prove the coherent spatiality of mental images. In fact, interest in imagery was quite indolent until two sets of experiments proved, or seem to prove, that mental images could actually be rotated and scrutinized as if they were spatially integrated pictorial representations in front of the real eye.

The experiment that set the alarm bells ringing was first published in 1971 by Roger Shepherd and Jaqueline Metzler, although the preliminary results were privately circulated in a short paper entitled 'On Turning Something Over In One's Mind'. In their experiments subjects were asked to judge whether paired projections of block-like figures were identical or not. The results indicated that the subjects were mentally rotating the image of these remembered figures until they were in a position that allowed a reliable comparison of the two shapes to be made. In fact, the time taken to arrive at an assessment of identity or otherwise increased in relation to the size of the angle by which the two figures were out of register when they were first presented to the real eye. The rate was the same regardless of the plane of rotation. It took just as much time to achieve rotation in the plane of the screen as it did in the fore and aft axis. Here, it seems, was incontestable evidence in favour of a spatially organized pictorial representation inside the imagination.

Meanwhile, at MIT, Stephen Kosslyn and his associates were carrying out experiments the results of which led them to the conclusion that mental images played an important part in the retrieval of visual information. Kosslyn's experiments were inspired by the introspective reports of people who often insist they have to form an image of a room or a house before they can say how many chairs or windows there are in it. Kosslyn designed an experiment to test this informal situation. He asked his subjects to memorize a picture of a motor launch. He then asked them if there was an anchor or a flag at the prow. Having fixed their attention on the prow or the front end of the craft, he then asked them questions about the furnishings on the bridge and on the stern respectively, and found that the speed of their answers was proportional to the distance between the prow and the target about which he then questioned them. It seemed that the mind's eye was scanning a mental image and taking longer to go from prow to stern than it did to go from prow to bridge. He also tried to see how altering the size of the mental image influenced the speed of the report by inviting some of his subjects to visualize an animal as if viewed from close up, and then as seen from far away. He then asked them to report the presence or absence of certain features such as whiskers, claws or a split upper lip. The results he obtained were once again consistent with the idea that a pictorial image was being looked at.

The reports were recognizably and repeatedly faster where the subject was asked to report a larger image than it was when he was being asked to visualize and report a smaller one. He obtained the same results when the size of the images was manipulated indirectly. He invited the subject to imagine a particular creature alongside an elephant or a fly and found that it was easier to retrieve certain requested features from an animal whose image was proportionately enlarged by being put alongside a fly, than it was when the target creature was shrunk by being placed alongside a much larger animal like an elephant.

It could be argued, and indeed the anti-imagists have argued, that these results have nothing to do with imagery as such. They point out that the order to visualize something *large* is automatically interpreted by the subjects as an instruction simply to form a *list* of features, and that it is by consulting this list, rather than by looking at a picture, that the subject succeeds or fails in the task. I do not think this will be an appropriate place to describe all the controls that Kosslyn and his associates introduced to meet these objections but having made systematic and ingenious allowance for them he still obtained results that favoured the idea that images were being looked at by the mind's eye. In the last fifteen years or so Alan Pavier at the University of Western Ontario has also obtained results that stress the functional importance of visual images, although his theory features an elaborate reciprocity between visual and verbal representations.

The opponents of imagery have not been persuaded by any of these findings. As far as they are concerned, there must be an alternative explanation that avoids the unacceptable philosophical implications of a mind's eye for which these rotations and inspections are pictorial events. This implies that there has to be a mind's brain to recognize what the mind's eye tells it, and so on in an infinite regress. What they offer by way of an alternative explanation is a theory that says that any information expressed in a pictorial format can be represented much more productively in a propositional form, and although these propositions may yield images these are a by-product and not essential to the mental work of the subject.

The idea of a proposition is derived in the first instance from the pioneer work of Frege, for whom a proposition was something that was expressible as a sentence, although it could not necessarily be identified with the features of any particular sentence. Unlike pictures or images, which represent objects, propositions express assertions *about* objects and the relationship between them. Unlike pictures they can be true or false and their truth value is to some extent invariant under paraphrase. The opponents of imagery insist that a propositional representation can do everything that a pictorial one does and more.

It may be unrealistic to regard these alternatives as mutually exclusive.

As I have already mentioned, Alan Pavier found it impossible to interpret his experimental results without assuming the co-existence of a verbal and a pictorial code co-operating with one another. In fact, without such a reciprocity it is quite hard to explain the way in which mental images tend to assert so much more than they visibly show. In the case of dreams, for example, what one sees in the intentional sense is often at odds with the visible appearance.

Here is a dream that illustrates what I mean. It is reported by the nineteenth-century physician McNish who was, incidentally, a close personal friend of James Hogg, the author of *The Confessions of a Justified Sinner*. McNish dreamed that he saw Versailles and that it was '*An immense architectural creation of the gothic ages with a hundred and ten thousand minarets sprouting up and piercing the sky with their pointed pinnacles. The whole was as visibly unlike reality as possible. And yet this never occurred once to my mind, and while gazing upon the visionary fabric it never occurred to me for a moment that it had ever appeared other than it now did. It was the same now as when I previously beheld it.*'

I assume that everyone is familiar with this sort of paradox, and that we all recognize how hard it is to give a coherent account of such experiences. Perhaps I can reinforce McNish's example with a dream of my own. I recently went up to Cambridge to deliver a lecture, and in my apprehension I had rehearsed my arrival in a series of increasingly alarming dreams. About four nights before, I dreamt that I was parking my car in what I knew to be Trinity Lane, although it was from its visible appearance also a narrow side street behind the Santo in Padua. At the end of the lane I could see the Master of Trinity waving hospitably at me, and he was the actor Michael Hordern. Now there was no sense in my dream that Hordern, the actor, was playing the part, or that he had 'popp'd in' between the election and anyone else's hopes. As far as I was concerned in the dream Hordern and the Master were one and the same in spite of the fact that I also knew, simultaneously, that the Master and Sir Andrew Huxley were identical. The rest of the dream was so humiliating, for which I blame neither Sir Michael nor Sir Andrew, that I shall draw a veil over it.

The fact that we can dream of something without its necessarily looking like what we know it to be means that there is at least one class of mental images whose members have what pictures and photographs do not – namely, intrinsic propositional content – something that says what the image is an image of. For someone who knows what Versailles looks like, the only way in which a photograph can justify its claim to be a photograph of Versailles is by resembling it; whereas when a dream image of Versailles comes before the mind, such a resemblance does not appear to be necessary. As Jerry Fodor says, '*Since it is my image, I am the one who gets to say what it is an image of*', irrespective of its appearance. Admittedly, self-contradictory images of this sort are confined to dreams and there is no conceivable way in which someone knowing what Versailles actually looks like could picture it as a Gothic pile. Asking someone to do this could make as little sense as it does to invite him to say the phrase, 'It is warm in here' while meaning, 'It is cold in here'. But this does not mean that waking imagery is devoid of propositional content altogether. On the contrary, to visualize something, as opposed to merely seeing a picture of it, is to 'see' it under some form of description, since it is under the auspices of such a description that the image comes into existence in the first place. This is especially noticeable when it comes to picturing something as a result of reading an account of it. Since the image is generated by language it wears its linguistic pedigree on its sleeve and has characteristics that distinguish it from the experience of seeing a picture of the person, object or scene to which the description refers. In other words, although photographs and paragraphs can share the same objective reference there is no way in which they can express the same objective sense. Even within language, the claim that two sentences are strictly synonymous is questionable to say the least, so that the possibility of pictures and mental images being synonymous is even more remote. Here are some examples of the way in which the images generated by a description differ from the experience of looking at a picture that shares the same reference.

No picture, still or moving, could express the visual effect of Thomas Hardy's description of Tess when she first appears at a May Day dance.

*Phases of her childhood lurked in her aspect still. As she walked along today, for all her bouncing handsome womanliness, you could sometimes see her twelfth year in her cheeks, or her ninth sparkling from her eyes; and even her fifth would flit over the curves of her mouth now and then.*

The effect of this description is undoubtedly pictorial, just as Henry James thought it should be, but it expresses both more and less than any picture might do. Hardy does not provide us with anything that one could properly call a likeness, and there are no details from which one could reconstruct an Identikit picture of the young heroine. Conversely, no photograph could even begin to assert the simultaneous presence of all the developmental stages that Hardy claims could be recognized in one face. A film-maker might cast an actress who conformed to such a description, but it is unlikely that an audience would recognize it – certainly not with the unencumbered force that the reader who has been privileged to read the description 'sees' it. And although it is impossible to give a coherent account of what it is to visualize something in this way, there is, as the philosophers would say, 'something that it is like' and there is nothing in a photograph that is even remotely equivalent to that 'something'.

This also applies to the way in which Hardy tries to capture the appearance of Tess's '*mobile peony mouth*'. At one level, of course, the effect of this description could be much more successfully achieved by a picture that matched the colour that Hardy is referring to, but even so the experience of visualizing the lips under the auspices of the evocative word 'peony' is inescapably different from seeing a photograph with peony-coloured lips. Because apart from the colour to which it corresponds, the word 'peony' has connotations of delicacy, fragrance and perishability, and although the predicates are not picturable, the image that is generated by the word is subjectively infiltrated by these implications and to a very large extent constituted by them.

Here is another example. In *Great Expectations*, Dickens describes Mr Wemmick as having a mouth like a letter-box, and he reinforces the comparison by insisting that the clerk posts his food as opposed to eating it. The mind's eye appears to have no difficulty in conjuring up a mouth that conforms to this description, but there is no way in which a picture could express such a comparison. Dickens has presumably seen someone whose mouth looked, for all the world, like a letter-box and since such people are rare but not unique, a conscientious casting director could presumably find an actor from whose appearance a vigilant and witty spectator might draw the same conclusion. But the metaphorical judgement would have been retrospective, and would have been extracted from all the other details that a photograph would be bound to show. Whereas the reader's mind working under the coercive influence of Dickens's metaphor achieves a single, unencumbered experience of a mouth-like-a-letter-box.

Both of these descriptions achieve their distinctive effect by exploiting the peculiar power of metaphor, for which there is no equivalent in a picture or at least not an explicit equivalent. It is only in language that one can state an explicit comparison between one thing and another – between lips and peonies, mouths and letter-boxes. Although a picture can be viewed with the knowledge that a metaphorical implication is intended, there are no communicative resources within the pictorial format for making such implications explicit. For example, only someone who was familiar with the dogma under whose sponsorship the picture was painted would recognize the fact that when the infant Jesus was displayed on a white napkin in a Flemish nativity, he was meant to represent the Host lying on the eucharistic corporal. In this case, the metaphor is contained in the image but is not actually stated by it, whereas the explicit assertion that Tess's mouth is to be compared with a peony creates an image that is actually constituted by it.

Apart from its peculiar success as a metaphor, the description of Tess's mouth is due to another peculiarity of linguistic representation. Deployed in isolation, without any accompanying details about the rest of the girl's face, it has the irresistible force of synecdoche; in other words it conveys the impression of the whole by forceful epitomizing of a part. We visualize Tess in the mode of her mouth-as-peony, and although nothing else is described or represented there is no sense of her being bereft of other features. Whereas a picture that left everything else to the imagination would have to look something like Tenniel's illustration of the diaphanous smile of the Cheshire Cat (*see below*). We are mystified but convinced by Carroll's description of this anomalous display whereas Tenniel's illustration of it is merely ludicrous.

These two examples raise another issue of which I was scarcely aware until I began to write about it, and that is the kinesthetic effect of linguistic description. Apart from the referential implications associated with the word peony, the imagery that is generated by reading the word has something that is necessarily absent from a picture. In seeing the word on the page, the reader voicelessly articulates it, and by rehearsing its delicate consonants, he finds himself receiving and delivering the chaste kiss that such lips deserve. Something similar happens when Dickens mentions the fact that Mr Wemmick's mouth is like a letter-box. In an effort to get his mind round such a comparison, the reader inadvertently enlarges his mouth so that it apes the postal rictus and, as a result of making this private grimace, the visual image is conjured into a vivid existence. This has something to do with the process discussed by Gombrich in an article on portraiture. He points out that artists sometimes have difficulty in capturing a likeness of the sitter's facial expression merely by looking at it. They cannot begin to paint what it looks like until they have rehearsed its feel on their own faces. If you stand behind the canvas and watch an artist painting a portrait, you will often see him aping the expression of his sitter as if the experience of putting on such a face enables him to see the expression for the first time. This has a bearing on yet another example.

In *Great Expectations*, Dickens describes the memorable stance of the stranger in the Three Jolly Swagmen as follows: '*His head was all on one side, and one of his eyes half shut up, as if he were taking aim at something with an invisible gun.*' Perhaps this description is vivid enough but, when I read it for the first time, it did not appear before the mind's eye until I had rehearsed the posture for myself. It could be argued, of course, that in understanding the description enough to be able to imitate it I was already in possession of the image to which the description corresponds. Nevertheless, the act of imitating it helped to confirm my intuition and the visual image was somehow consolidated by the kinesthetic experience of acting it out. One might want to say that one could get exactly the same effect by seeing an actor form the gesture in accordance to the description but, although the actor would generate his performance in the knowledge that what he was trying to do was an instance of looking *as if* he were taking aim along an invisible gun, the spectator who was exempted from the verbal instruction that guided the performance would not necessarily glean this implication, and in failing to do so he would miss the menacing experience of seeming to have an invisible gun aimed at *him* in his vicarious role as Pip.

Once again, the visual effect of these kinesthetic experiences is in no way jeopardized by the absence of supporting pictorial detail. On the contrary, although Dickens provides no further features, the head that is thus cocked does not seem incomplete. One way of explaining this is to say that Dickens has supplied us with the verbal equivalent of a sketch. But the comparison is misleading because the way in which a sketch or a cartoon is indeterminate with respect to detail is completely different from the way in which a sketchy description is. Both of them, admittedly, are epitomizing procedures, but the way in which they separately achieve their epitomes is altogether different. Which takes me back to the argument put forward by those who oppose the so-called imagery position. There is something about a mental image, whether it arises spontaneously or under the auspices of a description, that makes it altogether different from a picture. And the same principle applies to the representation of whole scenes and not merely to the person, and faces, that participate in them.

With the retentive accuracy of photography, film can scarcely avoid a replete reproduction of whatever there is to be seen on any particular occasion, whereas a novelist can summarize, generalize and particularize without creating a particular impression lacking the details that he fails to mention. In some mysterious way, the description of a scene appears to be fully occupied by what it describes, and never appears to lack what it fails to mention. This presumably is what Percy Lubbock means when he refers to the distinctive 'pictoriality' of the ball in *Madame Bovary*: '*The thing is "scenic" in the sense that we are concerned with a single and particular hour – but though it is thus a* scene, *it is* not *dramatically rendered. If you look at the dialogue, what there is of it, together with the actual things described, the people, and the dresses, and the dances, and the banquets and took these and placed them on a stage for a theatrical performance, the peculiar effect of the occasion in the book would vanish.*' Under the influence of a few carefully organized paragraphs which take no more than a minute or two to read, it is possible to endure and experience the full length of the festive evening, whereas a film-maker would have to show both more and less in order to convey the same effect. More, in the sense that by pointing his camera in any given direction each frame would find itself inescapably loaded with unnecessary detail. And less, in the sense that no detail could express what any one of them meant to Emma as she luxuriated in them – '*the peculiar effect of the occasion in the book would vanish*'.

In a single paragraph describing the dinner before the ball, Flaubert achieves effects that are inconceivable in the medium of film. At the outset, we are within the heroine as she enters. '*She felt herself*', Flaubert tells us, '*plunged into a warm atmosphere compounded of the scent of flowers and of fine linen, of the savour of meat and the smell of truffles.*' A film-maker has only two choices: he can show Emma entering a scene to which this description corresponds, but then we are forced, whether we like it or not, to see a particular girl with features conspicuously omitted in Flaubert's description – one visible person amongst many visible others – or he might, in the effort to capture the scene from her point of view, leave her out and track into the room along what the spectator was supposed to identify as her point of view. But neither of these would capture the evocative effect of that word '*plunged*' with which Flaubert expresses the sense of her inaugural immersion, and what picture could express the reflection of the candles which '*glowed on the silver dish-covers with elongated flames*'? No doubt the wicks could be trimmed to accommodate this description, and the flames would lengthen by the requisite amount, but nothing could reproduce the sensuous onomatopoeia of the phrase '*elongated flames*'. And in some odd way the description works by exploiting the very thing that makes language a supposedly inadequate way of representing the simultaneous co-existence of many things. As Lessing points out in *The Laocoön*, only pictures can instantaneously display all that there is to be seen looking in any given direction, and by being inescapably consecutive language is forced to enumerate them in the form of an inventory. And yet this is exactly how Flaubert's description achieves its overwhelming effect of luxurious superfluousness. '*The pieces of cut glass had steamed over, and reflected a dull glimmer from one to the other. Bunches of flowers were set in a row down the whole length of the table, and on the wide-rimmed plates stood serviettes folded in the form of a bishop's mitre, each with an oval-shaped roll inside the fold. The red claws of the lobsters lay over the edge of the dishes*' and on it goes item by item accomplishing an effect that is altogether different from the one that would result from showing all of this at the same time.

In fact it is by virtue of the consecutive enumeration that the effect of luxury is heaped into the reader's imagination. And as a result of the words that are employed to describe each item the visual image is mysteriously invigorated and transfigured. By telling us that the serviettes were '*folded in the form of a bishop's mitre*', as opposed to showing them in their already folded state, we experience the seductive rasp of the starched linen and the accomplished skill of the deft attendant who laid the table long before the arrival of the guests. '*The pieces of cut glass*', we are told, had '*steamed over.*' In that imperceptible pluperfect we enjoy not only the blurred reflection subsequent to the condensation but the crisp glitter that they would have reflected previously, and so on. In fact, it is difficult to overstress the subtle effect of transitive verbs used to describe the way in which something achieves its static appearance. Flaubert tells us, for example, that '*Luscious fruits were piled on moss in open baskets.*' The experience that results from this description is partly the result of the active verb, which tells us how the format was achieved. The fruit was not merely in a pile, it had *been* piled with all the plutocratic implications of unlimited wealth, and of there presumably being more where that came from. And then there is the elusive effect of abstention. Emma sees that the '*quails still had their feathers on them*'. All that a film could show is feathered quails but the sentence employing that tiny word '*still*' can imply some peculiar withholding of the plucker's hand. That is to say, that they are not merely quails with their feathers on but quails that owe their feathers to the deliberate act of leaving their feathers on. In such a sentence, Flaubert can automatically convey the impression that such a spectacle makes on the mind of a provincial girl who is presumably accustomed to having her quails served plucked. The effect is comparable to a sentence that occurs in the next paragraph when Flaubert tells us that '*Madame Bovary noticed that several of the ladies had not put their gloves in their glasses.*' A wealth of social innuendo is expressed by this anomalous abstention, and by the fact that Flaubert tells us not merely that it had not occurred but that it was noticed by Emma as not having occurred.

Think, too, of the way in which Flaubert introduces us to the town of Yonville. The whole enterprise is vividly visual and yet it would be difficult to imagine how film could accomplish any of the effects. In his first mention of the church, for example, Flaubert can tell us immediately that '*Rot has set in on top of the wooden roof making hollow patches of black on its blue surface.*' In order to show this, a film-maker would have to get his cameras on to the roof by some method that would tell the viewer that he was there rather than somewhere else. Could one really endure the slow crane up and the track along the roof to the point where the hollow patches of black were to be seen? Apart from the fact that such a manoeuvre would take more time than it deserved, the suggestive implications of the slow approach might imply that something much more important was to be seen – Emma about to throw herself off the roof, for example. Whereas in the brief flash of a single sentence we have arrived without the labour of making an optical journey. And the same principle applies to his description of the interior. Details are enumerated without our having to undergo the time-consuming ordeal of a travelling shot. And when features of the interior are described, we once again see both more and less than any film could show. The little figure of the Virgin with '*a rich crimson on her cheeks, like an idol from the Sandwich Islands*': the image that results from this description is poised weightlessly in the reader's imagination and although we know very little about its look, we are told something that no picture could convey about what it looks *like*. By comparing it to an idol from the Sandwich Islands, we cannot avoid drawing conclusions about the religious simplicity of the absent worshippers.

Flaubert then moves us into the town square without our having to undertake the expense of a visual journey. He can offer with edited clarity the town hall with its '*three ionic pillars at ground level*' and an assertion to the effect that it was '*built "to the design of a Paris architect"*'. From the fact that this phrase was put in quotation marks we can safely assume that Flaubert means it to be read as the boast of a particular townsman uttered at some unspecified time, and we are thereby introduced to the provinciality of Yonville's inhabitants. And having enumerated no further architectural details, Flaubert tells us what no film could, '*And that is all there is to see at Yonville*'. This is the very thing that a film could not show since a photograph would unavoidably represent everything else that was to be seen at Yonville. By using the same technique, Flaubert can also compress the eventless passage of provincial time by telling us that '*Nothing, in fact, has changed at Yonville since the events about to be recorded.*' He achieves this by using a linguistic resource for which there is no equivalent in pictures – the word 'still'. '*The drapers shop still waves its two calico streamers in the wind . . . and above the big front door of the inn the weatherworn "golden lion" still displays its poodle's mane to the passer-by.*' Combined with that first phrase, '*Nothing, in fact, has changed at Yonville*', we are given to understand that each item described at the time of writing was there when Bovary first arrived, and that inanimate things indifferently outlive the human tragedies that are enacted in their shadow. The point is, that in showing more, a film unavoidably tells us considerably less than a novel; and the effect of translating fiction into pictures is comparable in many respects to giving us a photograph of the apple that Cézanne so carefully constructed out of paint.

But the distinctiveness of Flaubert's achievement is not confined to the purely visual effects of his prose. We live with Emma's feelings and not merely with the scenes that she perceives. Here is the description of her mood after Leon's departure:

> *Next day was a day of mourning to Emma. Everything seemed wrapped in a drifting, clinging darkness and sorrow sank deep in her soul with a muffled wailing, like the winter wind in a derelict château. It was the spell cast by the departed, the lassitude that followed the event, the pain caused by any accustomed motion breaking off or prolonged vibration abruptly ceasing.*

A film-maker who wished to convey this mood could do so only by showing Emma's face lost in gloom. Nothing could convey that drifting, clinging darkness, and in the metaphor of the winter wind in a derelict château we are unavoidably reminded, if only by contrast, of the warm, hospitable atmosphere of the festive château described earlier.

Then there is the description of the capricious purchases with which Emma tries to console herself:

> *She bought a Gothic prie-dieu, spent fourteen francs in a month on lemons for cleaning her nails, wrote to Rouen for a blue cashmir dress, and picked out the loveliest sash at Lhereux's to wear round her waist over her dressing-gown. So arrayed she reclined on the sofa, with the blinds drawn and a book in her hand.*

How could showing compete with such telling? The purchase of a

Gothic prie-dieu is accomplished in five words whereas it could only be achieved in a scene taking several minutes at the least. Separated by nothing more than a comma, we can accomplish the expenditure of fourteen francs in a month. And how could a film represent a decision to learn Italian followed by the action of buying dictionaries? Taking these sentences, one after another, the reader knows perfectly well that they refer to events on widely separated occasions but a film would find it very difficult to represent the intervening intervals, and although mixes or fade-outs could go some way towards representing the passage of time there is no way in which such 'trucage' could compete with the frictionless alternation of skilfully punctuated sentences. Which raises the vexed question of tense.

Although film has an unrivalled capacity for showing events as they happen, it has none of prose's fluent dexterity for representing the present in relationship to the past; the frequency of events or their uniqueness; or how things might have been in contrast to how they turn out to be. The absorbed reader is not immediately aware of the way in which his experience is being manipulated but by subtle alternations of tense, the novel creates in his imagination something that is closely equivalent to the containment of *'Time present and Time past in Time future'*. Flaubert is rightly credited with pioneering efforts to exploit the resources of tense, but the most daring consummation of these experiments is to be found in Proust. It is this as much as anything else that makes the attempts to render *Swann in Love* into a film such an obliquely banal enterprise. As Gerard Genette has argued, the distinctive effect of this masterpiece is based partly on the fact that its occasional episodes are embedded in a translucent medium of the habitual or frequentative. At the outset of *Swann in Love*, we are introduced to the Verdurins with an account of the customary ritual of *'the little clan'*. We are told, for instance, that *'the Verdurins* never *invited you to dinner. You had your place laid there. Monsieur Verdurin used to say "We are all friends here, Liberty Hall you know"*,' and although the phrase is given in inverted commas from which we are to take it that it was uttered by the character in question, we also assume that the utterance was habitual. In a film it would be necessary to convene a scene in order to have this line spoken and it would lose its effect in the midst of all the other recorded conversation. We are also told of the habitual methods of keeping the faithful in line and of the vetting procedures for testing new members: *'If the test proved satisfactory the newcomer would in turn be numbered among the faithful.'*

It is only when Proust has accumulated a thick, hospitable background of the way things were in general at the Verdurins' that he can afford to introduce the punctual arrival of Swann on a particular occasion. *'And so, that year, when the demi-mondaine told Monsieur Verdurin that she had made the acquaintance of such a charming man, Monsieur Swann . . .'* It is only set against

233

the described tradition that this singular moment achieves its effect. With its wealth of habitual, frequentative detail the atmosphere has become supersaturated with expectant hospitality neatly precipitated by the phrase '*And so, that year*'. Note also that Proust allows himself to represent an echo of Odette's locution by quoting the small phrase '*such a charming man*' which gives the reader the opportunity of sampling her distinctive diction without having to hear her actually say it. And yet the rhythm of the narrative is suddenly enlivened by precipitating Monsieur Verdurin's request to his wife in direct speech, '*My dear, Mademoiselle de Crécy has something to say to you. She would like to bring one of her friends here; a Monsieur Swann.*'

The scene is thus set for Swann's arrival but Proust artfully postpones the moment by giving us a long generalization about Swann's familiarity with grander society. In the course of this, Proust reverts to a previous time in order to explain how Swann had been introduced to Odette in the first place, telling us that he *had* found her at that time '*endowed with a kind of beauty which left him indifferent, which aroused in him no desire*'. He slips subliminally into an appropriate pluperfect from which we learn that '*She had struck Swann as not entirely devoid of beauty.*' And as the pluperfect tense extends we learn that '*Odette had written to Swann asking whether she might see his collections which would very much interest her . . .*' Again Proust gives us an indirect sample of her diction, adding that, '*She felt she would know him better once she had seen him in his home, imagining him to be so comfortable with his tea and his books.*' Nested inside this pluperfect tense we hear Odette both directly and indirectly and although a flashback might achieve some of this effect, it would disperse everything that was accomplished by representing it against the background of the Verdurin tradition. So the affair between Swann and Odette develops alternating moods and tenses with an opalescent subtlety that is altogether absent from the dismal film of the same name.

The format of film is hermetically sealed against yet another of Proust's characteristic exertions of intelligence. Throughout the episode of *Swann in Love*, the author represents Swann's perceptions against a background of his art-historical knowledge, and the appearance of living characters is repeatedly alluded to in terms of their perceived counterparts in painting. Odette is scarcely described in person but she is represented by reflection, as it were, in Swann's recognition of her premonitory presence as Zipporah in Botticelli's Sistine painting of *Jethra's Daughters*. This enables him to '*find in an old masterpiece anticipatory and rejuvenating allusions to personalities of today*'. She reappears in yet another allusive refraction when Proust tries to describe the effect of her smile: '. . . *the life of Odette at all other times, since he knew nothing of it, appeared to him with its neutral and colourless background, like those sheets of sketches by Watteau upon which one sees here, there, at every corner and at various angles, traced in three colours on the buff paper innumerable smiles.*' The same allusive indirectness brings an arrogant footman into a visibility with which no filmic representation could hope to compete: '*A few feet away, the strapping great fellow in livery stood musing, motionless, like that purely decorative warrior whom one sees in the most tumultuous of Mantegna's paintings, lost in thought, leaning upon his shield, while the people around him are rushing about slaughtering one another.*' The film's director, Schlöndorff, was obviously aware of these allusions – since his set dresser took the trouble to decorate Swann's apartment with reproductions of most of the pictures mentioned in the text – yet there is no way in which these images can be made to exert their metaphorical force upon Swann's perception. In the film we see an enlargement of Zipporah's head prominently displayed under a connoisseur's lens but, without the coercive force of a sentence to assert the comparison, Botticelli's artwork never attaches itself to the object of Swann's yearning, and the only conclusion to be drawn from the presence of such specimens is that Swann is one hell of an aesthete. But the most conspicuous omission from this, or indeed any conceivable film, of *A la Recherche du Temps Perdu* is the accuracy and wit of Proust's 'thick' descriptions of behaviour.

The term 'thick description' has become fashionable amongst ethnographers in their effort to explain what might be meant by the interpretation of human behaviour. The phrase was originally introduced in an essay by Gilbert Ryle when he took pains to point out that there was a fundamental difference between the involuntary blink of an eyelid and a deliberate wink. As Clifford Geertz argues in his appreciative essay on 'Thick Description', although the distinction between the two is not readily expressible in a photograph, the difference is vast '*as anyone unfortunate enough to have had the first taken for the second knows*'. Taking his inspiration from Ryle, Geertz goes on to point out that '*the winker has done two things, contracted his eyelids and winked, while the blinker has done only one. Contracting your eyelids on purpose when there exists a public code in which so doing counts as a conspiratorial signal is winking.*' In other words thick description, unlike photographic representation, takes account of the intentions of the performer, and the social context within which the physical movements he chooses to realize these intentions might or might not be recognized. Admittedly, in a well-acted film the spectator is usually able to derive these thick descriptions of what is going on for himself, just as he can when he is immersed in social reality. But the novelist can go deeper and guarantee more forceful explanations of the meaning of any behaviour he chooses to represent.

Consider Proust's description of the foolish Dr Cottard. Without pausing to give us any details about Cottard's appearance, Proust accurately epitomizes his convivial idiocy. Dr Cottard, we are told:

*was never quite certain of the tone in which he ought to reply to any observation, or whether the speaker was jesting or in earnest. And so, by way of a precaution, he would embellish all his facial expressions with the offer of a conditional, a provisional smile whose expectant subtlety would exonerate him from the charge of being a simpleton, if the remark addressed to him should turn out to have been facetious. But as he must be prepared to face the alternative, he dared not allow the smile to assert itself positively on his features and you would see there a perpetual flickering uncertainty in which could be deciphered the question he never dared to ask, 'Do you really mean that?'*

While an accomplished actor guided by a tactful director could display behaviour from which a thick description, similar to the one provided by Proust, could be derived, this interpretation could not be guaranteed. In Proust's words, it is infinitely more amusing than it would be if merely displayed. This is because the author enjoys at least two advantages that the film-maker cannot. He can enter what passes for Cottard's mind and identify the anxiety that such a ninny feels when he is confronted by conversation he scarcely understands. He also has the privilege of understanding Cottard's motives more distinctly than the character himself could even aspire to. As a visitor to Cottard's mind he can see how it works more accurately than its proprietor. But there is another point: Proust derives his interpretation of Cottard's behaviour from many occasions. By seeing him or someone like him at one Verdurin party after another, he succeeds in epitomizing the theme of his conduct. As a writer, there is no need for him to represent either one or any of the scenes from which the generalization was made. He can compress many occasions and several scenes into a single, frequentative generalization: '*And so, by way of a precaution, he would embellish all his facial expressions with the offer of a conditional, a provisional smile.*' By imperceptibly deploying verbs cast in the iterative tense, the fact that this was a characteristic of Cottard is established and explained in a flash.

Here is another example of awkwardly self-protective behaviour. This time it is a description of the pianist's aunt:

*As she was entirely uneducated and was afraid of making mistakes in grammar and pronunciation, she used purposely to speak in an indistinct and garbling manner, thinking that if she should make a slip it would be so buried in the surrounding confusion that no one could be certain whether she had made it or not. With the result that her talk was a continuous, blurred expectoration, out of which would emerge at rare intervals a few sounds and syllables of which she felt sure.*

In both these passages of 'thick description' Proust is developing intuitions that have been helpfully generalized by the work of Erving Goffman. According to Goffman, the significance of many passages of human behaviour, both verbal and non-verbal, remains quite opaque until we take account of the agent's intention to correct the worst possible interpretation of his or her action. This presupposes that the participants in the social scene recognize the existence of certain norms, or standards of performance, and that any interaction with others involves a certain risk of falling short, and of therefore representing ourselves in an unfavourable light. In some cases the faulty performance represents an offence against others, an inadvertent encroachment upon their dignity or privacy, and in the effort to make amends, if socially sensitive, the offender repairs his or her reputation by some form of remedial behaviour, a shrug, a self-deprecating glance or a murmured apology. As long as the tactful remedies are acknowledged by reciprocal signs of acceptance, the offender can rest secure in the knowledge that their image has been restored in the eyes of the world at large.

As Goffman points out, these remedial processes can be compared with the formal structures of law which also sets standards below which it is impossible to fall without making amends. As in law, there is an orderly sequence of offence, remedy and reconciliation. But he goes on to point out that the offender is often the first to recognize that an infraction has occurred, and usually initiates the appropriate repair work without having to be prompted or called to account. An even more important distinction is the fact that the remedial work is expressive rather than productive, and the performance is usually designed to restore a favourable impression of the offender as opposed to giving compensation to the offended. This is because many of the infractions that I am referring to are not so much offences against others, but errors of performance that reflect badly on the offender. For example, the man who trips in the street to his own, and no one else's, inconvenience often retraces his steps and ostentatiously examines the surface of the pavement – as if to establish the impression that the fault lies in the pavement and not, as might otherwise be suspected, in the nervous system of the person concerned. Such behaviour is completely inexplicable unless we take account of the fact that the walker recognized that there are certain motor standards to be upheld and that if he falls below these, without giving a satisfactory account of why he did so, he will advance through the social scene accumulating the reputation of being a careless bugger.

In some cases, however, the remedial behaviour may be preventative rather than reparative. Someone who recognizes that his or her social inefficiency is likely to produce a suite of embarrassing mistakes will cover his approach under a smokescreen of ambiguous conduct in which he hopes that it will be difficult for the onlooker to distinguish the culpable errors. And this is exactly what is happening in the two examples I have quoted from Proust. Without such an explanation, it might be difficult to interpret the blurred expectorations of the pianist's aunt.

If we were to see her in a film, without the privilege of reading Proust's explanation, we might be led to believe that she simply had catarrh or a cleft palate. And the same goes for Dr Cottard's hesitant flickering smile. With Proust's 'thick description', derived presumably from hours of careful observation and conjecture, this otherwise puzzling demeanour is made transparent to the reader.

The difference between a play and a novel is that the actions in the latter are often explained in the very process of representing them, whereas in a play the performance may be guided and directed by such an interpretation in the hope that the spectator will glean such a conclusion by hindsight. This perhaps is one of the reasons why the process of rehearsal is often so interesting to the uninitiated visitor. In the discussions that lead up to the final performance of this or that line, and in the competing justifications for a variety of inflexions, the spectator visits the play in the mode of fiction and hears what might have been included in the script if the author had decided to turn it into a novel rather than a play. To some extent there is an almost reciprocal relationship between visibility and intelligibility: in the novel, the explanation and interpretation of behaviour takes precedence over its visible representation. Both Cottard and the pianist's aunt can exist intelligibly in the reader's imagination without having to be fully visualized. We are intelligibly acquainted with them without having been visually introduced. Although we know next to nothing about their 'look' they have a forceful psychological presence, and the same is true for Odette and for Swann whose appearances go by default. Whereas as soon as these characters come into visible existence riding piggy-back, as it were, on the names by which Proust refers to them, they seem to loom large without a scrap of mental life. They are like those visitors to a fancy-dress party who arrive at the festivities and find it necessary to tell the host that they have come as Swann and Odette, and can be seen throughout the evening going through the motions mentioned by the novelist.

The same principle applies to almost any character in a novel on whose behalf an actor makes a presumptuous fancy-dress appearance in a film. The disappointment or indignation that one experiences is usually explained in terms of some contradiction between his appearance in the two media – 'That's not what Mr Rochester looks like' or 'That's not *my* Mr D'Arcy'. But these objections miss the point. The shock is not that of finding that Mr D'Arcy or Mr Rochester look like this or that, but in discovering that they have any sort of look at all. They have acquired, as it were, an impudent visibility and we are tempted to cut them dead as showbiz counterparts of the Titchborn claimant.

The fact that someone is in a novel, as Mr D'Arcy is in *Pride and Prejudice* or Odette is in *Swann in Love*, does not mean that they are *in* the novel in the same way that someone else might be *in* Birmingham or *in* a cubicle. They cannot be taken out of the novel and put in a film of it. Mr D'Arcy and Odette are made out of the same material as the novels in which they occur, and they cannot be liberated in order to make a personal appearance in another medium. What is so valuable and memorably peculiar about Mr Carker, with his teeth and his wickedness, is the fact that he is in *Dombey and Son* and cannot get out.

\*

From what I have just said, it may look as though the principal objection to taking a character out of a book and putting him into a film is that he leaves the inexpressible features of his inner life behind, like a refugee who is forced to leave his assets at home and can only take away the clothes he stands up in. But that is not the point either. Even for literary characters who have no recognizable inner life, their representational existence is such that there is no conceivable way in which they could pursue an alternative existence in another medium. This is because they are descriptive fixtures of the text in which they occur, and due to the distinctive compressions and ellipses of responsible prose they cannot be paraphrased into a synonymous appearance elsewhere. Mr Wopsle, for example, makes two widely separated appearances in *Great Expectations* – as the opinionated minister at the beginning of the book, and as the ridiculous thespian towards the end. But because of the peculiar way in which Dickens represents him, he is constitutionally incapable of extricating himself from his literary habitat and taking up residence in a filmic one. Consider the way in which Dickens represents his behaviour at the Christmas dinner:

> *A little later on in the dinner, Mr Wopsle reviewed the sermon with some severity and intimated – in the usual hypothetical case of the Church being 'thrown open' – what kind of sermon he would have given them. After sobering them with some heads of that discourse, he remarked that he considered the subject as the day's homily, ill-chosen, which was the less excusable, he added, when there were so many subjects 'going about'.*

Like a fossil, which is not merely embedded in the rock but is actually made out of the same material, Mr Wopsle's existence is materially continuous with the indirect narrative in which Dickens represents his speech. We only *hear* his voice through two sets of inverted commas enclosing the phrases 'thrown open' and 'going about', but we are acquainted with the rest of his discourse in Dickens's witty representation of his gist. A film would have to unpack this indirectness and expand it into fully extended speech and we would lose the double-sided representation of that phrase, '*After favouring them with some heads of that discourse*', which tells us everything without having to show us anything. Then Dickens majestically syncopates the scene by allowing Mr Pumblechook's diction to emerge with unpetrified directness:

> 'True again,' said Uncle Pumblechook, 'you've hit it, Sir, plenty of subjects going about, for them that know how to put salt upon their tails, that's what's wanted. A man needn't go far to find a subject if he's ready with his salt-box.'

There is no way in which a film could do justice to this artful alternation between indirect and direct speech. And in the dismal realizations of Dickens that now infest the screens of domestic television we are assaulted by pretentiously picturesque usurpers.

The point is that although it is tempting to think of the novel as a medium in which we can recognize a visible image of an imagined reality, and to suppose that this image can be projected on to any surface that is capable of reflecting, it is misleading to think of description and depiction as interchangeable modes of representation. What the novel offers us is a transcription of thought and although the thoughts of an author necessarily take objects, people, and scenes as their arguments, as soon as these are rendered into a dramatic form, where the visible representation of actions replace the descriptions of them, the essential subject of fiction disperses into thin air.

None of these objections had occurred to me seventeen years ago when I undertook to adapt *Alice in Wonderland* for the screen. With hindsight, I can recognize that I made the problem even more difficult for myself by tackling a work that dealt with dream. As I have already described, the paradoxical experiences of dreaming cannot be reproduced literally in the form of explicit visual images, and yet it was the effort to convey the dream experience in a visual form that tempted me to make a film of *Alice* in the first place.

Unlike Henry James, who recoiled from the possibility of illustration, Carroll not only co-operated with Sir John Tenniel in the production of illustrations for the novel but also provided drawings of his own. In writing the book to entertain a Victorian child it seems unlikely that Carroll was self-consciously aware of writing about dream as such, and likely that he chose this form as a way of creating a medium in which miraculous events could take place without having to resort to the traditional format of the fairy tale. It is only in its afterlife as a novel that these distinctively dream-like features have become prominent. And perhaps it is only to the modern reader that the events described in *Alice in Wonderland* – like Kafka's fictional events – express the peculiarity of action as presented to the dreaming imagination. It is in the structure of his narrative that Carroll succeeds in expressing this distinctive peculiarity, and although film would seem to offer an unprecedented opportunity to show the transition and transformations that are only to be had in dream, these are the very devices that usually defeat the enterprise.

In the effort to represent the inescapable oddness of dream, film-makers usually exploit optical effects, failing to recognize that it is not the look of things that makes dream images different from waking ones but the attitude that one has towards whatever it is one sees – if seeing is the right word to use. For the reasons that I have already mentioned, dreaming is not a case of looking at something, nor is it, as Gilbert Ryle suggests, pretending to look at something – it is another way of being. In dreaming one participates in the action instead of being an objective spectator of it. In that sense film can never succeed in re-creating the experience accurately, and the introduction of trick photography simply confirms that the viewer is looking at a peculiar picture rather than living through an odd event.

A year before I decided to adapt the book, however, I had seen Orson Welles's masterly translation of Kafka's *The Trial* – a dream book if ever there was one. For the first time I was convinced that *Alice in Wonderland* was possible as a film after all, and my determination to go on with the project was reinforced by my recognition that Alice was a precursor to Joseph K. In both novels the protagonists find themselves involved in a legal process whose accusations remain obscure. The overwhelming impression of Carroll's novel is that *people had been talking about A . . .* What gave Welles's film the unarguable quality of a dream was the inexplicable concatenation of events, and not the peculiarity of any one of their appearances.

I recognized that I could only succeed with *Alice* if the film realized the characteristically disjunctive grammar of dream. The strange juxtaposition of elements in a scene that never strike us as odd when we are dreaming, should occur as almost passing details in a film. When visualizing the law court in *Alice* we furnished it with lodges and stage boxes in which spectators could be seen hastily dressing, casually shaving or having Christmas dinner, as the trial proceeded. As Alice runs through the garden on her flight from the White Rabbit's house she was shown passing an enamelled bath-tub in which a naked man is carefully washing himself. These items are normal in every respect except the context in which they appear before the eye. When it came to representing The Pool of Tears, the film showed fully clothed figures seen floundering in water through a hole in the floorboards. The camera must treat all of these events with a perfunctory casualness comparable to that of the dreaming McNish who knew, without finding it paradoxical at the time, that Versailles was gothic, and had always been so.

Apart from the way that things are inappropriately juxtaposed in the same scene, dreams are characterized by the way that one scene gives way to the next without any of the transitions that lend ordinary narrative text its coherence. Just as we are both controller and victim of the dreaming so, at the Mad Hatter's Tea Party, which reaches an inconclusive end, Alice's voice was heard on film without her appearing to speak. Suddenly her voice came from somewhere else saying 'Why are you painting those roses?' In the very next cut she walks towards the gardeners painting the rosebushes, although we have not seen her leave the Mad Hatter's tea table.

In this scene I did not want men literally pretending to be playing cards and looking like pantomime characters. This suggestion in the book seemed to me to resemble the experience in which we know something to be other than it appears to be, so that we think of people as cards although they are not. We achieved a comparably absurd transformation in the film by having the gardeners painting real roses with very small camel-hair brushes, but in order to do this correctly they took as their model not a red rose but a picture, and the assistant gardener held open a book of Redouté roses on which the real roses could be based. It gave a surreal effect that was made to seem quite humdrum by the exasperated Head Gardener who crossly asks his assistant to hold the book straight so that he can see to paint.

The problem for a director filming a book, for which there are already famous and well-loved illustrations, is the strong temptation to reproduce these literally. In most of the previous adaptations of *Alice* there had been slavish replicas of rabbit-headed men and courtiers dressed like playing cards. But Tenniel's pictures were designed for the printed page, and images that sit quite comfortably in the medium of the engraved line become absurd when translated into the realistic medium of photography. As Charles Rosen and Henri Zerner have pointed out, in *Romanticism and Realism*, when the artist exploits the device of the vignette, in which the margins of the picture bleed off into the whiteness of the page, the reader has the impression that the illustration is made out of the same material as the text that yields the description. Paragraph and picture are inseparably associated on the surface of the page. Instead of imitating Tenniel I had to deny his existence altogether, and the White Rabbit had to sacrifice his visual identity as a rabbit and become a man in whom one saw a rabbit.

It was necessary to turn in a different direction altogether to find the visual details appropriate to a Victorian dream. The hallucinatory realism of the Pre-Raphaelites gave me the appearance and effect that I wanted in the film. The fatal newness of the furniture in *The Awakening Conscience*; the darkening hush of the storm in Millais's *The Blind Girl*; and the doom-laden seaside of Dyce's *Pegwell Bay* inspired the look of the film. By recognizing rather than ignoring the book's Victorianism, and by stripping off the traditional disguises of the characters, other themes began to surface from the novel that I thought I knew so well. The nineteenth-century preoccupation with childhood, and the glorious

'Alice', drawing by Lewis Carroll

'Alice', from an engraving after Sir John Tenniel

*Sir John Everett Millais*, The Blind Girl
(left)

*William Dyce*, Pegwell Bay, Kent –
A Recollection of October 5th 1858
(below)

freshness of infant vision before it becomes clouded and obscured by the duties and responsibilities of growing up, helped me to think about Alice's changes of size. These can acquire interesting meanings for a child who is not yet an adult but on the edge of becoming one. Growing large and being small are vivid experiences that are bound up with questions of access and prohibition. Bigness and maturity prevent our return to the rose garden, while smallness and minority carry with them connotations of weakness and obedience.

By the time I was editing all this material and when the first show print came back from the labs I realized that if the film succeeded at all it was by avoiding direct adaptation. Like Robert Lowell's translations, it was an ironic *imitation* of *Alice in Wonderland*, and it is only as a travesty that it has a relationship with the original novel.

*Anne-Marie Mallik as Alice* (left)

*Malcolm Muggeridge as the Gryphon, Sir John Gielgud as the Mock Turtle and Anne-Marie Mallik as Alice join hands to dance the Lobster Quadrille in the BBC production of* Alice in Wonderland (below)

# Index

Page numbers in *italic* type refer to illustrations
and captions to illustrations.